P9-DCW-641

BERNARD MAYBECK

BERNARD MAYBECK

Artisan, Architect, Artist

KENNETH H. CARDWELL

➔

Gibbs M. Smith, Inc.
Peregrine Smith Books
Salt Lake City
1983

Copyright © 1977 by Peregrine Smith, Inc.

Library of Congress Cataloging in Publication Data
Cardwell, Kenneth H   1920-
   Bernard Maybeck: artisan, architect, artist.
   Bibiography: p
   Includes index.
   1. Maybeck, Bernard R.   2. Architects—
California—Biography.
NA737.M435C37   720'.92'4 [b]   77.13773
ISBN-0-87905-148-5

Manufactured in the United States of America

Contents

First Church of Christ, Scientist.
Roy Flamm photograph.

Introduction

There is something bigger and more worth while than the things we see about us, the things we live by and strive for. There is an undiscovered beauty, a divine excellence, just beyond us. Let us stand on tiptoe, forgetting the nearer things and grasp what we may.

Bernard Maybeck—1923

In 1940 I was a student of architecture at the University of California. Roaming the hills of Berkeley looking for examples of the modern work of William Wurster, Gardner Dailey, John Ekin Dinwiddie, John Funk, and others, I, like a generation of architectural students before me, noted some distinctively individualistic designs which were obviously older houses yet seemed amazingly fresh and attractive in their use of materials and their placement in the hillside landscape. Upon returning to the drafting room I learned from the seniors that these were the work of Bernard Maybeck. Some said that he had long been dead, others not so positive believed that, although he might still be living, he was much too old and too eccentric to be approached.

Upon a return visit to the area, I noticed an elderly man with flowing white beard and intense blue eyes dressed in baggy denim trousers and loose, peasant-like smock. On his head he wore a magenta crocheted beret and in his hands he held a gnarled walking stick and some letters. Hesitantly, I told him of my interest, as a student of architecture, in the design of the houses about us and inquired if he knew the name of their architect. He responded with the request that I post his letters in the corner box and, without identifying himself, invited me into his garden to talk. As he settled in a makeshift outdoor studio strewn with papers and drawings, he asked about the training I was receiving as an architect and continued with comments on modern buildings and the opportunities I would have to experiment with new materials.

I sat entranced as he spoke of his scheme to connect the bridges of San Francisco Bay with a broad avenue through the city and showed me drawings illustrating how buildings in the path of the new construction would be floated on barges across the Bay to be used in newly developing communities. After more than an hour of conversation, I left. He had not told me his name, we had not discussed the architecture of his buildings. But I would return many times during the next seventeen years and during that time Bernard Maybeck and I became warm friends.

Our visits were interrupted by my entry into the armed forces in 1941. I returned to Berkeley in 1945 to continue my architectural studies and I also renewed my acquaintance with Maybeck. One purpose of my visits was, as before, to learn more about him and his work. I invited him for rides in my Buick convertible to look at houses in the surrounding neighborhoods. He enjoyed riding in the open car. It reminded him of his own favorite mode of transportation, a Packard touring car, which he had used extensively during the 1920s. I would drive by a house which I suspected he may have designed and ask if he were its architect. He would quickly answer "yes or no" and change the subject of conversation to another topic.

I soon suspected that my device for supplementing my list of his work was faulty, and decided to test his memory by going to houses which I knew he had designed and to others which I knew had been designed by other architects. The results were revealing. I found that his memory was not at fault; he knew which houses he had designed, but he craftily would admit to be responsible for only the ones that pleased him. In fact, if one of the houses designed by another architect delighted his eye, he would, by default, also let me credit him for its design.

In 1947 I had the good fortune to acquire an old Berkeley house reputed to have been designed by Maybeck although it lacked any obvious design signatures such as a large fire-place, a venturi chimney cap, colorfully stained timbers, or beam ends carved as dragon heads. For several years I was uncertain of its authenticity; it was on no list of Maybeck work that I knew. I later invited Bernard and Annie Maybeck to tea to meet Catherine Bauer Wurster, whose husband William Wilson Wurster had assumed the duties as Dean of the College of Architecture at the University in 1951. Much to my delight Mr. Maybeck assured me he had designed the house and, in addition, was very critical of the approach to its entry.

He explained that my house was one of the three structures he had built for Professor Isaac Flagg on quite a large piece of property. At the time of its construction in 1912, the house had been approached from the southwest. Later subdivisions of the Flagg property had required the development of an entrance walk from the northeast which made the arriving guest reverse his direction to reach the front door. Maybeck recommended that I remodel the entrance porch to suit the changed conditions. I concurred with his idea but said that the support of a young family precluded an immediate change.

It was a pleasant visit, and one recorded in my memory by subsequent events. The following week, a sketch of the revision I was to make arrived in the mail. It was drawn from the memory of his short visit, showing the old house and a new stairway descending to greet the arriving guest. But, more significantly, it indicated by a date that perhaps in twenty years or so I could accomplish the change.

In 1950 I had returned to the Department of Architecture, this time to become an Instructor in descriptive geometry, paralleling Maybeck's own association with the University almost sixty years earlier. It was natural that some of the rides with Maybeck took us to the University campus and the Architecture Department to inspect the work of the students. Maybeck was particularly interested in a geodesic dome which the students had built under the direction of Professor John Rauma in preparation for discussion with Buckminster Fuller who was coming to spend some time at the department as a visiting critic. When Fuller learned of Maybeck's interest in the structure he expressed a desire to visit him.

After greeting Fuller, Maybeck questioned, "Well young man, what is your interest in architecture?" Fuller told of his geodesic and tensegrity structures and explained them as investigations in the separation of tensile and compressive forces in construction. Maybeck was intrigued and remarked that, he too, had experimented with that idea a number of years ago. I was fascinated by the rapport that developed between two individuals reputedly so dissimilar, one a romantic architect, the other a technocratic engineer.

Shortly thereafter, Maybeck's creative eclecticism was forcibly revealed to me. Several weeks after the conclusion of Fuller's stay at the University, Annie Maybeck telephoned to report that Ben was most anxious to see me. She said, "It has something to do with that man and his domes." When I arrived at Maybeck's studio, he had spread before him a copy of *Life* magazine showing Sir Basil Spence's proposal for the reconstruction of Coventry Cathedral as a war memorial. Maybeck was visibly agitated. "Look, look," he said, "a reconstructed Gothic cathedral is not what is needed; what should be done is to preserve the bombed ruins as a memorial." He then suggested that a large glazed geodesic dome covering the ruins would be the perfect solution and urged me to contact Fuller to initiate such a project.

In 1956 Maybeck gave his office records and drawings to the College of Architecture of the University of California, Berkeley, which subsequently was to become the College of Environmental Design. All the early Maybeck records of practice in the Bay area had been destroyed in the San Francisco fire of 1906, and most family memorabilia had been lost in the Berkeley fire of 1923. However, with the aid of a grant from David Pleydell-Bouverie, I undertook the cataloging of his drawings of the years 1906 through 1940, making a record which was completed in 1958. It was my original intention that this catalog be published with drawings and photographs, but no one was interested in the project.

It became apparent that Maybeck's work needed fuller explanation and, through the award of a Graham Foundation Fellowship for 1961, I expanded the catalog to a book which would include early buildings and events of Maybeck's professional career. It had always been my hope to be as documentary as possible in this endeavor, wanting as I did to avoid amplifying the many myths that exist about Maybeck and his work. He wrote that his buildings are his expression and that "they will tell you who I am and what I am." I have avoided contrasts and comparisons to contemporary architects with whom Maybeck had no contact. He was six years younger than Louis Sullivan and seven years older than Frank Lloyd Wright and, while he certainly knew of their work by the mid 1920s he was not influenced by either. I have tried to give emphasis to only those architectural details and experiences which broaden the knowledge of the man and his work.

Maybeck's long life may lead us to forget that the greater part of his work belongs to the era of our grandfathers. He was a part of that time when architects neither shunned technological developments nor forsook the fantasy and delight achieved in older architectural forms. His ability to resolve the conflict between the demands of individuality and continuity, between craft production and mechanization, make his work valuable for its insights on problems comparable to contemporary ones.

This volume would not have been possible without the generous assistance of many people. First and foremost are Annie and Bernard Maybeck. Kerna Maybeck Gannon and Jacomena (Mrs. Wallen W.) Maybeck have provided invaluable information and support. Jean Murray Bangs, through her early efforts in gathering materials on Maybeck and recording his work with the photographic firms of Stone and Stecatti, and Minor White, enriched the collection of documents given to the University. Catherine Bauer and William Wurster were always encouraging and helped in securing financial support from David Pleydell-Bouverie and the Graham Foundation.

My early interest in Maybeck was stimulated by Professor Winfield Scott Wellington and I gained much valuable information from him. Librarians Arthur Waugh and James Burch assisted in the development of the College of Environmental Design Documents Collection and their continuing help on bibliographical items has been a great assistance. Many other colleagues, academic and professional, have shared pertinent items and have provided helpful critical comment. Among these are Elizabeth Kendall Thompson, Theodore Bernardi, David Gebhart, Robert Betts, Barbara Silvergold, and Richard Longstreth. The photography of William Ricco and Roy Flamm, Maybeck students in their own rights, fortunately documented much work which has since disappeared. Alan Williams drew many of the plan drawings for publication. Gibbs and Catherine Smith of Peregrine Smith, Inc. believed in the book which Richard Firmage edited and designed. To all the others unnamed, the owners of the houses, who graciously allowed me to visit and to take photographs, and the many individuals interested in Maybeck who provided relevant information, my heartfelt thanks.

K. H. Cardwell, Berkeley, 1977.

Bernard Maybeck, watercolor sketch of chateau, (no date).
Documents Collection, C.E.D.

I

The Finest Lesson

My father talked to me from childhood about the importance of doing what I wanted to do, of being true to myself. He urged me to let my art rather than any financial consideration have first place in mind and heart always. That was the finest lesson my father taught me. It has become my religion.

Bernard Maybeck—1927

We are shaped by that which surrounds us. A man is favored who is surrounded by that and those which radiate a wholesomeness and beauty. We, in turn, attempt to shape that which surrounds us. A man is blessed who truly strives to make himself and his surroundings truly better. Bernard Maybeck was favored and blessed. And he was wise enough to realize his fortune; energetic enough to exercise his talents and intelligence. He remembered himself as a happy and active child, though sometimes given to long periods of daydreaming. But whether active or pensive, he was always very independent, and remained so throughout his life. He once told a story of his schoolboy days:

> I was a poor scholar at first until a turning point came. My teacher of mathematics told the class that a certain formula represented the best way of solving a particular mathematical problem. "Take it for granted," he said. "How the formula was obtained does not concern you." I never have liked to take anything for granted. That teacher incited me into taking an aggressive interest in study.[1]

Bernard Maybeck came naturally by his questioning and independence, being reared in an artisan family whose heritage included free thinking and action. His father, Bernhardt Maybeck, was born in Oelde, Germany, in 1833, the second son of a master builder prominent in his community and active in the political life of his country.[2] Bernhardt started to train as a sculptor in Munich, but the revolutionary events in Germany in 1848 put an end to his studies. His father, discouraged by the failure of his compatriots to establish a new democratic regime, decided to send Bernhardt and his brother, Henry, to America where they would have the opportunity that his own generation had been denied.

Upon arriving in the New World, Bernhardt and Henry were apprenticed to a cabinetmaker in Staten Island and trained in the craft of Flemish and Dutch furniture making. As a new immigrant, Bernhardt gravitated to the German-American settlements where he met Elisa Kern.

Elisa Kern was born in Morscheim, Germany in 1832, the fourth daughter of Eva Hoffman and Christian Kern.[3] The Kern family was among the most esteemed and active in the village. Family stories tell of Christian Kern's imposing house being used as an underground station to aid in the escape of refugees from the revolution. Because of his political involvement, Kern was arrested and imprisoned in Zweibrücken in 1849. When, in the following year, political prisoners were released under a general amnesty, Christian Kern lost little time in liquidating his holdings in order to take his family to America. A widower, he and his five unmarried daughters set sail from Le Havre in 1851.

1. Bernard Maybeck interview with Mark Quest.
2. B. R. Maybeck MSS, "Family," Documents Collection, College of Environmental Design, University of California, Berkeley (hereafter cited as C.E.D. Docs.).
3. *Ibid.* Hyppolyte Guerner, a maternal cousin of Maybeck, provided helpful information on the Kern family.

Not long after his arrival in the United States, Kern was established in a comfortable two-storied stone house in the German community of Yorkville on Manhattan Island. During his years there, many German expatriates came to visit and discuss philosophy, art, and politics. Among them was Bernhardt Maybeck. Christian Kern was delighted when the young man, whose intellectual beliefs were sympathetic with his own, proposed marriage to Elisa.

Bernhardt and Elisa Maybeck set up housekeeping in 1860 on McDougal Street, near Bleeker, in the heart of Greenwich Village. At the time the village was filled with modest single-family terrace houses. The early nineteenth century development of lower Manhattan subsided during the Civil War, and the village maintained the quiet air of a suburban center while the city grew vigorously and expanded rapidly to the north. Bernhardt started a small cabinet shop on nearby Broadway with Joseph Reinal. At the shop he devoted his time exclusively to the carving, while Reinal executed the joinery of the custom furniture they manufactured. In a little over ten years, Bernhardt and Elisa achieved the independence in America that fulfilled their young hopes. The birth of their child, Bernard Ralph Maybeck, on February 7, 1862, completed the dream.

But neither Bernhardt nor his young son had long to enjoy the idyll of family life. Elisa died in 1865 when Ben was three years old, and throughout his life his mother remained a haunting image of a lovely lady urging him to be an artist.[4] Bernhardt, faced with the problem of caring for a young son and earning a living, gratefully accepted Christian Kern's offer to come to Yorkville, and there Ben spent most of his youth. Even after his father married Elizabeth Weiss, the family, which was completed by the birth of Ben's half-sisters Irene and Julia, continued to share the old house on the hill.[5]

The few known facts of Ben's early life indicate a pleasant childhood which was enriched by the cultural interests of his family. Grandfather Kern took a special delight in young Ben, teaching him French and stimulating his imagination with stories of the revolutionary events in Germany. His father encouraged him to draw after school and took him on Sunday outings to do watercolor sketches. Along with art, family singing and musical performances formed a part of the household activities.

Several changes had taken place in the Maybeck household by the time Ben entered public high school in 1875. Grandfather Kern had left New York to make his home with

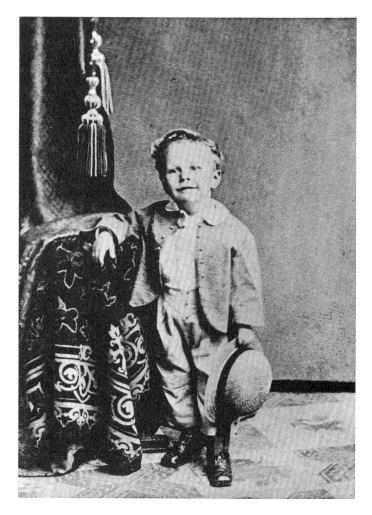

Bernard Ralph Maybeck, three years old (ca. 1865), New York City.
Documents Collection, College of Environmental Design, UCB.

4. "Ben" was used by family and friends to distinguish him from his father Bernhardt. It was used throughout his life. Elisa kept a diary which Ben treasured. Unfortunately it was later destroyed.
5. B. R. Maybeck DWGS, "Drawings," C.E.D. Docs. contain a sketch of Grandfather Kern's house drawn from memory by Maybeck late in his life.

14

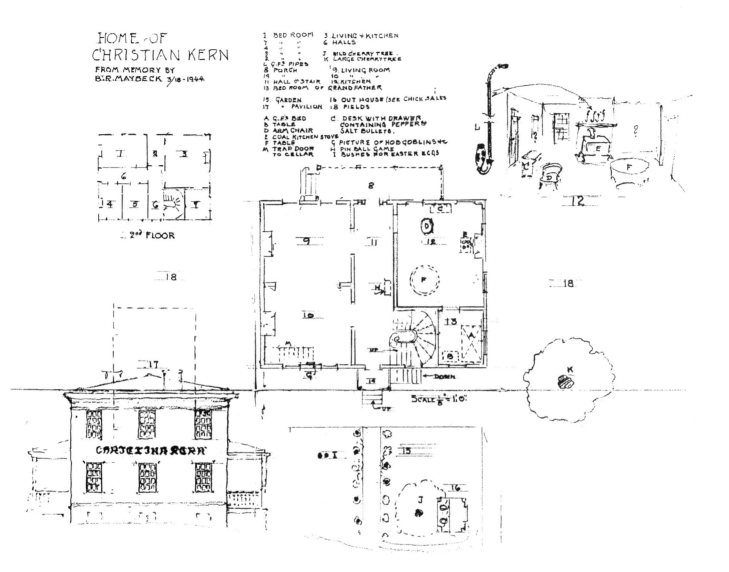

HOME OF
CHRISTIAN KERN
FROM MEMORY BY
B.R. MAYBECK 3/18-1944

1 BED ROOM   3 LIVING + KITCHEN
7 "   "   6 HALLS
4 "   "
5 "   "   J WILD CHERRY TREE
L C.F's PIPES   K LARGE CHERRYTREE
8 PORCH   9 LIVING ROOM
14   "   10   "   "
11 HALL & STAIR 12 KITCHEN
13 BED ROOM OF GRANDFATHER

15 GARDEN   16 OUT HOUSE (SEE CHICK SALES
17 " PAVILION   18 FIELDS

A C.F's BED   C DESK WITH DRAWER
B TABLE   CONTAINING PEPPER &
D ARM CHAIR   SALT BULLETS.
E COAL KITCHEN STOVE
F TABLE   G PICTURE OF HOBGOBLINS &c
M TRAP DOOR   H PIN BALL GAME
  TO CELLAR   I BUSHES FOR EASTER EGGS

2nd FLOOR

Bernard Maybeck, pencil sketch (1944), home of Christian
Kern drawn from memory.
Documents Collection, C.E.D.

his daughter in New Haven and Bernard's father had given up his shop to go to work for Pottier and Stymus, a large firm with shops in Paris and New York City that specialized in architectural carving and custom furniture design. Bernhardt soon became foreman of carving.

Ben attended two private schools as a boy. In the Benjamin Franklin School and Deutsche-Americanische Schule he learned French and German and was introduced to philosophy and mathematics. While he did not excel in any particular field, his progress was satisfactory. In high school his budding independence received stimulation from a "frail but stern Yankee named Pettigrew" who introduced him to Emerson's philosophical thought.[6] Impressed by the high sense of responsibility that underwrote Emerson's life and writings, Maybeck began to make some demands upon himself—he began to learn how to think. From high school he entered the College of the City of New York, where he pursued a liberal arts course with emphasis in languages and science. However, chemistry was his downfall; what was required was not his understanding of the theory involved but a repetition of the accepted formulas, and he failed miserably.

With his lack of success in higher education, Ben decided to follow his father's trade. He, too, went to work for Pottier and Stymus, serving as an apprentice for the prestigious firm that did the furnishings for the Pullman Company's parlor cars. His work consisted of running errands and making tracings of shop drawings. However, his propensity for daydreaming and his youthful enthusiasm for improving the designs put before him did not please his foreman, who wanted no more than a routine response to the job. Unhappy in his apprenticeship, Ben started the design of a reversible Pullman seat on his own, and this whetted his appetite to be a designer rather than a draftsman. His father had always stressed the importance of doing what one wanted to do, of being true to one's self. Desiring that his son should succeed in a career of his own choosing, he arranged for Ben to study in Paris at the studio of Mr. Pottier's brother.

What was the nature of the young man who prepared to go to the Old World which his father had left thirty years before? Maybeck reported that as a boy "I was a fathead!...so self-concerned that I couldn't sense the beauty of the other fellow. I was too critical of other people, too much interested in myself." He was undoubtedly harder on himself than he needed to be. His family described him as "witty and fun loving,"

Bernard Maybeck, prior to departure for Europe (ca. 1881). Documents Collection, C.E.D.

remembering the "twinkle in his eye." His sunny disposition delighted those around him.[7]

In addition to the genial manner that would win him many friends at school, Ben was backed by a broad liberal education which had been supplemented by discussions of art, politics, and philosophy at home with the friends of his father and grandfather. He had attained skill in drawing and sketching

6. Phrases used by Maybeck in letters, interviews and in conversation are indicated by quotation marks. The source is cited when a significant amount of additional information is available.
7. B. R. Maybeck MSS, "Family," C.E.D. Docs.

through the constant practice required by his father, and his apprenticeship had taught him the fundamentals of descriptive geometry, plus the invaluable experience of seeing drawings take three-dimensional form in the shop. Perhaps most important, his philosophical idealism was established. All that he would see, all that he would learn in Europe, would be tempered by the prevailing German transcendental metaphysics that he had been exposed to in his youth.

In 1881, at the age of nineteen, Ben sailed for Europe. He made his way to the Paris studio of Pottier and Stymus where he at once went to work. Located a short distance from the École des Beaux-Arts, the studio provided Ben with a daily view of the students as they pushed their drawings on carts from the surrounding ateliers to the judgment halls. The tall silk hats they wore reminded him of an architect at home, "an elegantly dressed young man, with pot hat and kid gloves," who had arrived each morning in a carriage to bring his drawings to his father's shop. Maybeck decided that he, too, would become an architect, and he wrote to his father, asking permission to enter the École des Beaux-Arts.[8]

It was a good time to seek admission to the school. The unrest and confusion that such well-known students as Henry Hobson Richardson had experienced in 1863 had climaxed with the dismissal of the romantic medievalist Viollet-le-Duc in 1867. But the triumphant classicists of the Academy had compromised, and they added to their traditional training in the classical orders the study of gothic structure. Henry Lemmonier began lectures paralleling Viollet-le-Duc's theory of building and emphasized the humble and humane elements of history; and Emmanuel Brune initiated a course that translated the emerging mathematic theory of modern structure into practical examples. Each of these men exerted a strong influence on Maybeck.

Another significant change that had taken place as a result of reforms was the inclusion of three *ateliers libre* to the formal structure of the school. Jules-Louis André had taken over the direction of Henri Labrouste's independent atelier in 1860, and, when it was made an official part of the École, it meant a recognition of the "free classic" style of Labrouste and a victory for his advocates. By the time Maybeck sought entry to André's atelier, it had an excellent reputation.

How Maybeck prepared for the stiff entrance examinations of the École is unknown. He did not have financial means that would permit private tutoring, but he was well prepared in

drawing and reasonably fluent in French and German. And he had a better than average knowledge of French history and philosophy from discussions his father had arranged with the French carvers in his shop. Jules André may have received him into his atelier prior to the examinations of the École, which would have been his privilege if he wished. In any event, Ben passed the entrance examination in March, 1882, ranking 22nd among the 250 applicants, 50 of whom were admitted to the school.[9]

Life at the atelier and in the École was exciting for Maybeck. His natural amiability and humor stood him in good stead for the customary ragging of the *nouveaux*. One of the *anciens* of the atelier was Thomas Hastings, who had entered the preceding year. Hastings was studious and lived modestly and quietly. He neither drank nor smoked, and Maybeck found in him a genial companion. For a time they shared rooms on the *Boule Miche*, not too far from the École. The *étrangers* at the school tended to form a natural group and, in addition to Hastings, Maybeck made friends with Ambrose Russell from Kansas City, Rudolph Dick of Vienna, Enrico Ristori of Florence, and Robert Sandilands of Glasgow, all of whom he would see again in later years. He was fascinated by these young men of the world whose backgrounds were so different from his own.

Maybeck was an intense student in the atelier from the beginning.[10] On one of his first assignments he took special care to place his sheet of Whatman's paper squarely on his board. He worked furiously, placing glue under all the edges and rubbing his sheet vigorously to make a smooth working surface. *"Pere"* André, attracted by Maybeck's activities, crossed the studio, looked at the blank sheet, and commented, "Believe me, my dear sir, you will never do better." But the sarcasm did not deter Maybeck, and he took his pencil and worked carefully and cautiously until he had made a drawing

8. Maybeck's statements about his decision to become an architect varied. I have used the version that seems most consistent with external facts.
9. David de Penanrun, Roux, et Delaire, *Les Architects: Éléves de l'École des Beaux-Arts*, 2nd. Ed. (Paris: Librarie de la Construction Modern, 1907).
10. See Ernest Flagg, "The Ecole des Beaux Arts, Parts 1 and 2," *Architectural Record* (Jan.-Mar. 1894), p. 302ff, for a description of student life at the school during the latter half of the 19th century.

of which he was quite proud. "It had cleanness of line and there was not a smudge on the entire sheet," he later commented. André returned and shocked him by grasping a pencil and making smudges all over it. Then he commenced working on it in earnest. Maybeck finally saw "that out of all the mess there was emerging strength." His original had perfection of detail, but André's "changes added character and beauty."[11]

While at the École, Maybeck developed an admiration for his *patron*. Though at times André's cynicism was in direct contrast with his own high spirits, Ben learned from him an appreciation of the classical values of architecture. André never allowed Maybeck to forget that rhythm, balance, proportion, and scale must also figure in the resolution of modern architectural problems. In addition, André had a strong feeling for natural forms, and he urged Maybeck to use the landscape and its design to enhance and unify his architectural designs. Perhaps the greatest thing André did for Maybeck was to encourage him to reflect American taste and culture rather than merely the French mode. Proudly referring to the work of his former student, H. H. Richardson, André called attention to a developing American style which he believed could be matured by the application of Gallic rational thought to solve architectural problems in the New World.

Besides the theory and criticism of André, other experiences enriched Maybeck's education during his years in Paris. Stimulated by Henry Lemmonier's lectures on the Middle Ages, Maybeck visited many of the Romanesque and Early Gothic churches in the city and surrounding countryside. The direct form and structure and rude ornament that he saw delighted him. In the churches Maybeck sensed the sincerity which, Lemonnier had said, was a characteristic of the populace immediately after the first millenium A.D. His experience was a lesson not taught at school, and from this time on whenever he visited works of architecture, he consciously tried to relate feeling to form. Even his daily routine brought new insights. On his way from the atelier to his favorite restaurant, Maybeck would take a short cut through the transept of St. Germain des Prés. One time he was attracted by some "lovely singing" as he passed through the church and he stopped to listen. The music brought over him "the most awesome feeling, as though the architecture and the music had blended." It was an experience he would never forget, and it permanently focused his attention on the affective qualities of architecture.

11. Conversations between Maybeck and the author.

Atelier, École des Beaux-Arts, Paris (ca. 1884).
Documents Collection, C.E.D.

Unidentified photograph from Maybeck collection. Possibly Thomas Hastings and Bernard Maybeck seated front row, center.

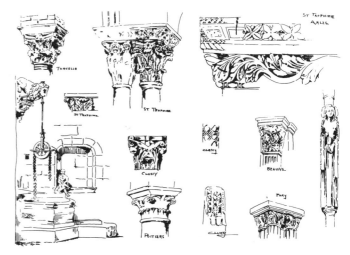

Bernard Maybeck, pen and ink sketches (no date), details of French Romanesque churches.
Documents Collection, C.E.D.

Between school sessions it was customary for many students to tour the classical antiquities of Greece and Rome. But Maybeck's limited means kept him close to Paris, although one summer he was able to visit the family homesteads of Oelde, Westphalia and Morscheim in Germany's Saar Basin.[12] One of Grandfather Kern's sisters, Katharina Bauer, lived in nearby Oppenheim, and there Maybeck found a job with the imperial Government working on a project to restore the medieval *Kathurinen-Kirche*. With this summer work and his modest allowance from home, he was able to continue his studies.

Although none of Maybeck's student drawings has been found, it is known that by 1884, he received two *mentions*, whereupon he was promoted into the *premiére classe*. André, too, was honored in 1884 by being elected as a member of the *Institut*. Throughout his life Maybeck was proud that his teacher had become "one of the forty immortals." Such recognition confirmed his belief in the École and its teachings.

Yet Maybeck's style developed from his individual sifting of the architectural theories he was exposed to at the school. His mature forms and ideas would at times reflect André's free classic style and at other times the structural determinism of Viollet-le-Duc's theory. But the neo-baroque forms of another hero of the École, Charles Garnier, would eventually become more apparent in Maybeck's work than either of these influences.

In 1886, after more than five years of training in Paris, Maybeck returned to the United States. The École did not award the *diplome* to foreign students until 1887; but Ben had completed work equal to that of the French students who received it. Eager to test his academic knowledge in practical situations, he hoped he would be able to continue the development of American design which André had noted in Richardson's work.[13] Maybeck had left New York as an eager fledgling with a sparse mustache, dressed in an ill fitting suit and stiff collar. He departed from Europe physically mature, confident of his ability, and dressed in a stylish cape pulled close to his open collared shirt and flowing silk tie. He wore a full beard, and his prominent forehead was made even higher by his thinning hair. If any doubts assailed him, he could place on his head the coveted "pot hat."

12. B. R. Maybeck MSS, "Family," C.E.D. Docs.
13. See John Mooser, "Search for American Style," *American Architect and Building News* 21(Jan. 8, 1887), p. 16. This was a recurring quest of architects of the last decades of the 19th century.

Bernard Maybeck, watercolor sketch of father's birthplace, Oelde, Germany.
Documents Collection, C.E.D.

Bernard Maybeck (ca. 1886).
Photograph courtesy of Jacomena (Mrs. Wallen) Maybeck.

II

Its Promise Should Be Fulfilled

Styles called Queen Anne and, by some, Victorian have died because of their dreadful absence of beauty. The Richardson heavy Romanesque has died out. But Trinity Church in Boston is a monument to an ideal. An ideal that the Romanesque was an unfinished art and that its promise should be fulfilled in the development of the architecture of the United States.
Bernard Maybeck—1927

Upon arriving in New York from the Ecole des Beaux-Arts, Maybeck at once started to work for the newly formed firm of Carrère and Hastings. Maybeck's school friend, Thomas Hastings, had entered the office of McKim, Mead and White after he left Paris in the spring of 1884. The following year Henry M. Flagler, friend and parishioner of Hastings' father, the Reverend T. S. Hastings, proposed that young Hastings take charge of the design and construction of a large luxury resort hotel he wished to build in Florida. Eager to take advantage of this unusual opportunity, Tom prevailed upon another McKim, Mead and White draftsman to join him in the ambitious undertaking. John Mervyn Carrère had also studied at the École des Beaux-Arts, but in a different atelier than Hastings and Maybeck.

Initially the venturesome young architects worked in a back room rented from McKim, Mead and White, but they soon outgrew these quarters and, by 1886, opened an office in lower Manhattan. Here they were situated among a row of old colonial dwellings which had been remodeled to house the many steamship companies of the time. They could look out the windows of their third floor quarters and see the Broadway skyscrapers, the newest and tallest being the ten-storied Wells Building.[1] By the time Maybeck joined the firm, designs were already underway for Flagler's hotel, the Ponce de Leon, and soon the project was expanded to include another hotel, two churches, and a large residence.

Flagler's dream was to create an American Riviera along the east coast of Florida, and it began to assume tangible form with the opening of the Ponce de Leon on January 10, 1888. The hotel and its grounds cover six acres in the heart of the old Spanish city of St. Augustine. The building, axially planned, follows the principle of functional organization which Maybeck and Hastings had learned in André's studio. The spaces are grouped into categories of use, and each group is

1. Thomas Hastings, "Reminiscence of Early Work," *American Architect and Building News*, 96, (July 7, 1909), pp. 3-4.

Hotel Ponce de Leon, St. Augustine, Florida.
American Architect and Building News, August, 1888.

Architectural features of a central dome and roof garden terraces reappear in Maybeck's later work.

The Alcazar, St. Augustine, Florida.
American Architect and Building News, August, 1888.

A pen and ink drawing by Maybeck, indicating his familiarity with Renaissance forms.

housed in a simple architectural block. Minor spaces, or circulation areas, link one block with the next. The four-storied main structure is built on three sides of a quadrangular court with the fourth side extending across the front of the building as a one-story portico with a central gateway protected by massive medieval iron gates. From within the gateway one can view Spanish tiled roofs, open galleries, roof gardens, loggias, sunny courts, cool retreats, fountains, corbels, gargoyles, and terra cotta ornament depicting the history of the city. It is evident that the young architects let their fertile imaginations run freely as they designed to fulfill a rich man's dream for the world's wealthiest families.

The interior of the hotel is no less lavish than the exteriors. Marble, oak, onyx fireplaces, Tiffany stained glass, crystal chandeliers, and murals decorate the floors, walls, and ceilings. The principal architectural feature is the central four-storied rotunda supported on great piers and carved oak caryatids. Its covering dome is penetrated by a star-shaped lantern supported by copper columns. The extensive architectural carvings came from the shop of Pottier and Stymus. Maybeck's father travelled to Florida to oversee their installation while his son supervised the construction of the building.

Applying their Beaux-Arts training to use regional materials with modern technology, the architects selected the local *coquina*, which the Spanish had used for construction and mixed it with Portland cement to make a concrete which was literally rammed into place in three-inch layers in wooden forms. Their experiment produced the first large multi-storied

Ponce de Leon Hotel, west tower and courthouse.
K. H. Cardwell photograph.

Lights in the mouths of the lion head gargoyles provide soft illumination of the courtyard at night.

Ponce de Leon Hotel, entrance detail.
K. H. Cardwell photograph.

The layering of the *coquina* concrete is visible in the shadowed areas. Mosaics, terra cottas, brick, bare bulb lighting, and Tiffany glass create rich ornamental patterns around openings in contrast with the unadorned concrete wall surfaces.

concrete building constructed in the United States.[2] In addition, their decision to leave the concrete surface unadorned revealed a sympathy for the nature of materials unappreciated by their contemporaries who chose to score concrete work with joints in imitation of masonry construction.

While Maybeck participated in the building of the Ponce de Leon and its companion hotel, the Alcazar, his specific contributions to the designs are not known. It is assumed that he and Hastings were the primary designers while Carrère handled the business details for the firm. When an article on the Florida hotels was published in 1888, sketches by both Hastings and Maybeck were used as illustrations.[3] The verbal descriptions of the hotels are unsigned, but their somewhat poetic qualities are easily identifiable as Maybeck's.

2. Carl Condit, *American Building Art* (New York: Oxford University Press, 1960), pp. 228-229.
3. "Plans of the Hotel Ponce de Leon, the Alcazar and the Methodist Episcopalian Church, St. Augustine, Fla.," *American Architect and Building News*, 24, (August 25, 1888), pp. 87-88.

He describes the Ponce de Leon as "a design in the style of the early Spanish Renaissance, which was strongly influenced by the Moorish spirit," and the materials used for the building as:

> a shell composite of light mother-of-pearl color, that glitters in the sun and turns to dark blue the shadows cast upon it by the deep reveals. In contrast with the main coloring is the bright salmon of the terra cotta, which is the material of the ornamentation.

He also pictures the interior in a lyrical vein:

> You pass...into a room as large as many an opera house. This is the great dining room. If ever dining is a fine art, it surely can be made so here, if one is fortunate enough to get a table near a window that overlooks the orange groves, sweet with flowers, brilliant with leaves and fruit, and vocal with the hum of innumerable bees.[4]

The dining room ceiling is decorated with historical pictographs and inscribed with folk sayings in Spanish. Perhaps the muralist, George W. Maynard, selected the texts: *De la mano ala boga se pierde la sopa*; *Oveja que bela bocado pierde*; and, *Remuda de pasturage haze bizerros cerdos*. But suspicion falls on a young architect whose sense of humor included the art of gentle ridicule. The proverbs translated read: "There's many a slip betwixt the cup and the lip"; "The sheep that bleats loses its mouthful"; and, "Change of pasture makes fat rams."

Whether or not Maybeck furnished ideas for or merely directed the completion of the hotel, it remains, even today in its use as a private college, a remarkable, fascinating building. And although only a decade after its innovative construction it was engulfed by the dry examples of proper good taste based on the works of Imperial Rome and Greece, the Ponce de Leon fortunately remains a rich and happy example of that creative eclecticism which shouts the joy of its creators.

4. *Ibid.*

Ponce de Leon Hotel, dining room ceiling detail.
Documents Collection, C.E.D.

Clerestory lighting through lunettes of Tiffany glass illuminates the painted ceiling of the dining room.

Ponce de Leon Hotel, arcade portico detail.
K. H. Cardwell photograph.

A terra cotta pier capital and stucco ornament foreshadow the rich patterns of the hotel's interior.

As work on the hotels and the adjacent Grace Methodist Episcopal Church (also designed for Flagler) diminished, Maybeck contemplated his future and assessed his position in the firm. His concept of medieval or Gothic design as a basic architectural expression for development and interpretation by the modern architect with his technology ran counter to the taste of John Carrère, who saw in the works of his former employers, McKim, Mead and White, an emerging style based on Renaissance forms. Even Hastings, whose philosophy of design was very similar to Maybeck's, rejected Gothic forms even for ecclesiastical structures. He interpreted Gothic architecture as an expression of a morbid, mystic life, and, influenced by his strong Protestant background, accepted early Renaissance forms, developed as a result of the Reformation, as the beginning of Modern architecture.[5] In short, the battle of the styles which had simmered at the École reached into the office.

The different direction Maybeck would move in is illustrated by a small house the firm constructed in 1888 for E. H. Johnson of Greenwich, Connecticut. It was a picturesque cottage composed with field stone and shingle walls in the prevailing mode of country house design.[6] But its design showed an unusual strength in the use of open planning and integrated volumes which H. H. Richardson had helped to introduce to American residential construction. Maybeck may have been its designer, for, although the published perspective sketch was signed by Hastings, the plan of the house appears to have been lettered by Maybeck. Moreover, the volumetric composition depicted for the Johnson cottage eventually became a hallmark of Maybeck's residential design, while later houses of the firm of Carrère and Hastings returned to a more traditional approach, formal in order and lacking the spatial continuity shown in this small building.

5. See David Gray, *Thomas Hastings, Architect* (Boston: Houghton Mifflin, 1933), for a collection of papers written by Hastings on his philosophy of design.
6. "Gate Lodge for E. H. Johnson, Esq., Alta Crest, Greenwich, Conn." *American Architect and Building News*, 24, (August 11, 1888), p. 63.

E. H. Johnson House, Alta Crest, Greenwich, Conn.
American Architect and Building News, August, 1888.

The integration of the English hall with the living spaces of a residence is more adroitly handled in this plan than in most small house designs of the period.

Perhaps the work on the Episcopal church had brought the fundamental differences in point of view to light; but there were other disparities in the firm. Both Carrère and Hastings associated with young men of wealthy New York families. Maybeck's world was dominated by men of a crafts tradition, and his complete lack of any social ambition separated him from his socially prominent colleagues even more than did his ideas. It was unlikely that he would ever become a principal in the firm, and Maybeck decided that, if he were to be his own man, he would have to establish a private practice. Impulsively, he sold his patent rights to the Pullman seat design he had perfected, and, with high hopes and little money, searched for a place away from New York where a freer social order would offer broader contacts with people ready to accept experimental and inventive ideas.

Maybeck's selection of Kansas City as a place to establish a practice was logical and practical. The Midwest, through the works of Adler and Sullivan, Burnham and Root, and William Le Baron Jenney, had begun to earn the distinction as the fountainhead of a new architecture. Moreover, of all the western communities that were expanding at the time, Kansas City, the principal railhead for the transcontinental railroads, showed the greatest activity. Maybeck also had an offer of rent-free space from his École classmate, Ambrose J. Russell. Unfortunately, Maybeck's move in 1889 coincided with the nationwide economic depression of the late 1880s. He was unable to obtain any commissions nor even find work as a draftsman.

The only evidence found of Maybeck's architectural involvement in Kansas City is a notation in the report of the jury of an entry submitted for the St. Louis City Hall Competition. The first place was awarded to the design entered by the St. Joseph, Missouri, architects Eckel and Mann. Among other winners were the entries "Faith," by Carrère and Hastings, and "Civic," by Fassett and Russell, each of which, as third and fourth place designs, received one thousand dollars. A second entry by Fassett, Russell, *and* Maybeck, with the nom de plume "Draeq," received comment but no financial award.

William Robert Ware, the professional advisor for the Competition, reported to the commissioners the merits of each design. He admired the entry "Faith" for an exterior of "monumental outline and decoration," but added that the design "fails singularly in the treatment of the windows." He commended the planning of "Civic," but found its exterior "uninteresting and monotonous." And although Ware had very harsh words for the planning and functional inconvenience of "Draeq," the entry submitted including Maybeck's name, he praised the elevations as a whole, finding them "dignified and imposing, though cut up by a strange confusion of levels of windows and cornices." He added that "the architectural treatment, especially of the rotunda, is so imposing and the central feature of the dome, with its four flanking turrents is so praiseworthy for elegance and dignity of line, that it is only fair to award this design, in spite of its grave and fundamental defects, a special honorable mention."[7]

During the Competition Maybeck had joined Fassett and Russell in their office. E. F. Fassett was president of the Kansas City Architectural Society, which sponsored a sketch club for the young draftsmen of the city. It was probably through the activities of the club that Maybeck met John White and Daniel Polk and became acquainted with their families. Not only did Maybeck's friendship with Willis Jefferson Polk, Daniel's older brother, have its beginnings in Kansas City; a meeting of greater significance was his introduction to Annie White, John's sister, who soon gained the young architect's affection.

As Ben's fondness for Annie deepened and he thought of marriage, he realized that he must make further plans for his professional career. Henry White, Annie's father, had been in California after the Civil War, and he assured Maybeck that the West was the land of the future. Reports of the architectural opportunities in the area also reached Maybeck from

Annie White, (ca. 1888).
Documents Collection, C.E.D.

the ebullient Willis Polk who was in San Francisco. Ben certainly could not ask for Annie's hand in marriage with the meager prospects of livelihood that Kansas City afforded him. So, immediately after the announcement of the awards of the Competition for the St. Louis City Hall, he boarded a train to California.

Upon arriving in San Francisco, Maybeck went to the office of A. Page Brown, where Willis Polk was employed.[8] Brown had no openings, but promised Maybeck a position within six months. Consequently, he took a temporary job with the firm of Wright and Sanders, who were busily engaged in work

7. Wm. R. Ware, "St. Louis City Hall Competition," *Inland Architect and News Record*, 15, (March 1890), pp. 35-37.
8. Accounts vary, some say he went to work for A. Page Brown. In conversation with the author Maybeck said that he worked for Wright and Sanders and was promised work in Brown's office.

for the Union Pacific Railroad. Late in the spring Maybeck was sent to Salt Lake City to supervise the construction of a company project. While engaged in this work, he designed a lady's fan with variously shaped openings and a quasi-mechanical arrangement for pushing air in one direction only. The drawing, patented by Maybeck in Salt Lake City in May 1890, is the first documented work of his design.[9]

Maybeck's patent was not the first nor the last indication of his interest in invention. He had designed, perfected, and sold his idea of a reversible coach seat, which in later years gained widespread use in trains and streetcars. His patent drawing for the fan screened his primary interest in the invention of a workable wing detail for an ornithopter. Maybeck grew up in a time when new inventions had the power to stir the mind out of all proportion to their value. And he viewed invention as adaptation, as change and improvement. His later devices of air-exhausting chimney caps, built-in range tops, and lightweight concrete roofs were studied experiments and, as such, inventions.

Maybeck assigned half of the patent rights for the fan invention to Annie White, who had remained foremost in his mind since he had left for the West. At the conclusion of his work in Salt Lake City, and with prospects of work in A. Page Brown's office, he journeyed to Kansas City to offer Annie the unconventional wedding gift of his patent. It was a tangible statement by the young designer, who was still short of money, that he intended to share equally the fruits of his talents. Annie fully understood his offering, and their marriage in Kansas City on October 29, 1890, marked the beginning of sixty-five years of devotion and companionship that enabled Bernard Maybeck to make the most of his creative ability. Once again, but this time accompanied by his bride "Doddy," Maybeck boarded the train en route to San Francisco.[10]

9. U.S. Patent Office, *Official Gazette* (July 22, 1890).
10. "Doddy," for Annie, was a White family childhood name of endearment.

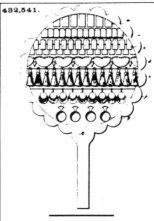

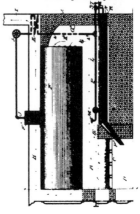

Patent drawing, *Official Gazette*, 1890, U. S. Patent Office.

Maybeck's patent drawing for a reversible train seat has not been located by the author. It is possible that since he sold his rights to the design, it may have been patented under another name.

Willis Polk, pen and ink drawing, 1900. View of San Francisco
from the roof of the Mark Hopkins mansion, looking southeast.
Documents Collection, C.E.D.

28

San Francisco in 1890 was a city of 300,000 people with another 100,000 inhabitants in the communities ringing the edge of the Bay. Robert Louis Stevenson, in a description written in 1882, captured the magnetizing qualities of the city in his article "San Francisco—A Modern Cosmopolis":

> A great city covers the sand hills on the west, a growing town lies along the muddy shallows of the east; steamboats pass continually between them from before sunrise til the small hours of the morning; lines of great seagoing ships lie at anchor; colors fly upon the islands; and from all around the hum of corporate life, of beaten bells, and steam, and running carriages, goes cheerily abroad in the sunshine.... The town is essentially not Anglo-Saxon; still more not American. The Yankee and the Englishman find themselves alike in a strange country.... In the course of a generation this city and its suburbs have arisen..such a swiftness of increase, as with an overgrown youth, suggests a corresponding swiftness of destruction.[11]

San Francisco was a city that had never been a village or a town. The gold rush, the silver bonanza, and the opening of the West by the railroad brought succeeding waves of people, and among them trade, finance and industry developed. The expanding economy of the city produced a wealthy society that first sought entertainment and then aspired to culture. It drew people who were young, aggressive, and cosmopolitan, a fact borne out by the biographical information of its architects. Of twenty men listing themselves as architects in the *California Architect and Building News* of 1890, none had been born in San Francisco, although four of them had arrived as children. The remainder were between the ages of twenty and thirty-five upon their arrival and represented such diverse national origins as Switzerland, Ireland, Scotland, England, Canada, France, Germany, Russia, and the eastern United States. For each of these twenty men there were two more, untrained and unskilled, who called themselves architects. Their antecedents are not known, but they were undoubtedly as young and from as varied backgrounds.

The influential architectural offices were directed by men who had arrived in the sixties and seventies. For many years the profession remained divided between established practitioners and "newcomers" whose number had been increasing since the completion of the transcontinental railroad. John Wright and George H. Sanders, for whom Maybeck had gone to Salt Lake City, were typical of the organized professionals.[12] The firm's practice was widespread in northern California where they designed many public buildings in the Romanesque and Gothic Revival styles. Their work was not distinguished, but in a period of excess their restraint was commendable. The single established professional from the École des Beaux-Arts was Albert Pissis, who built well proportioned Classical Revival buildings. Typical of his work is the Hibernia Bank Building (1891) at McAllister and Jones Streets which, at the inception of its construction, won the praise of both old and new members of the San Francisco architectural fraternity.

Not always to the liking of the established architects, young newcomers began to leave their mark on the city's architecture. Ernest Coxhead, an Englishman, came in 1889. He had located originally in Los Angeles but soon moved to San Francisco. Coxhead had attended the Royal Academy and had become an Associate of the Royal Institute of British Architects in 1886. His best work consisted of small churches and residential designs which drew heavily on medieval English precedents. The most successful of the newcomers was A. Page Brown. Born in New York City in 1859, he was educated at Cornell University, after which he apprenticed in the office of McKim, Mead and White. In private practice, he designed Clio and Whig Halls (1890-93) and the Museum of Historic Art (1885-89) at Princeton University. He came to San Francisco at the age of thirty to work for the Charles Crocker family, gathering about him a staff of young men whose names would be intimately connected with the development of San Francisco architecture. Included among them were Willis Polk, Charles M. Rousseau, A. C. Schweinfurth, Edward H. Swain, and, ultimately, Bernard R. Maybeck.

When Annie and Ben arrived in California, they set up housekeeping in a small apartment in Oakland. But the work for the Crocker estate that A. Page Brown had expected had not yet materialized, and Maybeck was faced with the problem of finding immediate employment. With his usual directness, he started at the foot of San Francisco's main thoroughfare, Market Street, intent on taking the first job to be had. A "Draftsman Wanted" sign in the office window of the Charles M. Plum Company was the first that he saw, and he entered

---

11. Cited in Katharine D. Osbourne, *Robert Louis Stevenson in California* (Chicago: McClurg, 1911), pp. 53-55.
12. Wright and Sanders had been instrumental in establishing the San Francisco Chapter of the American Institute of Architects in 1881.

to make an application. The employer asked for references and experience to which Maybeck confidently answered with sketches he drew on the spot. They convinced Mr. Plum of his ability and he began work in the drafting room that afternoon.

The Charles M. Plum Company, which made custom furniture and designed interiors for the carriage trade, lost no time in making Maybeck its principal designer. His colored sketches of interior furnishings for the Nob Hill clientele brought immediate approval. The most complete installation of furnishings made by the company during Maybeck's stay was in the East Bay community of Piedmont for Francis Marion Smith, nicknamed "Borax" Smith after the chemical which contributed to his fortune.

Maybeck was considered by Mr. Plum to be an excellent designer, but his effectiveness as a salesman in the store was of lesser value. His lack of interest in commercial enterprise is illustrated by his experience with a customer who admired a bolt of fine material and asked for its price. Maybeck sold it for its tagged price of six dollars and fifty cents. It was a grave error, as he later learned from Mr. Plum; the bolt he sold contained over six yards of cloth and the tagged price was the price per yard.[13]

Maybeck stayed with the Plum firm for over a year. By then the volume of work in A. Page Brown's office made it possible for Maybeck to return to architectural projects. Brown's principal work was the Crocker Building, which was well along in the design stage when Maybeck joined the staff in 1891. Evidence of Maybeck's participation exists, however, in the detail of the ornament devised for the frieze below the cornice treatment. Here the letter "A" was worked in flowery form, another comment by Ben that Annie was a partner in his efforts.

In 1892 and 1893 Brown's office was engaged in three architectural competitions: a Mission style design for the California building at the World's Columbian Exposition of 1893 in Chicago, a building for the California Midwinter Exposition the following year in Golden Gate Park, and a design for the French Hospital of San Francisco. The office designs won the first two competitions. Maybeck's own designs which he had submitted for the California Building and the French Hospital were less successful.[14] But if he failed to place, he did not fail to arrest the imagination of at least one admirer. A local correspondent of the *American Architect and Building News* said that if Maybeck's design for the California Building had been accepted, it would at once "conjure up sweet memories of blue skies, eternal sunshine, the dark olive green of nature, woods, and golden balls of fruit, all peacefully lying in the Western sun."[15] It is possible that this ornate praise was written by the biased Willis Polk; but whoever the author, he caught the essence of Maybeck's eclecticism which interpreted the spirit of Mission architecture without copying the details of a specific historic building.

Maybeck's contribution to Brown's design for the Columbian Exposition can be judged by the motif of the central dome which had as a prototype the one he or Hastings had designed for the Ponce de Leon Hotel. The nationally known critic, Montgomery Schuyler, wrote favorably of the building

13. B. R. Maybeck MSS, "Edgar Ormsby," C.E.D. Docs.
14. Unfortunately, these designs have been lost with the exception of one plan drawing of the French Hospital, which was published in *California Architect and Building News* (Jan. 1893), p. 7.
15. "San Francisco," *American Architect and Building News*, 35, (March 19, 1892), p. 187. Reference by courtesy of H. Kirker.

Crocker Building, San Francisco, 1891, A. Page Brown, Architect. Bancroft Library, UCB.

in the July 1893 issue of *Architectural Record*, pointing out that its dome, "the central and dominating feature,"

> gives the greatest architectural value to the subordinate parts, from which also in turn it derives much of its own impressiveness. While a quite original feature, it is distinctly in the color of the architecture it crowns....The roof garden that fills out the angles of the square assists the expression, at once festal and tropical, of the architecture, and completes one of the most attractive and appropriate of all the buildings in Jackson Park.

Maybeck was sent to Chicago to supervise the construction of the California Building. His reports of the Fair were laudatory; he liked the scale and vigor of its buildings, feeling as did many of the architects of the period that the Americans had demonstrated an ability in design comparable to their European contemporaries.

California Building, colored lithograph, World's Columbian Exposition, Chicago, 1893, A. Page Brown, Architect. Documents Collection, C.E.D.

A comparison of the central dome motif with that of the Ponce de Leon Hotel reveals many similarities.

California Building, "Roof Garden."
California at the World's Exposition in 1893, 1894.

The roof garden restaurant was one of the Fair's most popular eating spaces. The ornamented capitals of the piers and the coved eaves repeat a decorative scheme used in the Ponce de Leon Hotel.

In 1894 Brown's office was commissioned to design the Church of the New Jerusalem at Lyon and Washington Streets in the Pacific Heights district of the city. The persons connected with its construction are as interesting as its architectural features. Among them were Joseph Worcester, pastor and amateur architect; William Keith, noted painter of the California landscape; Bruce Porter, artist and designer of stained glass; and A. C. Schweinfurth, architect and draftsman who assisted Maybeck with the design.

The Reverend Joseph Worcester had more than an amateur's interest in the construction of the church. A subscriber to the leading architectural journals of the day, he maintained scrapbooks that reveal a strong interest in Romanesque architecture and in the works of H. H. Richardson and Bruce Price. And while some building elements are said to follow sketches made by Bruce Porter of a village chapel near Verona, the simplicity and natural decorative features must have been designed at the pastor's request. In Worcester's words:

The church is extremely simple, massive and its heavy tile covered roof supported by simple trusses of madrone trees with the bark on. The only architectural feature of the exterior is the bell-tower with its marble column and surmounting cross. The narrow window in the tower is filled with leaded glass that was part of Westminister Abbey hundreds of years ago. The side of which the tower forms a part is south, looking down upon a large garden, with grass and seats and a masonry basin for birds. It is surrounded by a wall which quite secludes it from the street, and through it you pass to enter the church.[16]

The church interior was furnished with handsome chairs, their seats woven of local "tule" grass. On the walls were paintings by William Keith depicting the cycle of nature through planting, harvesting, and ploughing in preparation for planting again. The furnishings and the use of the native California madrone tree as knee braces for the open framed roof trusses were symbolic for the church members of the Presence of Nature and the Omnipotence of God. The Church of the New Jerusalem, familiarly called the Swedenborgian Church, combined direct structural expression, use of native materials, and consciously developed symbolism to create a picturesque, harmonious whole. The image that the building conveyed was unique for urban San Francisco, although its emphasis on craftsmanship gained admirers from the west coast Arts and Crafts followers who subscribed to the dignity of labor, the appreciation of nature, and the simplicity of architectural form.

16. Cited in Othmar Tobisch, *Historical Recollections, The Swedenborgian Church of San Francisco* (San Francisco: 1950), p. 10.

Church of the New Jerusalem, interior view, San Francisco,
1894, A. Page Brown, Architect.
Documents Collection, C.E.D.

The interior furnishings were most likely designed in the
architect's office. Maybeck used similar rush bottom chairs in
furnishing the Phoebe Apperson Hearst retreat "Wyntoon,"
and in the W. P. Rieger house.

The Swedenborgian Church marked a change in, or at least a diversion from, the normal office design. Several years earlier, Brown's office had caught the attention of *The Wave*, a San Francisco weekly of social comment with editors and contributors which included the nationally known writers Frank Norris and Ambrose Bierce. Their caustic comments ranged from social satire to architectural aesthetics. "The dreadful order of A. Page Brown," the magazine asserted,

> is the designation attached to the round cornered structures rising here and there through the city. The vogue of this gentleman is prodigious and disheartening, his structures monuments to his incapacity, and prominent disfigurements to the city. Just as though home talent was not a sufficient plague, some malignant divinity let loose this exponent of crinkling shingles, round corners and flat windows upon us. The Towne House, at the corner of Taylor and California, is the crowning effort of the A. Page Brown School.[17]

However, the editors of *The Wave* had not reckoned with the fact that the A. N. Towne house had a stout defender in Willis Polk of Brown's office. Polk, whose firey tongue would become as well-known as his architecture, answered immediately in the *Architectural News*.

> Perhaps *The Wave* is a good reflector of the depraved taste of an indiscriminating public, or otherwise the above paragraph would not have appeared, and it is reprinted in *The News* simply to remind the egregious ass who wrote it that, had it appeared in a paper with any claims to respectability, it would have been the very essence of ignorant criticism based upon an utter lack of the simplest knowledge of architecture.[18]

The Wave's criticism of the Towne house had, in fact, helped precipitate the publication of the *Architectural News,* as did also the policies of the local architectural journal. The *California Architect and Building News* was owned by members of the San Francisco Chapter of the American Institute of Architects. They used it to advantage in the publication of designs by their members. The newcomers who had not joined the chapter found that their articles and sketches were not readily accepted for publication. This policy irked Willis Polk, Ernest Coxhead, and W. Redmore Ray, who had contributed drawings and articles to eastern magazines. Their solution was to start an architectural journal in competition with the local publication.

Although the *Architectural News* was shortlived, it recorded the scope and tenor of the newcomers' interests in national architectural news and ideas. The editorial comment of the first issue in November, 1890 dealt with the design of houses for the workingman and stated the editors' preference for this type of commission because "such a house could be expressive of the way of life of the laborer, direct and unaffected by the copying of architectural forms of another era which had lost their meaning and distinctiveness." Articles on the architecture of the missions of California by the staff, "Church Planning" by Ernest Coxhead, "Proportion and Formation" by W. Redmore Ray, and news from Boston, New York, Chicago, and Kansas City filled the pages of the new magazine. The name of Maybeck appeared in the prospectus of features for future issues. He was scheduled to do a series of articles on his translation of the German book *Der Stil* by Gottfried Semper; but the *Architectural News* failed after its third issue and Maybeck's articles were never printed.

The vociferous Polk was the editor of the young magazine, and, although his publication failed to survive the year, he ended in convincing the editors of *The Wave* that he and A. Page Brown were architects worthy of note. The Christmas issue of *The Wave* carried appreciative biographic sketches of both men and even recanted enough to say, in reference to a series of residences being developed by Brown for the Crocker Estate, "There is a peculiar appropriateness about this new style, and it might possibly become typical of San Francisco architecture."[19]

The newcomers in architecture, however, were not the leaders in any Arts and Crafts revival. The activities of these younger men centered, rather, in the Sketch Club of San Francisco which they had organized for discussion of design theory, for improvement of sketching abilities, and for general good fellowship. Ernest Coxhead and Willis Polk were its nominal leaders, and though the members shared a common idealism, they were diverse in their talents and their architectural designs remained individualistic.

17. *The Wave*, San Francisco (October 1890), p. 4.
18. *Architectural News*, San Francisco (November 1890), p. 5.
19. *The Wave* (December 1891), pp. 33, 34. The earliest published biographical sketch of W. J. Polk that the author has been able to locate. In later years Polk had a tendency to exaggerate his experiences and their importance.

Coxhead, Schweinfurth, and Maybeck—more experienced and better trained than the younger group—formed a natural friendship. In their work are found both similar and diverse elements of architectural expression congruent with their individual philosophies and experiences. Coxhead's domestic work reflected the revival of the Jacobean and Queen Anne revitalization of English domestic architecture begun by Phillip Webb and his contemporaries.[20] Schweinfurth was one of the first to find successful inspiration from the Spanish colonial past, as Richardson had done with Romanesque forms. Maybeck, on the other hand, applied the rationalism of the Beaux-Arts in designs that not only recognized the nature of the structure and material employed but also sought form expressive of the function to be served. There was no single strong influence from any one particular area that directed the development of architecture in the Bay Region in the 1890s. The work of the newcomers drew its greatest strength from the mixture of social and aesthetic ideas that abounded in its young heterogeneous practitioners.

20. Coxhead's work compares favorably with that of his American contemporaries. Cf. J. C. Stevens and A. W. Cobb, *Examples of American Domestic Architecture* (New York: 1889), and George Sheldon, *Artistic Country Seats* (New York: 1886).

J. D. Grant house, Burlingame, A. Page Brown, Architect. *American Architect and Building News*, June, 1895.

This bungalow design from Brown's office contrasts sharply with the Colonial Revival details of the A. N. Towne house built some five years earlier. Maybeck's Laura G. Hall house, built in 1896, was remarkably similar in form to this published sketch.

Hearst Hall, view from stage towards entrance.
Documents Collection, C.E.D.

III

Not For The Glorification Of The Architect

An architectural plan is not primarily made for the glorification of the architect. Neither is it a matter of elaborating buildings senselessly as a tribute to the vanity of human nature. If this were all, modern democracy would not hesitate to eliminate such an art by the simple expedient of neglect.

Bernard Maybeck—1917

At the end of 1892 the Maybecks moved from their apartment in Oakland to a small house located a half-mile north of the state university. Berkeley in the 1890s was primarily a university town. But near San Francisco Bay, a picturesque village housed the families of commercial fishermen who operated from its simple waterfront facilities. Grassy hills at the east were dotted with California Live Oak and rock outcroppings. Clear streams flowed in cool canyons hidden by native laurels and dense brush. Farms that supplied the daily needs of the nearby metropolitan areas of Oakland and San Francisco were scattered between the hills and the shore. The business district lay directly west of the university, which was set against the eastern foothills. To the north and the south of the campus were a number of Victorian country cottages. The majority of these were occupied by university personnel and students, though an increasing number of houses were being built in the area for the business and professional men who commuted to San Francisco by train and ferryboat. Maybeck was one of them.

During one crossing in the summer of 1894, through a chance meeting with Frank Soulé, Jr., Maybeck was presented with an opportunity that profoundly affected his professional career. Professor Soulé, who headed the Civil Engineering College at the University of California, told Maybeck that the newly formed Department of Instrumental Drawing was in need of an instructor of descriptive geometry. He was familiar with Maybeck's knowledge of the subject and urged him to

Bernard Ralph Maybeck, Instructor in Drawing.
Illustrated History of the University of California, 1895.

37

Berkeley, California, (1896).
Archives, Bancroft Library, UCB.

View over the campus to the Golden Gate from the eastern foothills.

apply for the position. Maybeck hoped to form an independent practice, but as the work in Brown's office on the Swedenborgian church was nearing completion and teaching would provide a source of income while he established his office, he applied for the position. He was appointed instructor in drawing for the fall semester of 1894. This was the first of a series of events linking Maybeck and the University. The long relationship culminated a decade later in the establishment of a complete curriculum in architecture.[1]

1. University of California, *President's Reports* (Berkeley: 1894).

When Maybeck began his teaching he encountered a number of engineering students whose interests were primarily architectural. For their benefit he instituted an independent, informal course in architectural design which met in his own home. John Bakewell, Edward Bennett, Arthur Brown, Jr., Harvey Wiley Corbett, Lewis Hobart, G. Albert Lansburgh, Julia Morgan, and Loring P. Rixford came to learn. The course combined the theory of design with a period of practical application during which the students worked on the additions to the Maybeck house on Berryman Street.[2]

2. John Bakewell MSS, "Correspondence," C.E.D. Docs.

University of California Campus, 1895.
O. V. Lange, photographer, Bancroft Library, U.C.B.

View from the north to the central campus area.

B. R. Maybeck house, Berryman and Grove Streets, (1892-1902).
The Simple Home, 1904.

The small, original one-story cottage to which Maybeck made additions can be identified by the double hung windows in the lower left corner of the building.

These students were the first of a large number of young people whom Maybeck urged to complete their architectural studies at the École des Beaux-Arts. It might have been to their advantage if Maybeck had been in a position to establish an atelier of his own and had expounded his beliefs. In his independent, questioning attitude Maybeck felt he had been able to ascertain creative principles of design from the analysis of buildings of historic periods. He did not foresee that students might not analyze what was taught as he had done, but would simply accept the training of the École as doctrine. Nor was he aware of the gradual erosion of the academic tradition of rational thinking that began in the ateliers soon after the death of Louis-Jules André in 1890. However, all of his students who went to the Beaux-Arts became leading architectural practitioners of the area within a few years. But only one, Julia Morgan, somewhat followed Maybeck—achieving at times in her work the same direct structural and expressive form that marks the best of his architecture.[3]

Besides his experience with teaching in Berkeley, Maybeck had an opportunity to impart his ideas about architecture through the newly formed Mark Hopkins Institute of Art. In 1893 Edward Searles had proposed that the University art school and the San Francisco Art Association, which had maintained a school of design since 1872, work together in administering a combined school in San Francisco.[4] Searles was anxious to put to good use the Mark Hopkins mansion which he had inherited from his wife, the former Mrs. Hopkins. Agreement was reached the following year, and the new quarters adjacent to the downtown area made it possible to open classes in drawing and sculpture to apprenticed architects and draftsmen at reduced rates. However, one or two energetic students of the school gathered the support of draftsmen in various city offices, and they agitated instead for a program in architecture. As a consequence, Bernard Maybeck was appointed as Director of the Architectural Section of the Institute in 1895. He chose as voluntary assistants H. T. Bestor for instruction in architectural sketching, George W. Percy of Percy and Hamilton for lectures on the nature and

3. After her return from the École, Morgan never worked for Maybeck, although they kept in close professional contact. The statement is based on an interview by the author with Walter Steilberg, a long-time associate of Morgan.
4. Wm. C. Jones, *Illustrated History of the University of California* (San Francisco: 1895), p. 222.

use of materials in building construction, and George Sanders to lead the class in architectural history. Maybeck himself taught a course titled "Practical Architecture and Design."

It was an excellent staff drawn from established professional men whom Maybeck had come to know and admire. Bestor was the new editor of the *California Architect and Building News*, which, under his direction, had begun to overcome some of its provincialism. Percy had supervised the construction of the initial portions of Stanford University and had gone on to design for the Stanford campus some of the first major structures in reinforced concrete in California. George Sanders had a broad interest in history and encouraged students to make their own investigations of the development of architecture. And, as reported in the *Architect and Builder*, August 1895: "The department under the general direction of Mr. Maybeck, who has for some years been practicing in this city where his taste is evident in some of the finest building, has the rare faculty of imparting his own enthusiasm to the students."[5]

Maybeck taught at the University and at the Institute until he left for Europe in 1897. When he returned in 1898, he was appointed to the position of Instructor in Architecture in the Department of Instrumental Drawing and Engineering Design. This was the University's first official recognition of architecture as a professional field, and the appointment regularized the informal teaching that Maybeck had been engaged in from the beginning of his employment. He continued teaching at the University until the spring of 1903, when it was proposed that the Department of Drawing offer a full curriculum in architecture with instruction given in the office of the Supervising Architect, John Galen Howard. Whether his resignation was because of the press of his practice, or because of the appointment of Howard as chairman of the newly named Department of Architecture, has never been determined.

In the first years in Berkeley, Maybeck made a start on an independent professional practice. His commissions were houses for friends and neighbors. It is impossible to know how many early houses he designed in Berkeley; the San Francisco fire of 1906 destroyed the drawings and office records, and the Berkeley fire of 1923 destroyed some of the buildings. At least four residences survived, however; built in the north campus area, they are described in a later chapter. While at the University Maybeck joined a group of young artists, writers, and instructors who met regularly for discussions with distinguished men of various professions. These included William Keith, the painter, and John and Joseph Le Conte, both scientists. For various members of the campus community of artists and scholars, Maybeck completed twenty or more projects prior to his leaving the University. Unfortunately, only a few drawings, photographs, and records of these exist.

Soon after the Maybecks bought the house on Berryman Street Maybeck, with the help of his students, began enlarging it. By 1895 they had added the drafting room which he used as his office. When Annie's father, Henry White, became ill and was forced to retire from his teaching position in Kansas City in 1895, the Maybecks invited all of the Whites to come and live with them in Berkeley. John White, an experienced architectural draftsman, would be a great help in the work Ben had undertaken. And Mark, the younger brother, could continue his education at the University. Also, Annie had begun to make a collection of her husband's ideas on architecture and hoped to attend classes to improve her ability in writing.

Late in 1895, Phoebe Apperson Hearst, who had always taken an active interest in the academic welfare of the University, told its president, Martin Kellogg, that she would like to have a building constructed as a memorial to her husband, George Hearst. Senator Hearst had made his fortune in the mining industry of the West, and Mrs. Hearst felt that a handsome building to house the Department of Mining would be a fitting tribute to his memory. President Kellogg contacted the Engineering College, and instructor-architect Maybeck was assigned the job of preparing a drawing of the proposed building. Maybeck had little time to prepare an adequate sketch, but, with the help of draperies and potted geraniums from his own house to frame his drawing, he made a presentation that he hoped would please Mrs. Hearst.[6] She was delighted by what she saw and wanted to be shown immediately where such a building could be erected on the campus.

5. *Architect and Builder*, San Francisco (August 1895).
6. Kenneth H. Cardwell and Wm. C. Hays, "Fifty Years from Now," *California Monthly*, 44, (April 1954), pp. 20-26.

A less thoughtful man than Maybeck might have proposed a site for the building. But Maybeck's prime concern was the total development of the University grounds. Soon after his arrival at the University he had taken an interest in campus expansion, discussing with his colleagues the need for a general plan. The University had had a landscape plan drawn in 1862 by Frederick Law Olmsted, but with the rapid increase in enrollment toward the end of the century, new buildings were already beginning to spread beyond the limits of Olmsted's pastoral siting.[7] Maybeck feared new construction undertaken without a plan for total development would mutilate the natural beauty of the landscape. Thus, when he was presented with the opportunity to select a site for the Mining Building, he saw a chance to argue for the creation of such a plan. His agitation resulted in the formation of a committee composed of himself, Professor William Carey Jones, and Regent J. B. Reinstein—the latter two both graduates of the University and past presidents of its Alumni Association. The committee was charged to investigate the ways a general plan could be obtained.

7. Olmsted's design was for the private College of California, a precursor to the University of California, Berkeley.

PROPOSED PLAN FOR STATE UNIVERSITY BUILDINGS AT BERKELEY.

(From a colored perspective by B. R. Maybeck, instructor in architectural drawing at the University, intended to illustrate Regent Reinstein's ideas. The proposition as made to the entire board met with unanimous approval, and it is probable that an effort will be made in the near future to put it into execution.)

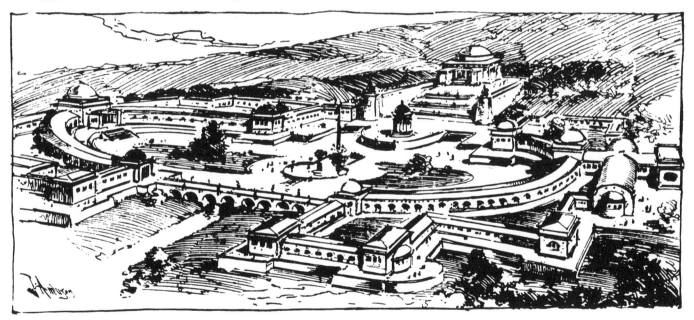

"Proposed Plan for State University Buildings at Berkeley."
San Francisco Examiner, April 30, 1896.

Maybeck's drawing is for a much smaller development than the program for the Competition eventually specified. Maybeck's great terraces, stairways, retaining walls, and bridges indicate the conflict between monumental symmetry and the natural sloping terrain which plagued most of the designers of the Competition entries.

Maybeck spoke in favor of securing the services of the best architect and landscape gardener of the country to design the plan. Since the laws governing the University required competitive bidding for work to be done on the campus, holding a competition seemed a suitable way to find the best designer. The committee solicited universities, professional organizations, and individual architects on a nation-wide basis, asking for opinions on the merits of architectural competitions. The replies ranged from total condemnation to qualified approval. Louis Sullivan regarded the competition idea as wholly fatuous. He declaimed "the assumption that you, I or anyone else can draw intelligent and just conclusions from a set of sketches submitted in competition," calling it "as false as it is specious and tempting."[8] Carrère and Hastings, whose answer was typical of the leading practitioners, suggested that "the best results will be obtained by inviting a certain number of architects of well-established ability and reputation to submit drawings and paying them a fixed sum for their drawings; then allowing all other architects not so invited to compete if they so desire," providing them "a certain number of prizes for an inducement."[9] The Regents of the University decided they were legally bound to advertise for plans and, accordingly, framed a two-stage competition. The first stage, which was to award ample prizes, would be open to all architects on a world-wide basis; the second stage would be a closed competition among the prize winners.

Maybeck has been identified with the idea of the plan for the University from its inception, and in the prospectus for the Competition his ideas were dominant. "The University," it states,

> is a city that is to be created—a City of Learning—in which there is to be no sordid or inharmonious feature. There are to be no definite limitations of cost, materials or style. All is to be left to the unfettered discretion of the designer. He is asked to record his conception of an ideal home for a university, assuming time and resources to be unlimited. He is to plan for centuries to come. There will doubtless be developments of science in the future that will impose new duties on the University, and require alterations in the detailed arrangement of its buildings, but it is believed to be possible to secure a comprehensive plan in harmony with the universal principles of architectural art.[10]

The aim of the plan was to simplify the complex function of a university, accommodating all of its many needs in a functional and artistic, as well as economical, way. It was to produce a convenient and beautiful arrangement suitable to the greatest number of students, while at the same time permitting growth. Maybeck did not expect perfection in the development of the University, but he thought the earnest and serious efforts of those responsible for its growth would in time "awaken love in the hearts of the men that behold it."[11]

Maybeck's writing in connection with the Competition revealed an aspect of his architectural philosophy which remained constant throughout his career. It set forth his conception of beauty as an attribute of ideal form, unobtainable by any single designer. A building approached ideal form by the combination of its pleasing shape, its effectiveness in fitting human needs, and its successful expression of human aspirations. With the premise that all historic architectures were beautiful to the degree of the universality of their abstract forms, Maybeck reasoned that there were universal principles of art. Therefore by using these principles the artists and architects of each succeeding generation could refine and interpret functional and expressive forms, coming closer to the attainment of ideal form and absolute beauty.

On October 24, 1896, a letter from Phoebe A. Hearst was presented to the Board of Regents of the University of California. It read: "I am deeply impressed with the proposition now before the Board of Regents, to determine upon a comprehensive and permanent plan for the buildings and grounds of the University of California, on the site of Berkeley and I heartily approve of the idea.[12] Completely convinced through Maybeck's enthusiasm and earnestnest of the need of the plan, she offered to pay for the Competition expenses and to provide the prize money with the proviso that Maybeck be released from his teaching duties for two years to prepare the Competition and to facilitate proper understanding of the ideas behind it in the eastern states and in Europe. The first step Maybeck took was to obtain the services of Julien Guadet, the brilliant École des Beaux-Arts theorist, to draft the architectural program for the buildings. His second step

---

8. "University Competition," *California Architect and Building News*, 17, (November 1896), pp. 122-23.
9. *Ibid.*
10. University of California. *The International Competition for the Phoebe Hearst Architectural Plan* (San Francisco: 1899), p. 10.
11. Bernard Maybeck, "The Planning of a University," *Blue and Gold* (University of California Yearbook: 1900), pp. 17-20.
12. University of California, *The International Competition* (San Francisco: 1899), p. 6.

THE INTERNATIONAL COMPETITION FOR THE PHOEBE ❧❧ HEARST ARCHITECTVRAL PLAN FOR THE VNIVERSITY OF CALIFORNIA ❧❧

Cover and title page, *The International Competition for the Phoebe Hearst Architectural Plan for the University of California,* (1899).

Maybeck's colophon "A" serves to identify him as the designer of the book's type face.

was to name a jury, and, with the aid of an informal poll of leading architects, he selected such internationally known figures as J. C. Pascal of France, Paul Wallot of Germany, Norman Shaw of England, and Walter Cook of the United States. Aiding these eminent architects in their deliberations would be the University's representative, Regent J. B. Reinstein.

In the spring of 1897, with the Whites in charge of the Berryman Street house and John in charge of the office work, Bernard and Annie Maybeck, accompanied by Regent Reinstein, left for New York and Europe to complete the arrangements for the Competition. The Maybecks took quarters in Paris where Bernard could distribute information about the Competition and at the same time aid Guadet in the preparation of the program. While in Paris he found time to visit various ateliers of the Beaux-Arts, where several of "his boys" of the Berkeley seminars were studying. John Bakewell and Edward Bennett had been admitted in 1895, Harvey Wiley Corbett in 1896, and Arthur Brown in the second class of 1897. Julia Morgan was also in Paris and Maybeck aided her in gaining admission to the École—a precedent-shattering event because she was the first woman to be accepted.

Maybeck also found both time to attend lectures on art history given at the École du Louvre and to accompany Morgan to the lectures given by Guadet on theory of architecture at the École des Beaux-Arts. At one lecture when Professor Guadet entered, the class rose as was customary and began applauding. The applause prevented him from beginning his lecture, and one by one the students filed out still applauding.[13] They were protesting one of Guadet's recent programs for the design of a factory. They felt that the study of a utilitarian structure was beneath the dignity of an architectural student. The tenor of student opinion reflected the work in the ateliers where the delight in ostentatious design had begun to supercede interest in rational academic theory.

Maybeck was required to travel extensively on Competition business, one of his duties being to visit the jurors to convey pertinent information to them. Annie, in her role as secretary, prepared reports of their progress and made arrangements for their travel. They visited many of the major cities of Europe to distribute details of the program and site to architects who wished to participate in the Competition.

In England, jurist Norman Shaw graciously invited the Maybecks to be guests in his Hampstead house. Maybeck saw much of Shaw's work and was particularly impressed by the quality of his early designs. He visited Oxford and traveled on to Glasgow to visit his École classmate, Robert Sandilands. The Glasgow School of Art, the major work of Charles Rennie Mackintosh, was under construction, but it is doubtful that Maybeck became aware of the Glasgow group. He renewed his acquaintance with École classmates Enrico Ristori in Florence and Rudolph Dick in Vienna. Dick took him to see recent developments of the Art Nouveau in Austria. Although the designs fascinated him, their lack of reference to traditional forms and their abstractions of plant life evoked a critical comment; he dismissed the style as fashionable and ephemeral.[14]

13. B. R. Maybeck, KPFA Tape, 1953, C.E.D. Docs.
14. Conversations between the author and Maybeck.

Bernard and Annie ended their travels late in September of 1898 in time to prepare for the judging of the initial stage of the Competition at Antwerp. Annie was expecting the birth of their first child. Maybeck was nonetheless completely engrossed with detailed preparations for the judging of the one hundred and five Competition entries and the more tedious responsibility of securing accomodations for arriving jurors. The casual manner with which Maybeck accepted the birth of a child contrasted greatly with the energy and attention he focused on the birth of an architectural project. Fortunately, friends traveling with Mrs. Hearst, who was present for the judging, took over the duties of preparing and arranging for Annie's confinement and, without interruption of the Competition, a son was born. Meanwhile the jury had met and selected eleven finalists, all of whom were invited by Mrs. Hearst to come to Berkeley and inspect the site at her expense prior to submitting their drawings for the second stage of the Competition.

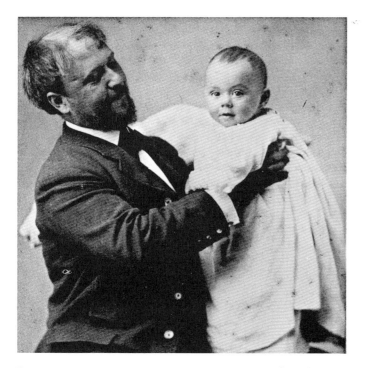

Bernard Maybeck and son Wallen White Maybeck, (1899). Documents Collection, C.E.D.

The four architects of the jury for the final stage of the Competition arrived in San Francisco on the morning of August 30, 1899, prepared to review the drawings.[15] Joined by Regent J. B. Reinstein and aided by Maybeck, they spent the following week in deliberation, in the Ferry Building where the drawings had been hung, as well as across the Bay on the campus site. On September 7 they reached their decision and awarded the first prize of ten thousand dollars to École-trained Émile Bénard of Paris. Second place was awarded to Howells, Stokes, and Hornbostel of New York, followed by Despradelle and Codman of Boston, Howard and Cauldwell of New York, and Lord, Hewlett and Hull, also of New York.

Maybeck was pleased with the decision of the jury. He could see in the Bénard design a general plan conforming to his own conception of a growing and developing building complex generally contained by the two natural water-courses of Strawberry Creek. The grand scale and rich architectural detail delighted him in much the same manner as had the World's Columbian Exposition. But responses to the results of the Competition were not all enthusiastic. A group of local architects felt strongly that commissions for buildings at the University should have been given to local practitioners. Led by English-trained B. J. S. Cahill and a German art critic, Max Jughaendel (possibly a pseudonym of Willis Polk), a newspaper campaign ridiculed the size, expense, and foreign style of the winning design. Even if the entire complex were built as planned, they questioned where California would ever find the eight thousand students to fill the grandiose halls.[16]

15. In the jury of the final competition, Mr. John Belcher of London took the place of Mr. Shaw who was ill. University of California, *The International Competition* (San Francisco: 1899), p. 12.
16. The competition program had called for planning for 8,000 students although the enrollment at the time was less than 2,000. In 1919 the 8,000 mark was reached; today the University has more than 28,000 students on approximately the same site.

Emile Bénard, wash drawing, "General Perspective,"
The International Competition for the Phoebe Hearst Architectural Plan for the University of California, (1899).

In January 1900, Bénard revised this plan at the request of the Regents to retain the natural stream beds which flow through the University grounds.

Bénard accepted the prize and came to California to revise his plan under the direction of the Regents of the University in order to give even more recognition to the natural areas of Strawberry Creek than his original design proposed. However, when offered the position of Supervising Architect to carry out his plan, Bénard turned down the opportunity. He had also won first place in the competition for congressional buildings in Mexico City, and the development there was more immediately promising than that at the University. The single building for which funds were available for construction was the Mining Building which Mrs. Hearst had proposed several years earlier.

Faced with selecting an architect to execute Bénard's plan, the Regents' interest turned to John Galen Howard of New York, whose entry had placed fourth. Howard had worked for Shepley, Rutan and Coolidge as supervisor of construction of Stanford University, and with this background he seemed a likely candidate to supervise the execution of the University plan.

Maybeck was sent to New York to extend the Regents' proposal to Howard. He immediately accepted, undertaking work on the design of the Mining Building even before moving his office and his family to Berkeley. Because of Maybeck's original sketch for the building and his position as coordinating architect, the design of Hearst Memorial Mining Building has often been attributed to him; however, since the original sketch does not exist and his participation is not documented, there is no way of determining his contribution to the design. He did act as Mrs. Hearst's architectural consultant on the building and undoubtedly reviewed the design, although his unorthodox ideas and proposals are reported to have brought howls of laughter from Howard's drafting room staff.[17] However, the Mining Building is freer from the restraints of academic classicism than any of Howard's later designs. The facade, the interior lobby handsomely framed in exposed steel members, and the multiple chimneys extending above the roof may have been more restrained without Maybeck's participation.

John Galen Howard, described by one of his first students, Warren Perry, as a man of great charm, culture, and dignity, came to Berkeley in 1901 to supervise the construction of the Hearst Memorial Mining Building. The following year he was appointed Supervising Architect and Professor of Architecture. Howard began work on studies to implement the Phoebe Hearst Architectural Plan. It is understandable that the result of this reworking culminated in a plan resembling more nearly the entry of Howard and Cauldwell than that of Émile Bénard, and resulted in the Howard plan for the University of California in 1914. It is to this plan that the University of today bears close adherence.

Hearst Memorial Mining Building, University of California, 1902, John Galen Howard, Architect.
Documents Collection, C.E.D.

Although Maybeck prepared preliminary sketches for this building, his contribution to the final design is not known.

Upon his return to Berkeley, Maybeck resumed his teaching and his architectural practice which had been interrupted by his duties with the Competition. His first task was to initiate the construction of a reception hall for Mrs. Hearst, who had outlined the needs of the building to Maybeck while he was in Europe. Maybeck apparently started the design for this structure in Paris: John Bakewell related that during the period Maybeck visited "his boys" at the École, criticizing and encouraging their efforts, he was also busy designing at his own flat. The building was to provide a space in which Mrs. Hearst could act as hostess for the many official receptions that would be held for the visiting jurors by the University and State officials concerned with the Competition. It was her intention to give the building to the University and have it moved to the campus at the conclusion of the Competition after the general plan had been adopted.

The ending of the Competition did not bring to a close the activities held in the reception hall Maybeck had built for Phoebe Apperson Hearst. In addition to its initial formal uses the building had been designed to be a place in which performances could be given and works of art shown, thus enriching the cultural life of students at the University. It contained space for musical and stage productions and a dining room large enough to seat five hundred people. With the opening of the fall semester in 1899, the building soon fulfilled the goal of its owner by becoming the center of the campus social and cultural life.

The reception pavillion, Hearst Hall, was built on the south side of Channing Way, adjoining Mrs. Hearst's residence on Piedmont Avenue. It was a building sixty feet in width and one hundred forty feet in length, with its principal axis oriented in a north-south direction on a site which sloped gently to the south and west. The structure—the engineering of which was worked out in collaboration with Maybeck's university colleague Herman Kower—was an exciting and bold concept that employed laminated arches and diaphragms to create sections of the buildings as independent, movable, and easily re-assembled units. Twelve wooden arches rising fifty-four feet above the ground floor level were paired to form six structural bays. Single arches were used at the walls of the end bays. These arches were constructed of laminated two-by-eight timbers, formed horizontally on the site by nailing the

17. William G. Purcell, MSS., "Bernard Maybeck," C.E.D. Docs. A paper prepared at the request of Jean Murray Bangs.

Reception pavillion, "Hearst Hall," Channing Way near College
Avenue, 1899. G. E. Gould photograph.
Documents Collection, C.E.D.

The original location of Hearst Hall. The tower at the right
contained the flue from the heating plant. It also embellished
the terrace roof garden gallery. To the left is the Phoebe
Hearst residence.

timbers to a radius of approximately sixty feet. Holes were
then drilled and bolts placed which were tightened after erection loads had been imposed. The arches were given lateral
stability by the floor of the main hall which was twelve feet
above the ground floor. It consisted of a diagonal grid of
beams and joists, which was left exposed in the ceiling of the
lower room. The arches were further tied, at approximately
half height, by a horizontal plane surrounding the exterior of
the arches, creating a floor for an outdoor gallery. The exterior walls of the building were curtain walls of stud construction
with columns at each arch. These columns were tied at the
middle to the arch by horizontal members which extended
through the exterior to support planting boxes.

Hearst Hall under construction.
Documents Collection, C.E.D.

Laminated arches and purlins in place; the framing of the main floor had just begun.

On the west elevation a ground floor-level band of windows lighted the dining area. The blank exerior wall of the principal room above was relieved by the cantilevered boxes planted with thin evergreen trees. They marked the location of the arches which framed the main room and were additionally accented by flagpoles that rose above the roof gallery. The gallery was lined with tubbed evergreens and, in addition to the surrounding view, the interior of the hall could be seen through the large dormer-like windows that rose from the shell of the main roof to provide clerestory lighting. The flue for the heating plant was built in a separate tower at the west side of the building and connected at the gallery level by an arch and balcony which afforded a superb view of the Golden Gate of San Francisco Bay.

The building was finished with redwood barn shakes, doubled in thirty-six-inch courses to create a horizontal pattern on the exterior surface. To the south, at the rear of the structure, were service facilities for the dining room and also a stagehouse covered by a large gable roof. The eastern elevation was similar to the west, with the omission of the tower chimney. A connecting bridgeway led to Mrs. Hearst's adjoining residence.

The entrance at the north consisted of a low-pitched gabled porte-cochere which abutted an arched vestibule, approximately thirty feet wide, the upper portion of which was entirely glazed. Stairways right and left led to the vestibule serving the dining room and joined in a single broad flight to the reception room above. The interior of the main hall was finished with redwood barn shakes similar to those on the exterior but treated with a sulphate of iron solution which rendered them a silvery-grey. Light came from clerestory windows covered by grilles of turned wood balusters of flemish derivation, typical of Maybeck's ornamentation. The alcoves formed by the spaces between the ribs of the arches were hung with Gobelin tapestries and various paintings from the Hearst collection. When the Hall was used for less formal occasions, such as afternoon teas given by Mrs. Hearst, a large canopy of Genoese rose velvet was suspended from the arches in the middle of the hall. The plain pine floor was covered by two large Chinese rugs of special design executed in grey-blue with a gold border. At night the room was lighted with more than a thousand incandescent bulbs. Two rows of colored lights were mounted directly on each arch of the room, and suspended from each arch were two rows of white lights with milk glass reflectors hung in an arch complementary to the structural members.

The Hall's excellent acoustics were realized through several conscious architectural devices. The all-wood interior and the special placement of the interior shakes, laid from the inner surface of one purlin to the outer surface of the next, formed excellent baffles. Screened by the wooden grilles, the large dormer spaces, or "sound hollows" as Maybeck dubbed them, were based on studies made by a German organist on the acoustical qualities of architectural forms.[18]

18. Conversations between the author and Maybeck.

Hearst Hall, set for a reception.
Documents Collection, C.E.D.

The acoustic hollows, which also admit the clerestory lighting, are clearly visible. The tapestries and paintings are from the Hearst family collection.

Hearst Hall, ground floor dining space.
Documents Collection, C.E.D.

Hearst Hall Gymnasium, exterior.
Documents Collection, C.E.D.

After the building was moved to the campus, Maybeck added
a trellised colonnade and bleachers surrounding a playing field
to the west of the entrance.

Hearst Hall was a remarkably good building. Maybeck took pride in the fact that its visitors were not conscious of the style of the room but of the works and performance of art it was constructed to serve. The forms from the exterior were indeed strange to a public more schooled in traditional architecture; yet the interesting spaces and expressive character of the whole made it a pleasing structure. The limited budget allotted for its construction tested Maybeck's belief that handsome architecture could be obtained by a direct expression of structure and simple surface treatments. Particularly notable was his careful consideration of light and sound as basic elements of his design. And although contemporary architects referred deridingly to the building as "railway Gothic," Hearst Hall achieved a unity of form, structure, and use that is characteristic of all successful architectural composition.

Once the University plan was determined, Hearst Hall could be moved to the University grounds, a project Maybeck undertook in the summer of 1901. At that time he had the building moved to the campus location designated for athletic facilities where it was converted to a gymnasium for women. Divested of the Hearst art and equipped with gymnastic paraphenalia, it served a generation of students until it was destroyed by fire in 1922. Besides serving as a gymnasium, it continued to function as a social center for the campus. Pageants, theatricals, and musicals were presented in the building. In its new location, Maybeck added a semi-circular trellis at the entrance and a playing field surrounded by open, wooden bleachers. The large native oaks on the site of the stadium were left in open wells among the seats to furnish shade for the viewers.

Hearst Hall Gymnasium.
Documents Collection, C.E.D.

Sofas and tapestries or vaulting horses and Indian clubs—the building accommodated either with equal grace.

51

Phoebe A. Hearst country estate, "Wyntoon," McCloud River, Siskiyou County, 1902-1903.
Documents Collection, C.E.D.

The great country estate, "Wyntoon," for the Hearst family, magnificently revealed Maybeck's imaginative ability to re-create a "mood" and to translate it into an architectural reality. The "castle" became a part of the primitive setting and atmosphere, not a disturbing, ultimately unsettling anachronism in the landscape.

Mrs. Hearst was very pleased with Maybeck's work and asked him to design a country house for her which would use many of the medieval furnishings removed from Hearst Hall. This country retreat, called Wyntoon, was situated on the McCloud River in the heart of a forested area in Siskiyou County between Mount Shasta and Mount Lassen. The building, constructed in 1902, was destroyed by fire in 1933. Fortunately, good contemporary photographs were published in the *Architectural Review* (Boston) in 1904, with a description by the architect. The article shows the literary mannerisms typical of Maybeck's writing. As one of his rare personal descriptions of his own building, it is quoted here in its entirety:

> The idea of composing this construction in the primeval forest on the McCloud River resulted from several causes First, the six trees in a semicircle. Second, the immense size of these trees. Third, the distance from railroad and expense of transportation. Fourth, climate. Fifth, forest fires. Similar conditions existed in the middle ages, and, consequently, without effort, the Gothic composition resulted.
>
> The spot is located at the foot of a mountain, the waters from which drain into a crystal torrent, a stone's throw wide. Although the air is dry, it was better to put the bedrooms high above the ground on account of the close proximity to the river. This was an advantage, for if the building had been only one or two stories high, it would have looked like a hovel in the hillside. As it is, the line of stone (lava flow quarried nearby) begins at the opposite side of the river at the beginning of the arched stone bridge to be built next year, and continues up, broken by trees and shrubbery, along the living room to the top of the tower and chimney. This tone color is blue-grey, verging on warm siennas.
>
> To have built a red tile roof on the building would have been fatal, so we put on a dead Paris-green glazed tile, which, from afar and against the trees, gives a misty color like the holes between the branches in the trees in the forest.
>
> The color of the woodwork is in the color of the bark of the yellow-pine trees, a violet brown. Now fill the windows, with leaded glass, and see the light through the dining room windows, which are large enough to light a cathedral. Imagine the clear blue and white foam of the river in the foreground roaring ceaselessly, and you have a picture of rest, and, at the dawn of day, an enchanted castle. I pointedly refer to the dawn, because the colors are pearly and do not suggest the evening light; in fact, the landscape is pearly.
>
> As you enter the house there is a rubble stone vestibule, with an archway to the living room. At one end of the living room is a fireplace as high as a man, and beyond it a copy of thirteenth century stained glass from the apse of the Lorenzen Kirke in Nuremburg. Old tapestries of the fifteenth and sixteenth centuries keep the moisture from the stone from making the room clammy. These tapestries are all historic treasures, and in texture and color bring the walls and ceiling into complete harmony. The dark height of the room, the unobstructed archways, the deep blues, reds, and yellows of the cathedral window, to which time had given maturity, the tapestries, the little flicker of fire, and the roaring of the river outside; and you, satiated, tired, and inspired by the day's trip among hazel, dogwood, great aged pines, rocks, cascades, great trunks of trees fallen years ago,—a dishevelled harmony,—here you can reach all that is within you. The dining room has a window at each end as high as two stories, with heavy wooden beam ceiling, and two massive rough, stone fireplaces, which are needed in the morning to keep the chill off.

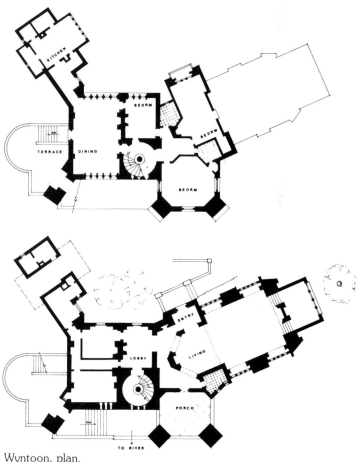

Wyntoon, plan.
Architectural Review—Boston, January, 1904.

The circular stone staircase leads to all rooms in the house, just as did the tower stairs in the middle ages.

It is perhaps, strange that, having the opportunity and the money, the architect did not do architecture. There are places where moldings and carvings are suggestive of pastry and perfume, and that is the case at the McCloud River; the only modern thing that could be introduced into a problem of this kind was that of proportions; given a 'hoary forest' and stone as a theme, make the work in exact accord with the sentiment and use, and give it a beautiful mass.

Wyntoon, interior.
Documents Collection, C.E.D.

Bark taken from trees cleared from the site is used for decorative ceiling panels between the roof trusses. The stained glass window was a copy of one in the Lorenzen Kirke, Nurnburg, Germany of the 13th century.

No architect was ever more conscious of the affective values of architecture than Maybeck. Cold rough stone, misty spaces, and dark height are more than poetic allusions; they are the very essence of Maybeck's contributions to our architectural heritage. His empathic response to materials, color, and space helped him create buildings always notable in their power to evoke mood. Wyntoon was built with the intention of conveying all the feeling of a medieval castle, ameliorated only by modern conveniences. Security from the elements and a simple and gracious way of life were Maybeck's interpretation of the essential qualities of a medieval retreat. His planning followed closely the early castles illustrated in Viollet-le-Duc's *Habitation of Man in all Ages.*[19] Wyntoon's towering roofs, recalling Teutonic origins, followed Maybeck's thesis that architectural forms would remain constant if geographical and technological developments went unchanged.

19. Maybeck's visits to restorations by Viollet-le-Duc probably included Pierrefonds castle.

Wyntoon, exterior view from the southeast.
Documents Collection, C.E.D.

The kitchen wing is in the left portion of the photograph.

To him it was logical that, given primitive conditions, primitive forms would result. When the building burned, William Randolph Hearst made overtures to Maybeck to rebuild it. However, he later abandoned these plans in favor of new construction on his San Simeon property, where he had been building for more than a dozen years with Julia Morgan as architect.

Wyntoon, refectory.
Documents Collection, C.E.D.

Deal tables and chairs as well as chandeliers were designed by Maybeck in association with Frederick H. Meyer, who in 1907 founded the California College of Arts and Crafts in Oakland.

Maybeck had eliminated himself as a participant in the Competition for the University general plan, but his experiences and travels well compensated for it. Two years of travel in Europe were of tremendous value to a young man developing his ideas and his practice of architecture. If the Competition did not bring him national fame, it gained for him the respect of the local community who admired the modest way in which he had played his part. Because of the reputation he had won in working on the Competition and in carrying out the commissions for Mrs. Hearst, Maybeck, at last, was able to establish his private practice on a sound footing. Already many townspeople had commissioned him to build houses and club buildings in or about the Bay Area.

View of Davis, Keeler, Rieger, and Hall Houses, Ridge Road
and Highland Place, Berkeley.
Photograph courtesy of Paul Rieger, Documents
Collection, C.E.D.

IV

Houses Simply Built

California climate demands a certain type of building. The roofs are to shed rain, but not snow; the windows are to let in all the sunlight possible, not to keep out the heat....Build around the hills on contour lines or step the houses up against the hill, one story back and above the other....Houses simply built depend on natural projections and their shadows for ornament.

Hillside Club—1902

Maybeck resigned from the University in 1903. The San Francisco *Chronicle* noted his departure with the comment that he was one of a group of promising young architects who came to California in 1890 and who, with A. Page Brown, were active in designing the Crocker Building of San Francisco and other handsome buildings of that time. The reporter further commented that the advent of this band of designers produced a number of aspiring architectural students and brought about an architectural revival.[1]

When the newcomers in architecture published their attack on the falseness and pretentiousness of workingmen's houses in the *Architectural News* in 1891, they drew heavily on ideas stemming from the Arts and Crafts movement in England. In their own work they attempted to correct the abuses in wood construction that abounded all around them. They used a shingled residential architecture which was uncommon in the region prior to this time. The isolated examples of Worcester's cottages, and simple summer houses in outlying areas were the exception to the over-elaborate structures decorated with spindle work and scroll saw ornament. Their work was done primarily for clients of modest means who wanted houses for everyday use, in contrast with the majority of the eastern Shingle Style works of McKim, Mead and White, Peabody and Stearns, Bruce Price, and others which were designed as summer retreats for wealthy families.[2]

The houses that the newcomers built in the nineties were similar to others found in many parts of the country at the end of the century. Interest was great in the design of the modest house as was attested by the rapid growth in circulation of the *Ladies' Home Journal*, which campaigned for small houses without "useless turrets, filagree work, or machine made ornamentation." Another successful magazine committed to the small house was *House Beautiful*, established in 1897; it added critical comments on the debased tastes of the rich.[3] What was significant for Maybeck was that in Berkeley the time and place were right to create an architectural expression of the modest house in a concentrated geographical area and on a scale extensive enough to be an influence in the community.

1. *San Francisco Chronicle*, May 11, 1903. However, by this date many of the promising young designers were dead. A. Page Brown was killed in a carriage accident; Edward Swain and A. C. Schweinfurth had succumbed to ill health.
2. Bruce Price designed at least one house for California. Cf. *Building*, (March 19, 1887), p. 109.
3. "Notes," *House Beautiful*, 4, (October, 1898), pp. 186-87.

In the last decade of the nineteenth century, the daily life of Berkeley centered around the University. Its rapid expansion required an increase in personnel. Moreover, business and professional people, artists, and writers, who were attracted by the cultural environment, began to build on the adjoining hillsides. Their reaction against Victorian ornateness was evidenced in their buildings, and by 1900 the designs of Coxhead, Schweinfurth, and Maybeck were the leading examples of the new mode.

Maybeck designed nearly one hundred and fifty houses in California over a period of more than fifty years. The majority are found in Berkeley. They are not easy to classify by either style or period of construction. The designs of the first half of Maybeck's career reveal a strong interest in structure and the craft of building in contrast with those of the last half, which often seem to be the product of an artist-architect seeking beauty by the manipulation of forms, colors, and textures. There is a tendency in the San Francisco Bay region to identify any structure that has rustic or picturesque qualities as influenced by Maybeck, yet these are not the qualities that are the hallmarks of his work. It is a sense of delight in spatial relations, creative use of structure, and innovative planning that consistently mark his significant buildings.

Other architects in the Bay region used exposed framing members and unpainted surfaces in small houses. But Maybeck, more than anyone else, exploited the physical qualities of redwood to create a unity between the structural and finish elements. He often used redwood for horizontal as well as for vertical structural members because, although soft, redwood is stronger in tension and compression than many pines and firs. He also used the great width obtainable in redwood boards to create rhythms consistent in scale with his structural order. When others used redwood trim and interior panels, it was often painted or stained and varnished to resemble mahogany; but the finishes scarred easily, necessitating frequent retouching. Maybeck's use of natural wood surfaces eliminated the possibility of chipped paint and also made the most of a quality unique to redwood that is not adequately captured by photography. The pink tone of new lumber mellows rapidly to a rich red-brown which is highlighted by an iridescent gold caused by the refraction of natural or incandescent light falling on the spring wood of the boards. But the principal reason for the widespread use of redwood was its cost. Maybeck selected it for his early houses because it was abundant and inexpensive.

Feeling that wood was the logical material with which to build houses in California, Maybeck used it in systems that emphasized its natural qualities. He considered himself a modern artisan at work with products of the machine age, and when he exposed framing members for the ornamental value of their repetitive rhythms, he drew inspiration from the construction of medieval craftsmen. In fact, he referred to his early houses as "Gothic houses" and likened them to the multi-storied, timber-framed houses of his ancestral homeland, the Rhenish Palatinate.

Maybeck built at least six Gothic houses prior to his departure for Europe as the Competition advisor.[4] They were characterized by steep roofs, exposed framing, and intricate silhouettes. Inadequate records prevent the making of a totally accurate chronology of Maybeck's work; but three houses north of the campus, which escaped destruction by the Berkeley fire, provided a group that illustrated his initial approach to residential design. They were the Charles Keeler house (1895), the Laura G. Hall house (1896), and the Williston W. Davis house (1897).

These three buildings, although varied in room arrangements, were similar in external forms, structure, and finish details. They all utlized post and beam construction, with four-by-four redwood posts spaced approximately three feet on centers. The walls were horizontally sheathed with one-by-eight redwood boards nailed to the exterior of the posts and exposed as the interior finish. The exterior skin was made of redwood shingles, which also covered the high-pitched gabled roofs. The supporting members of the eaves and the rafters were visible in the principal rooms, and the structural system enriched the interiors with its rhythmical patterns. Although there was little ornamental carving or use of color on the interiors, pyro-gravure of the redwood was sometimes used for decoration. The sash was usually the only painted element of Maybeck's small houses. Moss greens or earth reds were the preferred colors. The interior redwood boards and exterior redwood shingles were left untreated to turn to deep, rich browns.

4. These included houses for L. G. Hall, W. W. Davis, C. Keeler, E. Kellogg, and two unidentified houses published in Werner Hegeman, *Report on the Municipalities of Oakland and Berkeley* (Oakland: 1915), one of which is most likely the first A. C. Lawson house.

Charles Keeler house, Berkeley, (1895), pen and ink by
M. S. Cardwell from an early photograph.
Documents Collection, C.E.D.

Charles Keeler house, library.
The Simple Home, 1904.

This photograph from Keeler's book shows the library with
the exposed wooden structural system.

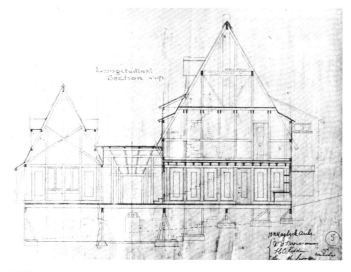

Williston W. Davis house, 2305 Ridge Road, Berkeley,
1897. (Destroyed)
Documents Collection, C.E.D.

This sectional drawing, reproduced from a fragment of a
blueprinted sheet found in the house prior to its demolition, is
the oldest construction drawing of Maybeck's work in the
collection.

Laura G. Hall house, 1945 Highland Place, Berkeley,
1896. (Destroyed)
Photograph courtesy of Paul Rieger, Documents Collection,
C.E.D.

The volumes of the structure are strongly revealed on its
hillside site in this contemporary photograph.

The Keeler house has been converted into apartments
and the exterior stuccoed; the only unaltered reminder of
Maybeck's original conception is its sharply pitched roofs
creating a distrinctive profile against the sky. Maybeck's
design for the Davis house was executed only in part; the
living room that was to be to the front of the entrance hall
was never completed. However, until the mid-1950s the Hall
house stood as the best example of Maybeck's early concern
for the integration of the separate living spaces of a small
house into a flexible unit. By the use of modularly spaced
studs, continuously banded casement sash secured without
frames to the structural members, and sliding doors, he
created an integrated design that was a precursor of the
best of modern domestic architecture. It combined a one-
storied living room and entry hall of generous proportions
with a two-storied block containing the dining and kitchen
facilities on the first floor. Bedrooms were above. The plan
is one of the few symmetrical organizations used by Maybeck;

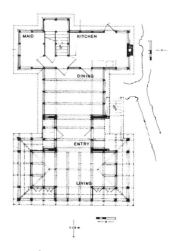

Laura G. Hall house, plan.
Drawn by Alan Williams from measurements by K. H. Cardwell.

Laura G. Hall house, dining room.
William S. Ricco photograph.

The table and bench are of the character of Maybeck's furniture designs. All of the construction members of the house were of redwood as were the paneled doors which were hung on the structure without frames or trim.

Laura G. Hall house, living room.
William S. Ricco photograph.

The fireplace, probably designed by Maybeck, was a later addition, but the window seat at the left which replaced French doors opening to an exterior deck was a change made by a late owner of the property.

but the house was not entered on the principal axis of the composition. An inclined path wound through an informal garden developed on the hillside site to reach the ground floor level of the house. To the left, the entry opened into a living room flooded by light from window walls surrounded by narrow balconies. To the right, the entry led to a dining room banked with windows on its north and south walls. The sliding walls of the entry, when opened made the three rooms one room oriented towards the panorama of San Francisco Bay.

After the completion of the Davis house in 1897, Maybeck's practice was interrupted by his trip abroad as advisor for the Competition. Upon his return in 1898, his initial concern was to prepare the entries in the Competition for judgment and to begin the building of the reception hall for Phoebe Hearst. As Maybeck resumed his teaching duties in the fall, his independent practice flourished. He was soon asked to design a clubhouse for a group of Berkeley women.

Through its use of structurally derived patterns, the Berkeley Town and Gown Club (1899), like Hearst Hall, is closely related to Maybeck's "Gothic houses." As a rule, Maybeck used the formulas he had learned at the École in the engineering classes of Emmanuel Brune.[5] Some of his drawings reveal calculations for bending moments in beams and columns, but in the design of the Town and Gown Club his approach seems more intiutive than rational, based on feeling rather than analysis.

5. After Brune's death his widow was urged to publish his lectures in book form. E. Brune, *Cours de Construction* (Paris: 1888).

Town and Gown Club, west elevation, 2304 Dwight Way, Berkeley, 1899.
Stone and Stecatti photograph, Documents Collection, C.E.D.

Cantilevered beams joined to the rafters of the broad overhangs by ties and struts lend an unusual air of grace and lightness to the structure.

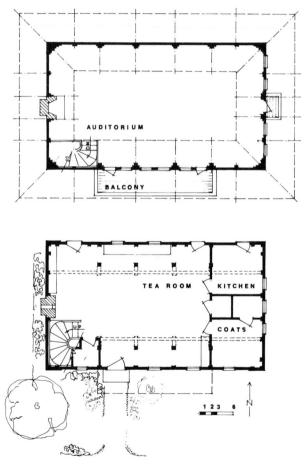

Town and Gown Club, plan.
Measured and drawn by C. Bell and L. Stoopenkoff, Documents Collection, C.E.D.

The clubhouse is a two-storied structure clad with unstained redwood shingles. The hipped roof has broad eaves supported by an intricate system of cantilevered beams which penetrate the walls and are balanced by ties and struts to the rafters. The timbering forms one of Maybeck's most interesting roofs; its light, cage-like construction provides a refreshingly unique covering to a room of handsome proportions and vigorous modeling. The volume of the room is constantly modified as the eye shifts from longitudinal beams to lateral ties or vertical struts overhead.

The building has always contained a first-floor lounge with a second-floor auditorium. However, by 1906, the club was enlarged to add a stage and additional seating space, and Maybeck's circular staircase leading to the upper room was removed. The building has been remodeled several times by architects other than Maybeck; but they have respected and conformed to the character, if not the detail, of the original structure.

Town and Gown Club building, interior.
Documents Collection, C.E.D.

Town and Gown Club, second floor meeting room.
Stone and Stecatti photograph, Documents Collection, C.E.D.

In 1899 a newspaper printed a description of the building under the caption "An Odd Clubhouse for Berkeley Women." It stated:

> Within a few weeks the finishing touches will be put upon a new women's clubhouse now going up on the corner of Dwight Way and Dana street, which is attracting much interest and curiosity on account of its peculiar oddity and eccentricity of design. The building, though partially complete, already shows its main points of outline, and these indicate a structure of the most unique kind, a radical departure from the conventional, bordering almost upon the freakish.[6]

Such criticism did not deter Maybeck. He went on to try new approaches to the composition of building forms. Even the first house he designed with the resumption of his practice indicated new directions. Whereas his previous houses were expressions of individual spaces delicately articulated, the William P. Rieger house (1899) on Highland Place was one bold pile, freely organized to show its various architectural spaces. To achieve an open plan and free fenestration, Maybeck adapted a board and batten structural system long used in California and known throughout the world. Common in early western building, the mildness of the California winters and the rapidity with which a space can be enclosed were contributing factors to its extensive use. True board and batten construction depends upon the strength of one-inch boards nailed top and bottom to a load-carrying plate. But the system's lack of lateral bracing and its susceptibility to penetration by the elements has made building codes restrict its use to minor buildings. Modern versions of board and batten are often merely skins covering wood framing.

6. From an unidentified clipping in the scrapbook collection of Julia Morgan, furnished through the courtesy of Flora Morgan North.

William P. Rieger house, 1901 Highland Place, Berkeley, 1899.
Pen and ink drawing by M. S. Cardwell from an old photograph, Documents Collection, C.E.D.

Bold massing of volumes and spaces lent a dramatic air to the freely organized plan.

In the Rieger house Maybeck took advantage of all that this structural system had to offer and, at the same time, conquered its inherent weaknesses. He used conventional framing up to the first floor level. Above this point, one-by-twelve boards were fastened to finished redwood two-by-sixteen top plates which performed multiple functions of lintels for doors and windows, ledgers for second floor joists, and a natural decorative frieze for all the interior spaces. Adding to the strength of the one-inch boards, stout posts at the corners and wall intersections were joined with the frieze members. The posts were diagonally braced with flat iron ties that were later concealed by the covering skin of shingles Maybeck used in lieu of conventional battens. This method was repeated for the second story. The roof had six-foot wide eaves and Maybeck used, as he had in the Town and Gown Club, a system of cantilevered beams and post brackets for their support. The rest of the detailing, such as exposed joists carrying the second floor and casement sash hung without frames, is similar to the construction found in his Gothic houses.

The Rieger house was a two-and-one-half story shingled structure with a gable roof of moderate pitch covering the main living rooms and extending in lean-to fashion over the service rooms at the rear. The second story was cantilevered over two sides of the first floor, partially sheltering a western deck adjoining the dining room. The deck was screened from the approach to the house by a boxlike vestibule at a level a few steps below the entrance hall.

The entry separated the dining room from the living room and, at its narrow end, opened into a stairwell that rose to the living space above. The wedge-shaped entry created a bend in the plan and shaped the building to fit the contours of the site. And, as in the Hall house, the fourteen foot long side walls of the entry hall slid open to unite the living and dining areas into one integrated volume. It was an unusual plan; it had few recognizable precedents.

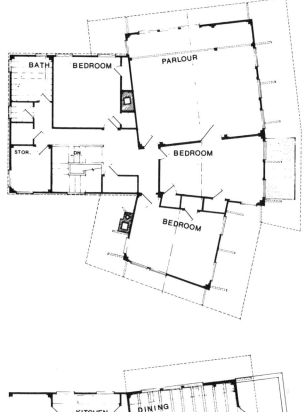

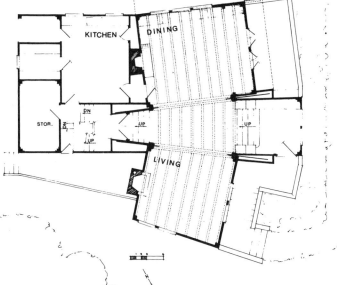

William P. Rieger house, plan.
Drawn by Alan Williams from measurements by K. H. Cardwell.

William P. Rieger house, under construction.
Photograph courtesy of Paul Rieger, Documents Collection, C.E.D.

The redwood board construction frames a distant view of a house designed by Ernest Coxhead.

Two houses that Maybeck built in Palo Alto for Emma Kellogg in 1896 and 1899 also illustrate his experiments with new forms. The first, a Gothic house, was constructed in a community much like Berkeley and in an area where the students and staff of nearby Stanford University resided.[7] Although very little is known about it, an article published in the *Palo Alto Live Oak* of November 6, 1896, described it as

> the quaintest residence that has yet been built in Palo Alto. It is not large, covering but 30 x 36 feet of ground space, being a story and a half and having five rooms; yet the odd design of the exterior, with its covering of cedar shingles, its casement windows and broken outlines, makes it noticeable. The architect R. B. Maybeck [sic], instructor in the State University, designates it Californian in style.

The second Kellogg house, built on the same site, replaced the original, which was destroyed by fire during Maybeck's absence. It is a bold, asymmetrical composition with a recessed entry porch open to the south and the west. A low flight of broad corner steps leads to the intersecting streets bounding the site. A cantilevered portion of the second story, once supported by large console brackets, shelters the entrance, and the entire building is dominated by a large gambrel roof.

7. B. R. Maybeck Photos, "Unknown," C.E.D. Docs. A photograph of a gable roofed house with surroundings similar to the second E. Kellogg house has not been identified or located.

William P. Rieger house, dining room fireplace.
William S. Ricco photograph taken after the upper portion of the house had been destroyed by a fire in April 1958.

The panel above the fireplace was made of two redwood boards joined with butterfly splines and pyro-engraved by Maybeck with a view of medieval Antwerp, the source of the perfume that Mr. Rieger's firm imported.

Perhaps Kellogg requested a house that would be less noticeable to the correspondent of the *Palo Alto Live Oak*. At first glance it seems an amazingly conventional house for Maybeck; but he might have been challenged by an expressed desire of the client to work with a traditional form. His inventive manipulation of a common shape, however, makes the roof distinctive. The junction of the planes is the reverse of the usual gambrel roof; the upper portion is overlapped by the lower to form a rain gutter. Its pitch above the second-story plate is so moderate that it disappears completely except in distant views. The lower planes which form the second story walls are extremely vertical and, by a slight flare at the eaves, leave the dormer windows an integral part of the first story. The roof enfolds and engages the walls of the building, creating a unified mass in contrast to the broken outlines of his earlier Gothic designs.

Emma Kellogg house, fireplace.
William S. Ricco photograph.

Emma Kellogg house (#2), 1061 Bryant, Palo Alto, 1899. Documents Collection, C.E.D.

The large gambrel roof of the second Kellogg house enfolds the walls and presents a unified mass in contrast to the broken outlines of most of Maybeck's earlier designs.

Only two designs for the year 1900 have been attributed to Maybeck. Both the Lillian Bridgman house and the G. H. G. McGrew house add to his experiments in form. They represent a pattern of practice set for an unknown number of Berkeley houses in which he did not act in his full professional capacity. Less marked by Maybeck mannerisms than other designs, a strong participation by the owner is claimed for both. Maybeck was always willing to aid friends and neighbors in building projects and the degree of his participation had little to do with contractual arrangements.

The Bridgman house is modest. Its most unusual feature is its informal plan which developed naturally from the pattern of living of the owner-designer. Upon inheriting a modest estate from her family, Lillian Bridgman decided to construct a home for herself and her sister. She began the design but was soon confronted with technical difficulties which led her to seek Maybeck's advice. In his selfless manner he proceeded to design the house, encouraging Miss Bridgman to execute the drawings while he gave expert criticism and advice. There are no drawings from which to evaluate the contributions of each to the design; but the organization of the house and the details show the experienced hand of Maybeck. Miss Bridgman was evidently very pleased with her experience, for she later forsook teaching physics for the study of architecture and developed a modest practice in residential design.[8]

8. A second house on the Bridgman property is a good example of her work.

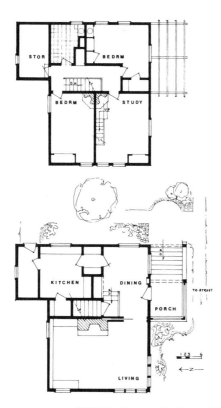

Lillian Bridgman house, 1715 La Loma, Berkeley, 1900. Plan, measured and drawn by K. H. Cardwell.

The informal plan developed from the living pattern of its owner.

Lillian Bridgman house, built-in bedroom furnishings. William S. Ricco photograph.

The details of the house reveal Maybeck's skillful contributions to the basic design of his friend's home.

The house of G. H. G. McGrew was designed by Maybeck and the owner with ideas contributed by their common friend, Charles Keeler. Its forms recall the Gothic house Maybeck had built for Keeler. The McGrew house is an ell-shaped building two stories in height with an attic room contained by a steeply pitched gable roof. Facing a side street, its entrance porch is recessed into the building block. The entry hall lies between the dining and living rooms and leads to a stairway with square hand rails, balusters, and large square newel posts. A spacious bay at the landing, lighted by a pair of casement windows, is used as a writing area and is visible from the first floor entry. The play of light and the continuity of the stairway's board and batten soffit as it rises in the open well to the ceiling of the second floor creates interest and delight without the addition of decorative details. After this date the use of the changing volume of a stairwell to enrich architectural passages consistently reappears in Maybeck's work.

G. H. G. McGrew house, 2601 Derby St., Berkeley, 1900. William S. Ricco photograph.

The McGrew house, designed by Maybeck in conjunction with its owner, became an example of what Charles Keeler termed "the Simple Home."

G. H. G. McGrew house, stairway. William S. Ricco photograph.

Maybeck used the changing volume of the stairwell to enrich the design and create interest without employing added decorative details.

The McGrew house and its predecessors became the examples of a "movement towards a simpler, a truer, a more vital art expression" when, a few years later, Charles Keeler assumed the spokesman's role for the modest house and "the simple life." His publication of a small volume entitled *The Simple Home* (1904) is illustrated with Berkeley houses designed by Coxhead, Schweinfurth, and Maybeck. It contains many suggestions for building that Maybeck had put into practice in his early designs. As a token of his esteem, Keeler dedicated the volume to his "friend and counselor Bernard Maybeck."[9] In 1902, Maybeck designed a studio for Keeler which was simply and beautifully detailed in wood and built to the north of Keeler's Maybeck-designed house of 1895.

Maybeck's Berryman Street house is pictured in Keeler's book and shows chalet characteristics which emerged in his experiments with building form upon his return from Europe. Keeler described it as a handmade home in which the timbers and planks of its construction, carpentry details, and furnishings made by the architect provided the interior finish. The exact dates of the transformation of Maybeck's house are unknown, but by 1901 it had become a simple, rectangular, two-storied block covered by a low-pitched, gabled roof with wide overhangs.

9. Charles A. Keeler, *The Simple Home* (San Francisco: Paul Elder and Company, 1904).

Charles Keeler studio, 1736 Highland Place, Berkeley, 1902. K. H. Cardwell photograph.

Charles Keeler studio, view from entrance.
William S. Ricco photograph.

Sunlight flooding through the windows upon the tastefully
executed woodwork reveals a room of natural elegance.

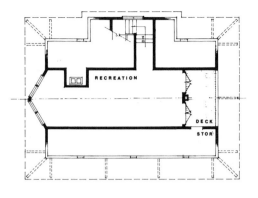

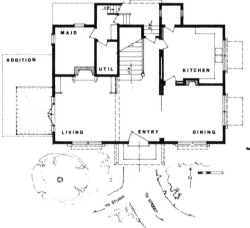

Isaac Flagg house (#1), 1201 Shattuck Ave., Berkeley, 1901.
K. H. Cardwell photograph.

Broad eaves supported by struts from the second-story walls
combine to give the house an air of strength and quiet dignity.

Isaac Flagg house.
Plan, measured and drawn by K. H. Cardwell.

Maybeck's experiments on his own house provided the prototype for several others that followed. The Isaac Flagg house (1901) was probably the first of Maybeck's adaptation of the chalet for a client.[10] Flagg was a professor of Classics and owned an acre at the north end of the Berkeley residential district a short distance from the Maybeck house on Berryman Street. Over the years Maybeck designed a number of projects for the Flaggs, three of which were built on the north Berkeley property.

The first house, a two-storied structure with a habitable attic under the low pitched gable roof, crowns a knoll of the site. Its broad, six-foot eaves are supported by struts that spring from the second story walls. The square struts are thickened at their middles to create a visual impression of strength. In their design Maybeck followed a concept advocated by Viollet-le-Duc—that structural members should reveal by their shape the stresses that occur within them. A very large trapezoidal opening in the east gable wall of the Flagg house provides fresh air for a sleeping porch, and a prow-shaped bay window of the west gable furnishes a view from the attic story. These bold elements, combined with the wide eaves and prominent struts, set the scale of the entire house.

In the interior, the spacious rooms, the wide stairway, and the huge fireplace echo the strong features of the exterior. The rooms are arranged as in a central hall plan, but without hall walls, thus combining the entry, the stairwell, and the living areas into an informal unified space. The living room fireplace is constructed of buff-colored brick, and the over-mantle is formed by short corbels bearing a wooden lintel which supports paneling sloped to the ceiling to cover the passage of the chimney through the floor above. Maybeck repeated this fireplace form, Jacobean in flavor, in numerous variations throughout his career. Executed in many materials—stone, brick, wood, and rough concrete—it became a hallmark of his residential designs.

Isaac Flagg house, fireplace and seat.
William S. Ricco photograph.

The basic fireplace form of the Flagg house with its heavy mantle and inclined paneling was used in various adaptations on many of his subsequent residential designs.

10. The Rieger house had overtones of chalet design, but its broken profile and massing were not characteristic of the style.

George H. Boke house, 23 Panoramic Way, Berkeley, 1902.
William S. Ricco photograph.

The original paired casement windows have been replaced by
fixed glass. Maybeck succeeded in reconciling horizontal and
vertical elements to create a building that still seems remarkably
exciting and contemporary.

The second house with chalet details was built for Professor George H. Boke in 1902 on Panoramic Way in Berkeley.[11] Even though it has a falsework of crossed logs at its corners in imitation of the nature of chalet construction, its actual structural order bears little relation to Swiss design. The house, on a sloping site, is entered on a half-level below the main floor. Its stairhall is built outside of the main rectangular form of the house, and is used as entry, circulation, and stairway for the principal living areas. The first landing of the stairway forms a vestibule for the living room. Double bolster blocks have been used on the columns between the stairhall and the living room to form a decorative entrance. A doorway at the second landing provides access to a large sleeping balcony the railing of which is ornamented by board balusters handsawn in a Swiss motif. The stairway then turns ninety degrees and leads to second-floor sleeping accommodations.

11. An exact copy of the Boke house was built in Oakland. Maybeck's office records also indicate duplicate plans and specifications of the Boke house were sent to Aberdeen, Washington in 1906 for the J. B. Elston house.

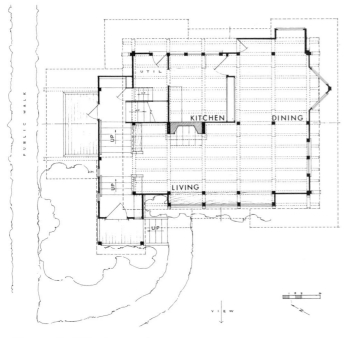

George H. Boke house, plan.
Drawn by Alan Williams from measurements by K. H. Cardwell.

The living room and dining room of the Boke chalet are one continuous ell-shaped space, separated by a single column of the main structural system. Its windows, originally paired casements with a single horizontal division, have been replaced in the living room by fixed sheets of plate glass. The fireplace is small and is faced with twelve-inch square matte-glazed tiles. It has a plain board mantle supported by brackets which repeat the design of the column bolsters. Filling

George H. Boke house, exterior sleeping porch.
William S. Ricco photograph.

In most of Maybeck's houses a sense of delight and variety is achieved through simple ornamental techniques. The basic sense of quality is achieved in the structural design and choice of materials.

out the block of the chimney above the mantle are two book cabinets fitted with leaded glass doors. All of the details, both structural and finish, are executed in redwood. The upstairs rooms are finished in board and batten with board-on-board ceilings. Short corbels penetrate the walls to support the large overhanging roof, and they are a good example of one device Maybeck frequently employed to extend the space of the house beyond the limits of the room.

The organization of the Boke house emphasizes the linear character of a post and beam framing system. Bolster blocks at the top of each column reduce the span and depth of the main beams. The basic unit is repeated ten times to create a rectangular building two bays wide and five bays long. The beams support purlins spaced two feet on center upon which rest one-by-twelve redwood boards that form the finished ceiling. The enclosing walls between the posts are of redwood boards or continuous casement sash. The curtain walls of some bays engage the columns while in others they project free from the frame, forming alcoves and window seats. In the Boke house Maybeck combined structure and plan to make an exquisite design for the modest house which for quality, limited by size and economy, has not been surpassed.

George H. Boke house, fireplace and entrance stairway. William S. Ricco photograph.

A "homey elegance" without elaborate treatments or finishes marks the Boke house as one meant to be delightfully lived in.

The Boke house did not bring to a close the designs that might be called chalets; but it did achieve the same integration of structure, plan, and spatial design which Maybeck had sought in his Gothic houses. Other experiments of the time made use of English vernacular forms as seen in the shingled cottage of 1902 for Professor Hiram D. Kellogg. Its living space was derived from the English hall, and was enriched by a two-storied bay window and a balconied corridor which led to the upstairs bedrooms. A fireplace reminiscent of American colonial designs with a highbacked settle of redwood created an inglenook and added a cosy note to the high-ceilinged room.[12]

12. In recent years the upper portion of the room has been floored to create additional bedroom space. The house has been moved to 2960 Linden St., Berkeley.

Maybeck's purpose in his use of forms, whether Gothic, Swiss, or English, was to extract the essence of their feeling rather than to achieve a coherent style. He classified architectures by their attributes rather than by their periods or national origins. To him Gothic architecture with its lofty spaces and steep roofs which pointed heavenward expressed aspiration, and its vertical lines indicated action—both desirable qualities for a vital expression in art. On the other hand, the classical styles with flattened roofs sloping towards the earth signified Greek ideals with an emphasis on human values; their horizontal lines indicated the repose that was a desirable attribute of the simple life. Maybeck's dilemma was that in interiors he preferred the quality of vertical space, yet on the exterior he sensed that the horizontality of classic lines was better suited to the surroundings.

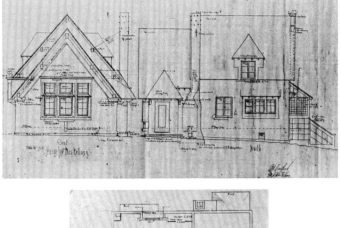

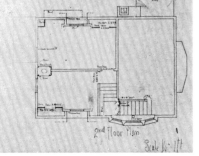

Hiram D. Kellogg house, 2608 Regent St., Berkeley, 1902. Plans and elevations, drawings courtesy of Mrs. R. Stoker, Documents Collection, C.E.D.

Maybeck's signature can be seen in the lower right corner of the original elevation drawing.

Hiram D. Kellogg house, exterior of building on its original site. William S. Ricco photograph.

Hip-roofed dormers, cantilevered bays and shingled mullions at the windows reveal Maybeck's delighted approach to architecture. Structural variety and richness immediately confront the viewer—nothing was static.

Faculty Club, University of California, Berkeley, 1902.
O. V. Lange photograph, Bancroft Library Archives, UCB.

The original plaster finish and form of the Faculty Club
suggests the old California Missions. Projecting trellis beams are
extensions of interior framing members. The small stucco
building to the rear housed the kitchen of the University Dining
Association.

The conflict between the medieval and classical idioms is well illustrated by the Faculty Club of the University of California with its interior vertical volume and structural lines contrasting with the horizontal fenestration and low-pitched gable roof of the exterior. The clubhouse was built in 1902; transformations and additions over the years have extended and refurbished the original facilities to meet the needs of an expanding faculty.[13] Nothing would have pleased Maybeck more than this organic growth of a building. It is a tribute to its designer that each architect has been able to leave the stamp of his own detail without changing the character of the original structure.

The rapid expansion of the University at the turn of the century brought to the campus a large number of men of diverse training and tradition. Even the geographical layout of the campus divided the staff into northsiders and southsiders. Faced with increasing divergence, a group of the faculty sought to establish a common meeting place for relaxation and recreation and "mutual good fellowship," where plans and policies affecting the University could be freely and informally discussed, where men could rub elbows and get clearer and closer views of one another than is possible "in the deadly atmosphere of an ordinary faculty meeting."[14]

13. Additions have been designed by J. G. Howard, W. C. Perry, W. S. Wellington, G. Downs and H. Lagorio.
14. "The Faculty Club," *University Chronicle* (October, 1902), pp. 196-207.

Faculty Club, plan.
Architects and Engineers, UCB.

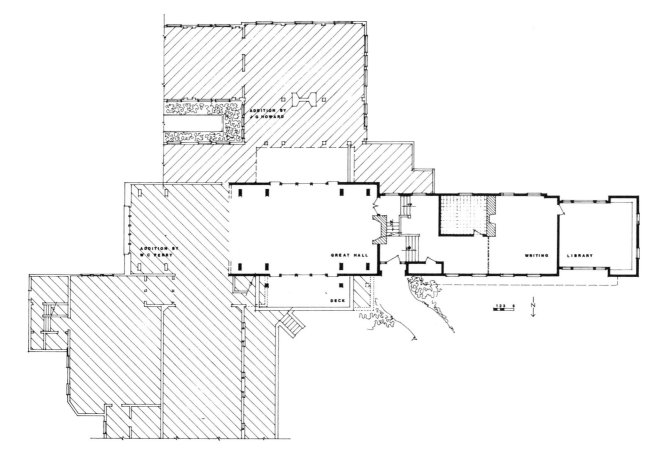

The program for the facilities changed even while Maybeck was designing the dining room and lounge area that had been called for. A number of the bachelor members of the faculty offered additional financial support if they could be provided with living accommodations. These were included in Maybeck's building which eventually consisted of a large hall, a billiard room, a writing room, a lounge, and living quarters. There was no kitchen, the dining room being served by a corridor from the facilities of the adjacent University Dining Association. Subsequent additions to the north, east, and south have more than doubled the size of the club building and have changed some of the uses of Maybeck's original rooms.

One room that remains essentially the same is the dining room, which the members call the Great Hall. Its interior framing is suggestive of Gothic timbering. Eight built-up columns of rough two-by-tens support a system of timbers framed as a half-truss for the low-pitched gabled roof. Each half-truss rises up and over to join its counterpart springing from the opposite side of the room. Balanced on the columns, the trusses are tied to the foundations by a steel rod. This ingenious framing, designed to give a high central space without any horizontal ties, is more readily understood in the later Unitarian Church at Palo Alto, which had a similar, though not identical, framing system.

The Great Hall has a sharply pitched ceiling carried by beams and purlins supported on the inner members of the trusses. Near the ridge, secondary truss ties create triangular spaces which are decorated with band sawn trefoils. The interior finish of the dining room is redwood board and batten, though in the gable end above the plate line of the wall framing the diagonal sheathing is exposed. A massive fireplace faced with matte-glazed tiles dominates the west wall. A large opening in the north wall is fitted with paired French doors leading to an exterior deck sheltered by a trellis. In Maybeck's original design the south wall was similarly treated. Above the French doors, transom windows are glazed with art glass interpretations of the seals of major universities. Adding to the Gothic allusion of the timber framing, beam ends projecting from the trellises into the room are rudely shaped to resemble heads of dragons. At one time Maybeck said the dragon's head found on many of his buildings was a tribute to his father's craft of wood carving.

The walls of the writing room were covered by stretched burlap, citron colored, and held in place by gilded, narrow half-round moldings. Its red brick fireplace was set flush with the halls. The upstairs residence rooms were reached by a hall in the form of an English long gallery whose continuous fenestration of simple casement sash and window seat along its north side afforded a simple, private lounge for resident members.

The exterior finish of Maybeck's section of the Faculty Club is principally a natural-colored sand plaster. Redwood shingles cover a portion of the second-story walls. The roof is of mission tile. Heavy wooden corbels and projecting trellis beams are extensions of the framing members of the interior. Arched entrance and window openings suggest California Mission forms.[15] The building with its fittings cost $4,400, and for that sum Maybeck was able to create the desired informal atmosphere while maintaining the vigorous scale and character of a men's club.

15. William C. Hays, "Some Interesting Buildings at the University of California," *Indoors and Out*, 2, (May, 1906), pp. 70-75. The earliest critical review of Maybeck's work including comments on Hearst Hall and the Faculty Club.

Faculty Club, "Great Hall," Archives, Bancroft Library, UCB.

In contrast to the exterior, the interior of the Great Hall with its great fireplace and wooden structural system was markedly Gothic in form and feeling. The building was used even before its interior was finished as can be seen in this photograph of the first annual meeting of the club.

The completion of the Faculty Club in 1902 ended a busy year for Maybeck. In addition to building the Boke and Kellogg houses, he had received at least five other residential commissions. And at home the birth of a daughter, named Kerna McKeehan after paternal and maternal grandparents, added to family responsibilities.

Throughout the decade in which he had been closely associated with the University, Maybeck had experimented with the craft of building. In his designs for his Gothic houses and the chalets that followed, he achieved the goal set by the newcomers to build houses that were expressive of a way of life; houses that were simply built and free from the meaningless details of another era. His designs, ranging in cost from $1,000 to $3,000, placed the modest house within the reach of those whose values emphasized the simple life. And while these designs led the way for a host of well-crafted houses constructed in the ensuing decade, it should be remembered that at the same time Maybeck was developing his simple houses, he was also engaged in the promotion of the grand scheme for the University, the erection of structurally innovative Hearst Hall, and in the construction of the romantic retreat, Wyntoon. Such contrasts in scale and costs of buildings would continue throughout his productive career. The early years set the pattern for what was to follow.

Faculty Club, detail of candle holder.
W. S. Wellington photograph.

The club building is another project for which Maybeck had the cooperation of Frederick H. Meyer as designer for the interior furnishings.

Grove Clubhouse, Bohemian Club of San Francisco, Bohemian Grove, Russian River, 1903.
Photograph courtesy of the Bohemian Club.

Superbly sited, the structure harmonizes with its setting while also providing a magnificient view of the area. Note the crossing roof battening, common to the wooden architecture of Switzerland, Sweden, and Japan.

V

Palette Of Time And Place

*Architecture is the handwriting of man. The architect is a
painter.... The history of architecture gives him his palette of
time and place. Each client fits into an era or in a mixture of
eras.... If the man is dressed in his own era, he is happy.
When you enter his domain you know... his dreams.*
                                        Bernard Maybeck—1930

When Maybeck opened his San Francisco office at 307 Sansome Street in 1902, he had little difficulty creating a flourishing practice. His reputation as a residential architect was well-established in his home community of Berkeley, and local residents continued to seek his services. The University Competition had brought him to the public's attention, and in 1899 he had joined the Bohemian Club, which was comprised of social and business leaders committed to the development of the cultural life of San Francisco. The commissions that came into his office were many and, although they were not large or lavish, they were spread throughout the San Francisco Bay region.

As in the first decade of his work, Maybeck explored his interest in structure and the craft of building, but he began to introduce new elements of color, ornament, and modeling into his designs of the second decade. The simple box-like shapes of the chalets and the articulated pavilions of the Gothic houses merged in experiments in molding spaces. His goal seemed to be to produce a greater variety of interior spaces. Maybeck's new designs grew more complex and, at the same time, his early simple homes, which Keeler had extolled, provided prototypes for the Arts and Crafts building in the area.

Even though much of Maybeck's early work received strong acclaim from people who were supporters of the ideas of John Ruskin and William Morris, he was not a proponent of a crafts revival. Maybeck started his designs on premises more sophis-

ticated than those attributed to the Arts and Crafts movement. Exploitation of structural order, application of visual phenomena, and respect for new materials and industrial processes, as well as a firm belief in the expressive qualities of form were the bases for his work. A building was designed in the manner that Maybeck felt was appropriate for the conditions of the problem given. So it was that the medieval castle for Phoebe Hearst reflected the primitive conditions of the area and of its construction. The unprecedented laminated wood arch framing of Hearst Hall was designed primarily to solve the problems of dismantling and reassembly and secondarily to provide a Gothic allusion of shape. The fact that Maybeck was ready either to adapt historic forms or to explore the boundaries of current construction technology went unnoticed by others advocating nature-inspired ornament and the infusion of handcrafts into the building process.

In California, the Arts and Crafts movement has been associated with the bungalow, mission furniture, art glass, and rustic buildings. It is unfortunate that the movement is more closely identified with the final phases of its dissolution than with its more illustrious beginnings, which can be traced to the wide-spread reaction against the debased design and the deterioration of the environment which developed during the Industrial Revolution. In the latter part of the nineteenth century in England, Europe, and America, groups formed through their common interest to improve the products and way of life of the new, industrialized civilization. They came to be recognized through their exhibitions and proposals for corrective action.

The thrust of the movement was two-fold—socio-economic and artistic. In the broadcast aspect it gave new impetus to city planning through the concepts of garden suburbs, new towns, and the "City Beautiful," which was originally a Beaux-Arts idea. It also made significant contributions to the aesthetic quality of product design through such groups as the William Morris workshops and the studios of Louis Tiffany. In architecture, particularly in the domestic field, architects produced designs with a basic simplicity and functionalism that have been identified as the beginnings of modern architecture.[1]

Maybeck's relation to the Arts and Crafts and the beginnings of the modern movement is obscured by his romantic individualism. He could create handsome pattern and design in his buildings without dependence on historical details, but when he felt a need to add enrichment he drew inspiration from past architectures, not from nature. The differences that his designs in an artisan tradition have with those generally referred to as "Craftsman," are well illustrated in the houses and clubs built soon after he opened his San Francisco office. In them can be seen imaginative siting, inventive use of structure, and sensitive detailing that distinguish his work from rough and awkward creations euphemistically called "rustic."

One of the first commissions to be executed in Maybeck's new office came about as a result of his association with the Bohemian Club. For a number of years the club had been holding a summer encampment in the redwood groves located along the Russian River north of San Francisco. In 1903 the directors of the club decided to build a permanent structure. A modest sum was raised by subscribers, and Maybeck was asked to design a clubroom that would serve as meeting place, dining room, and bathing facility for the campers.

The Club building, placed at the top of a high knoll overlooking the river, is superbly sited. The spot was probably chosen by the Grove committee; but, although dramatic, it posed a problem for its architect. Faced with making a very small structure hold its aesthetic position surrounded by trees well over one hundred feet tall, Maybeck wisely positioned one end of the building at the edge of the knoll with the rest supported by a substructure rising from the precipitous side of the hill. Columns made of tree trunks rose fifty feet to the floor of the club building above, establishing a strong vertical base set among tall trees. In this way the building achieved a scale in harmony with the giant redwoods and became an extension of the knoll, providing ample space for club members to enjoy the scenic view.

Broad eaves sheltering the balconies surrounding the building are supported by struts and rafters of unbarked logs. The arrangements of struts, columns, and knee braces are extremely handsome. The redwood saplings used for these exquisite details were very straight and tapered little from end to end, which allowed Maybeck to execute a precise design. In the interior, details of dressed lumber trusswork, planed board and batten walls, and glazed French doors contrast with the rough materials of the exterior. They mark Maybeck's sense of appropriate rusticity. The fireplace is worked in rough-cut local stone. Maybeck also designed a large deal table and three-legged chairs derived from seventeenth century Flemish forms to furnish the room.[2]

Along with his fellow Bohemians, Maybeck enjoyed the summer encampments for many years. He continued to contribute to the club activities—designing stage sets and costuming for several of their elaborate pageants. Today, after more than seventy years, the clubhouse spaces and furnishings remain as Maybeck designed them; only the kitchen and service facilities have been expanded.

1. Nikolaus Pevsner, *Pioneers of Modern Design* (New York: Museum of Modern Art, 1949), pp. 26, 27.

2. Conversations between the author and Maybeck. The chair design was derived from forms of Flemish milking stools.

Grove Clubhouse, interior view.
Photograph courtesy of the Bohemian Club.

The interior furnishings were designed by Maybeck. The chairs were patterned after Flemish milking stools.

B. R. Maybeck, charcoal and chalk drawing of original meeting place of the Bohemian Club, San Francisco, (no date).
Documents Collection, C.E.D.

It is inferred from the dimensions noted on the sketch that Maybeck's drawing was used to prepare scenery for one of the numerous Bohemian Club theatricals.

Outdoor Art Club building, 1 West Blithedale Ave., Mill Valley, 1904.
K. H. Cardwell photograph.

The roof structure adds visual interest to the building while revealing its structural character and providing a more ample interior space.

While most Arts and Crafts proponents argued for "honest construction," few took the structural frame of the building as a starting point for their designs. Maybeck, on the other hand, often created unusual shapes derived from his experiments in framing. His timbered roofs, inspired by medieval forms, were essentially new creations evolved from many past examples. While other architects were duplicating specific king post or scissors trusses, he was employing new ones aided by steel tension rods and standard lumber.

The design for the Outdoor Art Club (1904) in Mill Valley added a new roof variation. It has a simple, rectangular plan spanned by rafters trussed with a king post and collar ties. The ties extend through the roof covering and join a vertical extension of the wall columns, thereby strengthening the weakest part of the rafter chord between the tie and the support. Maybeck probably adopted this form for two reasons: first, the spaciousness of an uninterrupted vertical volume under a roof plane pleased him; second, the adaptation of a king post truss thrusting through the roof fulfilled his desire to indicate the nature of the building's framing from the exterior.

Outdoor Art Club, interior view.
Roy Flamm photograph.

Maybeck's play with building form by separating the principal structural members and the enclosing planes adds both interior and exterior interest to his design.

Even in residential construction Maybeck sometimes used special framing for architectural effects. An example is the living room of the J. B. Tufts house (1905) in San Anselmo, which was covered by a low-pitched gable roof supported on sloping beams with their thrusts restrained by concealed steel rods. The house, the first of three built for Tufts, is located on the side of a steep hill where it is virtually concealed. It is distinguished by the refined finish of its interior surfaces. The large living room is placed on the second floor to obtain views into the valley over the tops of the large oak trees on the site. Maybeck finished it with burl redwood paneling with heavily molded trim. Ornamental wood panels decorate the over-mantle of the fireplace and built-in storage units.

The Tufts house is of even greater interest for its use of artificial lighting. In his Gothic houses Maybeck had banked the casement sash to make good use of natural light, and in other houses had used skylights and unusually placed windows to create dramatic impressions. Bare bulbs and hanging lanterns adorned the early structures, but in the Tufts design Maybeck began to use indirect artificial light to enrich the interior. The ceiling, which follows the slopes of the low-gabled roof, is softly lighted by fixtures that are half-concealed by a wooden cornice. Wooden screens cover fixtures set into the stairwell walls and newel posts, creating additional ornamental lighting. The details are not so unusual or innovative as to make much of their design; rather, they indicate the direction of Maybeck's development as each new building added new subtleties to his architecture.

J. B. Tufts house (#1), 14 Entrata Ave., San Anselmo, 1905.
Covered deck adjoining second floor living room.
Roy Flamm photograph.

Virtually concealed in its verdant hillside setting, glimpses of the house reveal the interplay of light and shadow.

J. B. Tufts house, view from living room to entrance stairwell.
Roy Flamm photograph.

Gothic tracery housing indirect lighting combines with the natural elegance of wood to create a beautiful interior. Maybeck often spent time on the job to select and place unusual or finely-grained boards in strategic locations.

Isaac Flagg studio, 1208 Shattuck Ave., Berkeley, 1906.
K. H. Cardwell photograph.

The second story of this house does not appear to have been added by Maybeck.

Color became a strong feature in Maybeck's design of the Isaac Flagg Studio (1906). It soon became one of the distinctive elements of many of his buildings. Other than the moss green and earth red paints used on window sash, in the first ten years of his work color is little evidenced. The Faculty Club had walls covered with a green-gold burlap fastened with gilded half-round moldings. In Hearst Hall, Maybeck had installed red and blue lights to cast colored tones into shadowy recesses. But generally, plain, unstained woods provided the architectural background and color accents had been achieved by means of furnishings—tapestries in Hearst Hall and Wyntoon, oriental carpets and window hangings in the smaller buildings.

The Flagg studio, of chalet character, was originally a one-and-one-half-storied structure set in the garden of the large house Maybeck had built for Professor Flagg in 1901. It has since been enlarged to two full stories. The studio is framed by trussed redwood beams which rest on square eight-inch posts. Trusses and end walls support three six-by-six sub-beams spanning the length of the room. On these are laid two-by-two purlins which carry the ceiling. The east wall has panels of dark red plush set between flush fronted cabinets.

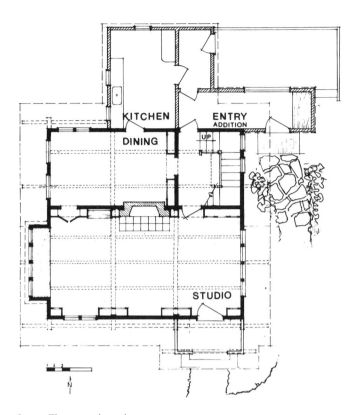

Isaac Flagg studio, plan.
Measured and drawn by K. H. Cardwell.

Isaac Flagg studio, living room.
William S. Ricco photograph.

Panels of red plush contrast with Prussian blue stained purlins and natural redwood beams.

A clinker brick fireplace on the west is surrounded by a wall of redwood casework and on the north and south continuous casement sash fills large openings. The entire room can be softly illuminated by indirect lighting units placed on top of the cases.

The beams of the studio are stencilled in gilt with geometrical patterns and carry purlins stained a Prussian blue. Gold purlins in the stairhall harmonize with dove gray woodwork, while Turkey red purlins of the dining room contrast with gray-green fir walls. The purlins penetrate the exterior walls and support the overhanging second story. On the exterior they are stained moss green with their exposed butt ends painted red-orange. The wall of redwood shingles and the redwood struts supporting the large overhangs were left untreated to age to blackish-brown tones. It is not surprising to find that Maybeck used a non-conventional framing system, nor that untreated redwood boards form bookshelves and flush case fronts. However, wooden structural members colored bright red and dark blue, ceilings of gold, and walls of plush do seem unexpected details for the simple home.

Maybeck had a practical reason for introducing color into the design of the Flagg studio. Its primary framing and trim members were redwood, but all of the secondary framing members were fir. In previous houses the ceiling materials had been all redwood and therefore had no contrast in color. When combining the redwood and fir of the studio, Maybeck selected stains to accent their differing grains and hues.

His aesthetic reason for his choice of colors was based on the fact that Professor Flagg was a Classics scholar. Maybeck knew from reading *Der Stil* by Gottfried Semper that the classical Greek structures were rich in polychrome ornamentation, and he chose color as a symbol of Professor Flagg's academic field. It is more than coincidental to find a similarity between Maybeck's color choices and Semper's plates illustrating the conjectural decorative painting of the Temple of Theseus at Athens. Several years later Maybeck drew a frontispiece for a publication of a Greek play entitled *Circe* which Isaac Flagg had written.[3] In his drawing Maybeck depicts Grecian structures in a wide range of hues.

3. Isaac Flagg, *Circe* (Berkeley and Ukiah: 1915), printed by the Roycrofters, East Aurora, N.Y.

Bernard Maybeck, tempera drawing, Frontispiece for *Circe*, by Isaac Flagg, 1915. Photograph, Art Gallery, UCB.

In the structural design for the Hillside Club (1906) Maybeck moved away from his simple artisan approach towards one that foreshadowed modern architects' separation of the structure and the skin of buildings in new spatial orders. His ingenious framing of the Faculty Club had started the experiment, but its interior was static and axially balanced. In the Hillside Club Maybeck created a fluid, asymmetrical composition of interior volumes. His goal was not to create new forms but to enrich old ones.

In 1902 Maybeck, along with Charles Keeler, had led in the formation of the Hillside Club which sought "to foster civic patriotism among the residents of Berkeley, to encourage parks, playgrounds, planting of trees, beautifying streets and gardens," in order to make Berkeley "an educational, art and home center.[4] Members believed that the achievement of the ideal community would be aided by improving its citizens through their cultural environment. Accordingly, they held concerts, sponsored lectures, and arranged for dramatic productions. In 1906 the club membership, by then about two hundred and fifty people, decided to have a building constructed in which they could meet and present their programs. Maybeck was automatically selected as architect. He had designed houses for many of the members, and from the start of the organization his ideas had formed a focus for their activities.

The scheme for the building is the most intriguing of all Maybeck's designs for small clubs. Photographs of the structure are rare, and both his original sketches and the building were destroyed by fire. Fortunately, one set of blueprinted drawings remains and, supplemented by members' verbal descriptions, it gives an adequate, if somewhat elusive image of the structure. Recollections of the old clubhouse always start with the quality of the light and sound of its interior. A detailed study of the drawings confirms that Maybeck gave special attention to the design in order to achieve innovative spatial, acoustical, and lighting effects.

A combination of post and beam, and column and truss systems formed the structure. Seven pairs of interior columns, spaced in alternating dimensions of five and ten feet to create three principal and three minor bays, carried beams and trusses for (and at places through) the roof. A grid system of

4. Hillside Club, "Minutes of Meeting," August 23, 1902. Bancroft Library, University of California, Berkeley.

girders and joists, hung on the columns, supported the floor and took the tension loads imparted from the cantilevered trusses through iron tie rods placed in exterior curtain walls of board and batten construction.[5] The entire structural frame was carried on the columns which rested on individual mat footings.

Steep gable roofs over the main room and transepts contrasted with flat roofs covering the adjoining areas. The edges of the low roofs were feathered into trelliage. Portions of the columns and trusses which were outside of the enclosing walls were also roofed with steep gables. The exterior was clad in redwood shingles; sills, exposed corbels, trellis members, and trim were also unstained redwood. Casement sash divided into square panes was used throughout the building and their paint was the only color accent.

The interior of the Hillside Club was redwood board and batten to the clerestory level. The upper portions of the walls were surfaced with rough split redwood barn shakes which had been dipped in sulphate of iron to produce a weathered silvery finish. The transepts had flat hung ceilings of shakes nailed to joists that floated free from the surrounding walls.

This permitted the passage of air and light into their attic spaces and produced the distinctive quality of light and sound which so impressed the membership.

The symmetrical nature of the structural system tended to give the building the picturesque outline of a small Gothic church. But Maybeck took advantage of his skeletal structure to introduce enclosing planes—at some places within and at others outside of the frame—that changed the interior volume from a static, axial order into a dynamic one. Nowhere was Maybeck's imaginative skill in plastic organization of spaces within and around a structural system better illustrated than in this building.

5. The Faculty Club and the Unitarian Church were other experiments in the separation of compressive and tensile forces in a structural frame.

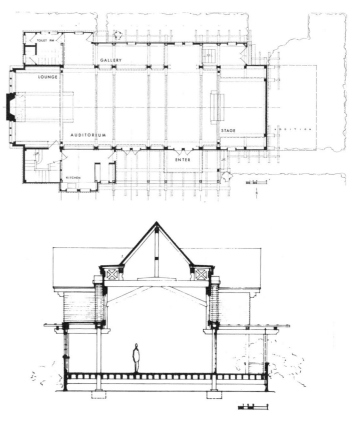

Hillside Club building, 2286 Cedar St., Berkeley, 1906.
(Destroyed 1923)
Documents Collection, C.E.D.

Although constructed on a rectangular grid pattern, the Hillside Club presented familiar but varied shapes on the exterior, and the unique quality of its interior space and volumes delighted the viewer within the structure.

Hillside Club building, plan and section.
Drawn by Alan Williams, Documents Collection, C.E.D.

Hillside Club building, members at dinner.
Photograph courtesy of F. H. Dempster.

Annie and Bernard Maybeck seated at the left, far side,
first table.

Early in the morning of April 18, 1906, San Francisco citizens were abruptly awakened by toppling chimneys and smashing crockery. Even persons in the suburban areas were aware of the severity of the earthquake, but no one, including the residents of the city who experienced the strongest shocks, could have known the serious consequent events that would mark the day forever in the history of San Francisco. Maybeck did not make his way by ferry from Berkeley to San Francisco that day. Those who did were stranded by the fire which soon swept the waterfront and business districts, destroying five hundred and twelve blocks in the three days it raged and isolating San Francisco from the eastern shores of the Bay. Anticipating the aftershocks that follow such a quake and wanting either to check buildings he had designed or the Hillside Clubhouse which was under construction, Maybeck stayed close to home. Even had he gone to San Francisco, his presence in the city would have made little difference to the preservation of his office drawings. The destruction of the city was so rapid and so complete that even its most vital records were destroyed, and Maybeck's office in Sansome Street was in the very heart of the most heavily devastated area.

After the fire Maybeck and White took temporary office quarters at 821 Eddy Street near the Civic Center. Mark White had been Maybeck's assistant since the office had opened on Sansome Street. He had finished his studies at the University in civil engineering, and under the guidance of Maybeck he began to adapt his knowledge to buildings. John White and an architect named George Howard had also shared the Sansome Street office with Maybeck, and although they had both worked for him at times, each had his individual commissions. At the new address they formed a firm as Maybeck, Howard, and White. The three did rehabilitation work on several commercial structures and several houses on the San Francisco peninsula. John White probably took the design lead in the firm, allowing Maybeck to continue his work with his original helper, Mark, under the old name of Maybeck and White. The new combination lasted for only fifteen months and by the time they all moved to a refurbished office at 35 Montgomery Street at the end of 1907, Maybeck and White (Mark) and Howard and White (John) had become the permanent alignment.[6] Maybeck and White practiced at the Montgomery Street address for the rest of their professional careers.

Charles Josselyn house, 400 Kings Mountain Road, Woodside, 1907. Maybeck, Howard, and White, Architects. K. H. Cardwell photograph.

A very large residence with many classical features including a columned courtyard, the Josselyn house was designed by the firm of Maybeck, Howard and White during the short time after the San Francisco earthquake that the firm existed. Maybeck's specific contribution to the design is not known although elements of the wood work recall some of his earlier work and classical details were later employed by him in some of his larger structures.

6. George Howard was not related to John Galen Howard. Composite and incomplete office records were kept in the initial year after the earthquake. The appendix lists the work by firms as determined from certificate books, drawings, and journals in the C.E.D. Docs.

One of the first commissions Maybeck received as a result of the fire was for the design of a temporary bookstore for the Paul Elder Company (1906), in the business district set up on Van Ness Avenue during the reconstruction of the city. The building was located on the site of a structure destroyed by the fire, and Maybeck ingeniously hung his framing from new interior columns placed within the limits of the old foundations. It was similar to the system he had used in building the Hillside Club, but here it gained economic and design advantages by saving the cost of removing old foundations and by freeing the plan arrangement from the constrictions of existing work.

Paul Elder, who had a lively interest in the arts, was more than a bookseller. In his store he exhibited paintings, sold Rookwood pottery and Tiffany glass, and sponsored lectures of cultural interest for the community. His firm also published works of local literary people in specially designed publications modeled after the work of the Kelmscott Press and the Roycrofters. Reflecting the interest of the owner, Maybeck chose to design the temporary Elder store in an Arts and Crafts manner. With rough-sawn lumber in exposed structural patterns varied by the light from skylights and clerestories, he integrated the columns, walls, ceiling, casework, and lighting fixtures into an appropriate background for the books and crafts.

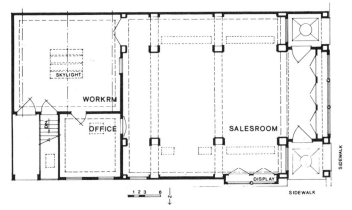

Paul Elder and Co. bookstore, plan.
Documents Collections, C.E.D.

Paul Elder and Co. bookstore, Van Ness Ave. and Pine St., San Francisco, 1906.
Photograph courtesy of W. S. Wellington.

For the temporary bookstore constructed after the San Francisco earthquake and fire, Maybeck designed the interior in an Arts and Crafts manner using rough-sawn lumber to create a harmonious housing for the books and crafts objects displayed and sold within the store.

Bernard Maybeck, pen and ink drawing, ca. 1906, Paul Elder bookstore.
Documents Collection, C.E.D.

Maybeck also designed the permanent Elder Book Store (1908) in the rehabilitated center of the city. Here he faced a typical architectural problem—to build an interior within an existing commercial structure. The space had the advantages of height and access to natural light along one side, ten feet above the first floor level. Maybeck developed the store as a central two-storied space with windows on one side. Flat, wooden arches spanned the ceiling in an unorthodox diagonal fashion, and at each end of the room mezzanine galleries adjoined the central space. The walls were paneled in wide vertical boards and finished with trim in Gothic profiles. Cylindrical light shades, hung from iron rings, formed chandeliers which were suspended from the ceiling by heavy chains. Ornamental screens derived from Gothic patterns carved in wood decorated the mezzanine levels. The book store was a well-proportioned galleried hall, and its Gothic ancestry would have been sensed even without its blatant decorative tracery.

It is surprising that Maybeck's tracery had little if any relationship to the building's structural order; he seemed to prefer to use it as a screen for space or light. Other decorative treatments—such as his trellis forms—often grew from basic framing members as they had in the Faculty Club. Even his exposed wood sheathing patterns developed from a simple repetition of lines into decorative schemes of boards contrasting in widths and accented by color. But in many designs his tracery and other bits and pieces of historic ornament were often incongruously placed or strangely scaled.

Paul Elder and Co. bookstore, 239 Grant Street, San Francisco, 1908. (Destroyed)
Photograph courtesy of W. S. Wellington.

High ceilings spanned by Tudor arches, coupled with clerestory lighting and Gothic tracery combined to create an unusually eclectic, intriguing interior for the permanent Elder Book Store.

Bernard Maybeck, ink and colored pencil drawing, "Children's Room," Paul Elder bookstore.
Documents Collection, C.E.D.

An angel graces Maybeck's drawing of the decoration for the children's section of the bookstore.

Howard B. Gates house, 62 S. 13th St., San Jose, 1904.
William S. Ricco photograph.

The elliptical lines of the facade arch are repeated in the steps
leading to the entrance. Baroque details are found in the
balconies resting on fat consoles and the balustered railings.

Although most of Maybeck's domestic work prior to the
earthquake has been associated with German, Swiss, and
English medieval vernacular forms, the fascination he felt for
the plastic modeling of volumes and spaces as seen in the
Hillside Club had previously found expression in the neo-
baroque details of the 1904 San Jose residence of Howard
B. Gates.[7] The street elevation of the Gates house displays
an adept asymmetrical composition with strong light and
shade effects and a vigorous modeling of the wall surface. The
house is actually three stories high, but by lowering the first
into the grade and nestling the bedrooms under a large gabled
roof, Maybeck created the impression of a one-and-one-half-
storied house. The illusion is heightened by his placement
of the entrance door at a split level between the ground and
second stories where an enlarged landing of the stairwell
forms the entry.

7. Arthur B. Clark, *Art Principles in House, Furniture, and Village
   Building* (Palo Alto: Stanford University Press, 1921), pp. 45, 46.
   The Gates house is illustrated and listed as the residence of Edwin
   Thomas.

Howard B. Gates house, stairway from main floor to bedrooms.
William S. Ricco photograph.

Richly composed of woods, the stairway to the lowest level is
circular with a railing of squat balusters of turned redwood,
while from the second to the third story, it is square with a
railing of tenuous spindles. Overhead light, accented by side
lighting from semi-concealed windows at each landing, floods
the stairwell.

Maybeck also produced residential designs with elements based on conjectural reconstructions of Greek and Roman houses. He loosely called their form classic, but this did not preclude his use of Romanesque, Gothic, or even baroque details. And, in the 1920s when other architects also turned to southern European examples for the California house, Maybeck's designs still remained uniquely individualistic. His complete disregard for archeological detail and proper "good taste" in historic style is evident in all of his works. Of course, with the ascendancy of the American Beaux-Arts movement, his mixed use of period prototypes caused his architecture to be labeled "eccentric."

The first construction to reveal Maybeck's conception of Greek or Mediterranean domestic architecture is the Oscar Maurer studio (1907) on LeRoy Avenue in Berkeley. The studio is sited near the bank of Strawberry Creek and faces a large oak tree which grows in the middle of the street. (Members of the Hillside Club had persuaded the city fathers to save the tree by paving around it when grading improvements had threatened its destruction.) Maurer was a portrait photographer and the building designed for him contained a small office and a display gallery in addition to living quarters. The various rooms of the one-story building nestle under low-pitched gabled roofs. Maybeck used changes in the floor level to accommodate the studio to the sloping site, and variations in room heights to add interest to its interior. The changes, clearly expressed on the exterior, create a picturesque silhouette dominated by the horizontal eave lines of the tiled roofs.

To reinforce the classical image of the studio Maybeck used two bits of ornament. One is found in the large window of the gallery which is sheltered by the deep entrance porch. A small wooden Corinthian column in the center of the window is intersected by the plane of the glass so that half of the column and its gilded capital lies outside the room and half within, creating a strong illusion that the gallery is open to the street and its sheltering oak tree. The second, a simplified classical frieze executed in plaster with guttae, but with neither tryglyphs nor metopes, is located as a sill and apron for the office window. The drawings indicate that it was intended to carry an inscription. In addition, the coloring, as in the Flagg studio, is suggestive of Semper's plates on the polychromy of Greek buildings. Walls of gray sanded plaster abut beams stained brown, and purlins colored blue and green contrast with the rose tones of the exposed roof sheathing.

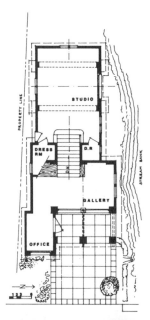

Oscar Maurer studio, plan.

Oscar Maurer photographic studio, 1772 Le Roy Ave., Berkeley, 1907.   Roy Flamm photograph.

Andrew Lawson house (#2), 1515 La Loma Ave., Berkeley, 1907. William S. Ricco photograph.

Dramatically different from his Gothic houses, the Mediterranean style of the concrete, "earthquake-proof" Lawson house is strikingly contemporary and reveals Maybeck's skill and architectural vision with widely differing styles and materials.

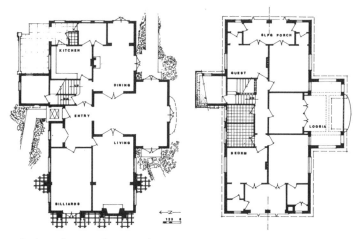

Andrew Lawson house, plan.

The interior spaciousness of the plan is augmented by vistas into the gardens through the rooms.

The design for the second Andrew Lawson house (1907) also has a Mediterranean flavor. The first, a Gothic house, had been located in the district south of the University, and when Professor Lawson later purchased a large tract of land on the hillside north of the campus, he again engaged Maybeck to design his house, which was to be constructed of reinforced concrete. Most likely Lawson's knowledge of geology spurred his interest in an earthquake-proof house; but certainly the San Francisco disaster added impetus to his decision for its building. Herman Kower, the engineer Maybeck had consulted for the design of Hearst Hall, was chosen to work out the structural details. But the early Roman flavor that the Lawson house evokes was the the result of a romantic historical connection Maybeck made between the destructions of San Francisco and Pompeii. He would design as would a Pompeiian architect, but with modern materials and methods.

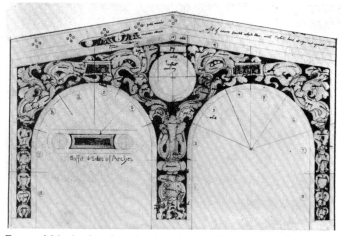

Bernard Maybeck, ink and colored chalk drawing, sgraffito study, Lawson house.   Documents Collection, C.E.D.

Andrew Lawson house, entrance detail.
Documents Collection, C.E.D.

Simple, clean detailing with the inlays and scoring of the plaster creates an entrance of subdued elegance.

The Lawson house is a two-storied rectangular structure placed on the upper portion of its hillside plot. A low-pitched gable roof, formed by concrete slabs covered with tar and gravel, continues in shed forms over portions that extend from the main block—a loggia covering the living space at the south and the stairwell at the north. On the exterior, at points where transverse concrete walls carry the second story, engaged pilasters one story in height support redwood trellises.

An interior spaciousness is emphasized by vistas into the garden through axially placed rooms. The entry hall leads at the right to a billiard room and ahead to a living area where large French doors open onto a terrace and garden. Flanking the living room are a study and a dining room with openings creating views through the length of the building. The second-story contains bedrooms which are connected by dressing closets to open sleeping porches. On the south, the exterior loggia affords a sweeping view of the city below and the Bay beyond.

Maybeck was familiar with concrete surfaces through his work with the Florida hotels; but instead of experimenting with the textures of the walls of the Lawson house, he plastered them. The exterior is finished with pink and buff colored sand plasters and smooth-cast white concrete. The simply molded cornice and various wall panels are ornamented with diaper line patterns and insets of small colored tiles. The interior of the house is plastered—with the exception of the billiard room, which was to be veneered with wood.

While Maybeck made no dramatic strides in exploiting the concrete forms of the Lawson house, his treatment of the cornice and openings around the upstairs loggia is not based on conventional masonry forms; and, even with its plastered surfaces, the house has a monolithic appearance. His use of rigid frames and two-way slabs contributed to the open interior of the house; but its spaces are more geometrically and axially balanced than are those of most of his wooden structures.

J. H. Senger house, 1321 Bay View Place, Berkeley, 1907.
Documents Collection, C.E.D.

The Senger house combined a shingled exterior with one of
stucco and half-timbering with the trim brightly painted in reds
and blues creating a curious and somewhat awkward composition in which the portions can even appear to be unrelated
structures.

The San Francisco earthquake and fire had created a wide
interest in reinforced concrete. The Art Gallery and the
Women's Dormitory at Stanford University, pioneering structures of Ernest Ransome, withstood the shock, while masonry
structures around them toppled. It seemed logical for this
new material to be used in new forms. However, the high cost
of steel in California hampered experimental work, especially
for residential building. A comparison of the cost of the Lawson house with that of the wood-framed Senger house—one
similar in size and built in the same year by Maybeck—shows
that reinforced concrete construction was more than double
the cost of building in wood.

In the 1907 house for J. H. Senger, a professor of German, Maybeck emphasized Germanic forms ranging from the medieval to the baroque to reflect his client's interests. Its exterior combines shingles and plaster with half-timbering, irregularly related to structural rhythms, which recalls rustic structures of the Rhineland. The design of the house is erratic—steeply pitched gable roofs supported on overly heavy corbeling are interrupted by dormers with broken pediment forms. In spite of awkward combinations, the house is worthy of study for the integration of its interior and garden. Maybeck's early houses often revealed his sensitivity to the nature of the land, but this was generally a contrasting relationship based on the size and placement of the structure on the site. The Gothic house broke sharply from a natural garden with few, if any, transitional elements from one to the other. The Senger house, like that for Lawson, uses a garden with paved terraces, trellises, and secondary structures to complement its interior spaces.

The entry floor level is more than a half-story below the living rooms although it is not separated from them. A short flight of stairs arrives at a landing and vestibule of the music room which has its own formal entrance from the western side of the property. The stairway switches back to land in an ell-shaped combination of living and dining rooms. This equivocal space is dominated by a large concrete fireplace cast in baroque forms and ornamented by ceramic tiles which Senger had purchased on a visit to Germany. Opposite the fireplace, at the end of the dining area, a raised platform designated by Maybeck on the plan as an *erker* (alcove) functions as a space for informal eating. Large glazed doors can be opened along the entire south wall of the dining room onto a bricked terrace sheltered by a free-standing pergola. The living room extends through glazed doors onto a terrace covered by the second-story. Views from the terrace into the garden, over the city, and across the Bay reveal one strong attraction for building on Berkeley hillside sites.

J. H. Senger house, plan.
Documents Collection. C.E.D.

J. H. Senger hose, view from terrace to garden.
Documents Collection, C.E.D.

The plan and interior of the Senger house were successful in integrating the living area with the terraces and gardens, revealing Maybeck's sensitivity to the natural surroundings.

J. H. Senger house, exterior detail.
J. Beach photograph.

The descriptions of the Maurer, Lawson, and Senger houses have emphasized the diversity of Maybeck's historical sources, and although he continued to use the Swiss chalet for a model, it too developed into new forms. The earlier chalets of Flagg and Underhill were single rectangular blocks.[8] But in the Albert Schneider house (1907) there is a shaping of the mass indicative of a more free room arrangement. Maybeck abandoned the rigid structural module of the Boke chalet in favor of conventional framing combined with a simple post and lintel system to span the living areas. Beams supporting the eaves and struts bracing the balconies butt against vertical two-by-eights that are an exterior indication of the building frame. The form does not return to totally articulated parts as in the Keeler and Davis houses, but combines open planning with a robust development of balconies and eaves to enrich the exterior.

On the Schneider house the roof form, short on the uphill side and long on the downhill one, echoes the character of the site. The ridge of its principal gable parallels the level lines of the ground, while a transverse gable over the master bedroom and balcony points west to the Bay. The eaves at the ridge project almost six feet and sweep down in diminishing breadth. The house, however, does not adjust itself to the contours as does the Maurer studio or some of Maybeck's later work; instead, it rises high as a vertical element in the landscape, modified only by the horizontal lines of the balconies and long sweeps of the eaves.

The house is entered by passing through a hillside garden designed by John McLaren, whose fame grew with his development of Golden Gate Park in San Francisco.[9] The steep garden path leads to an entrance vestibule which opens directly into the living area. The circulation way from the entry at the south to the stairwell at the north lies between the living room and the dining room and is defined by the free standing columns at one side of the living area. The flow of space from a sheltered terrace outside the dining room through French doors in the west wall of the living room marks a strong visual axis which composes with the one of the north-south circulation. Nine-foot ceilings and simple board and batten walls make the scale of the interior compatible with its bold composition.

8. The Underhill chalet on LeRoy Avenue, Berkeley, is listed in several publications as the residence of S. D. Hutsinpillar.
9. Cf. John McLaren, *Gardening in California* (San Francisco: A. M. Robertson, 1909).

Albert Schneider house, 1325 Arch St., Berkeley, 1907. Documents Collection, C.E.D.

The Schneider house sits high on its hillside site to afford views from its many balconies of the Bay and surrounding areas.

The Schneider house is a modest house constructed on a modest budget. The remarkable thing about the plan is its sense of spaciousness, although the main rooms are contained in a roughly rectangular space twenty-five by thirty-five feet. Its ample feeling was developed by Maybeck's skill in relating one volume to another, as well as by his astute placement of voids in the walls that define them. The house, without any arbitrary room arrangements, achieves a dynamic balance of planes and volumes around its axial lines.

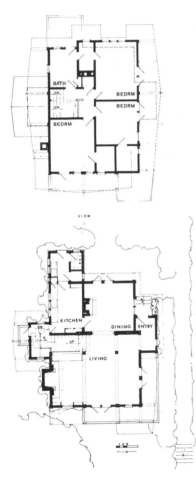

Albert Schneider house, view from living room to dining room. William S. Ricco photograph

Despite its modest dimensions, a sense of spaciousness is achieved through high ceilings and vistas through the rooms. The fireplace is a noteworthy variation of one of Maybeck's basic designs.

Albert Schneider house, plan.
Drawn by Alan Williams, Documents Collection, C.E.D.

The open plan complements the robust exterior of the design.

The William Rees house (1906) on La Loma Avenue in Berkeley, is said to be a copy of a chalet model the owner had brought back from Switzerland.[10] But the corners, detailed of crossed logs as in the Boke house, and the decorative detail of the balcony railings are probably the extent to which the design copied the model. An undefined space of the stairwell can be made into an entry by closing large sliding doors placed at right angles to one another, thereby separating it from the dining and living rooms. This singular and innovative plan arrangement is not to be found in any chalet. In addition, the stairway rises in an easy flight to an enlarged mid-landing which serves as a small sitting room with a view of the San Francisco Bay. The house is built on a steep and convoluted piece of property. Maybeck's design gained direct ground access at several levels, an attribute which a later owner took advantage of to convert the house into three independent living units. Like the Schneider house, it has a rich composition of balconies, large eaves, and uneven gabled roofs unlike conventional chalets.

Maybeck participated with developers or contractors in promotional designs throughout his career, and this may have been the situation with the Rees construction. There are no office drawings for this project, and it seems likely that Maybeck provided limited services and did the work outside of his regular San Francisco office routine. Remaining records of this type of collaboration are scanty; some such projects are no doubt unidentified and difficult to document as Maybeck's.

10. B. R. Maybeck Photos, "W. Rees," C.E.D. Docs. The Rees house has been published as the work of A. E. Hargraves.

William Rees house, entry and stairway.
Stone and Stecatti photograph.

William Rees house, La Loma and Virginia, Berkeley, 1907.
Stone and Stecatti photograph.

Although the Rees house has decorative details resembling a chalet, the plan arrangement was distinctive and original.

Frank C. Havens, the real estate developer of the subdivisions in which the Schneider and Senger houses were built, liked Maybeck's treatment of hillside sites, and in 1908 he asked Maybeck to design his own residence in neighboring Piedmont where he owned property. The site, which included a steep canyon studded with large California Live Oak trees, had its best building area lying fifteen feet below the level of the access road. Maybeck selected the spot for his design and arranged the plan to overcome the difficult grade conditions by entering the house at the second-story level. Although the house has been remodeled, a small bridge still spans the space from the entrance drive to the building where the entry once opened into a spacious hall. The hall led to bedrooms and a large deck bordering its south side. An open stairwell descended to the living and dining rooms below. The steepness of the site and the bridged entrance permitted all living spaces to be above ground. The living room still opens to a southern outdoor balcony which covers the terrace of the game room later developed as the lowest story. In addition to the main house, Maybeck designed servants' quarters above a garage for six cars, and it, too, was connected to the service element of the house by a bridge that spanned a minor lateral of the principal canyon.

Mr. and Mrs. Havens were in the East for an extended stay during the construction of the house, and Maybeck carried on a regular correspondence with them to inform them of the building's progress. In addition to technical and business details, he expressed his ideas on the relationship of a house, its owners, and its furnishing. "We believe that when you have seen the house and become accustomed to it," he wrote,

> there will be a thousand and one ideas come rushing to your mind to complete it....We therefore are getting an idea of the cost of things and when you have decided what you will do to put life into the rooms, you will make such a success of it that the thing as a whole will have that interest and personality which even as a plain business proposition will be a good investment....We also were under the impression that you could get your own personality into your house better if we stopped at the building proper, so as to leave you unhampered in the final work of furnishings.[11]

It may seem surprising that a designer as individualistic as Maybeck should encourage the owners to infuse their personalities into the design. It is a commendable attribute for an architect and one that many architects, acting as arbitrators of taste, find difficult to achieve.

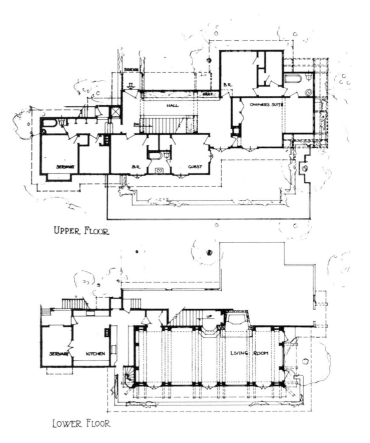

UPPER FLOOR

LOWER FLOOR

Frank C. Havens house, 101 Wildwood Gardens, Piedmont, 1908. Plan, Documents Collection, C.E.D.

The basic plan design is one of the few remaining original Maybeck elements of this greatly remodeled house.

11. B. R. Maybeck MSS, "F. C. Havens," C.E.D. Docs.

Frank C. Havens house, elevation.
Documents Collection, C.E.D.

Maybeck placed the large house in such a manner that all rooms were above the ground level of the steeply inclined site.

Mrs. Havens' interest centered on East Indian and Oriental artifacts, and while some of the carving which exists in the house was incorporated in the design by Maybeck, the major portion of the work was executed at a later date by East Indian craftsmen transported by Mrs. Havens from the Orient. At that time the house was virtually rebuilt. Maybeck's great living hall had rooms added in its lofty reaches, and redwood beams and surfaces were replaced by teak. Oriental details and complete rooms were imported to add to the structure. Leila Havens applied Maybeck's advice with such effectiveness that all that remains of Maybeck's design is the plan scheme, the proportions of the living room, and a few exterior details.[12]

12. F. C. Havens was a major client for whom Maybeck did not do repeat work. It appears that Maybeck's experiment with a concrete fireplace failed to draw properly and led to the invention of his "venturi chimney cap" which became a design characteristic after 1908.

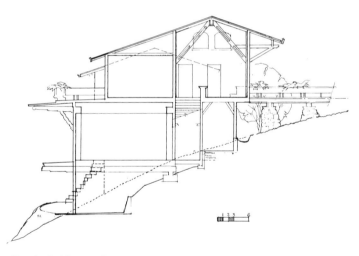

Frank C. Havens house, section.
Documents Collection, C.E.D.

Frank C. Havens house, living room.
K. H. Cardwell photograph.

Although the extensive alterations carried out in the 1920s have changed much of the interior and exterior of the house, some details and the character of Maybeck's design remain.

Bernard Maybeck, charcoal and watercolor drawing, Leon L. Roos house, 3500 Jackson St., San Francisco, 1909. Documents Collection, C.E.D.

Maybeck's rendering reveals the Tudor forms and details of the structure which was constructed on a gridwork of beams fastened to wooden piles driven into the hillside in an attempt to minimize possible earthquake damage.

But not all owners desired to devote time and energy in the furnishing of their houses, and when Maybeck was asked by a client to select or design furniture, he did so readily. Such was the case in building the Leon L. Roos house (1909) near San Francisco's Presidio Heights, an area which, even before the fire, had seen many large and expensive residences constructed in fine materials and academic styles. Maybeck chose to use Tudor forms and details, and while at first glance there seems to be little relation between the Roos design and his earlier Gothic houses, there are many similarities.

Maybeck articulated the spaces of the Roos house following the pattern he had used for the Hall house. A one-story living room is joined by an entry hall to a two-story block containing the dining room and kitchen areas with bedrooms on its second floor. Each block is surmounted by a steeply pitched gable roof, tiled in slate, which allows a richly timbered truss over the living area and provides space for servants' quarters in the attic over the bedrooms. The basement level is used for utility, storage, and recreation rooms. The townhouse is unique with its handsome level portico and graceful skylighted

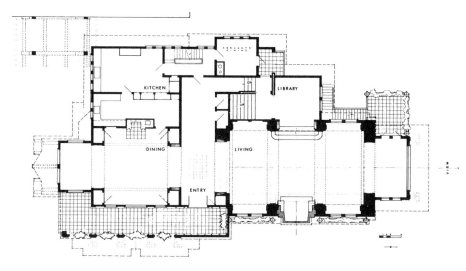

Leon L. Roos house, plan. Drawn by Alan Williams.
Documents Collection, C.E.D.

entry hall, and contrasts with the columned porches and formal entries of nearby residences.[13]

The living areas are well proportioned and handsomely detailed. The large spaces are composed around strong axial lines, and the smaller areas, designed for intimate occasions, add interest and delight to the overall design. Panels of mauve plush edged with gold gimp harmonize with redwood walls. Redwood battens and moldings have Gothic profiles. Indirect lighting and diffused light from wall fixtures softly illuminate surfaces and details, while hanging chandeliers sparkle against the dark heights of the roof timbering. Tables of dark oak and chairs cushioned with rose velvet supplement the furnishings selected from the owner's collection of medieval pieces. Wall coverings, light fixtures, and furniture—even the heraldic crest of the owner's initial ornamenting the entrance door—were fashioned from designs by Maybeck.

The Roos house is the largest of the townhouses that Maybeck designed. The trussed rafters of the living room rise to a height of thirty feet at the ridge, and their horizontal ties penetrate the roof in a manner similar to those of the Outdoor Art Club. The steep gable of the two-storied section paralleling the street is complicated by the addition of low-pitched roofs, projecting balconies, dormers, and wide eaves which are supported by cantilevered beams and post brackets ornamented by carved quatrefoils. And, although the walls are treated in

a strong rectangular pattern of plaster and half timbers, the various angles of the roof planes and the projecting and retreating surfaces of the minor architectural details create an erratic exterior.

The Roos house was constructed on a gridwork of beams fastened to wooden piles driven into the hillside. Although there is no record to indicate why Maybeck employed a foundation system unusual for residential construction, it is probable that he selected it to mitigate any possible damage by earthquakes. One of the oldest San Francisco masonry buildings to withstand the earth tremors had been built on a similar system, and the only damage suffered by wooden-framed structures in 1906 had been caused by sliding from foundations.[14] In any event, the firm and flexible bearing assured adequate ground anchorage, and Maybeck avoided the great bulk of foundation work that is commonly found in large San Francisco hillside houses.

13. Over the years Maybeck made several changes and additions to the Roos house. The last and most extensive was in 1926. At that time the principal staircase was modified, a small second-story living space was added, and additional rooms were developed in the attic story.
14. Cf. Washington Block (Montgomery Block), San Francisco, 1853, G. P. Cummings, architect, which was constructed on pilings and a grid beam footing.

Leon L. Roos house, entry passageway.
Roy Flamm photograph.

Fine materials and detailing are evident in this more expensive
residence.

Leon L. Roos house,
view from living room to dining room.
Roy Flamm photograph.

The chair in the center foreground is one piece of an upholstered set designed by Maybeck for the owners.

Leon L. Roos house, dining room.
Roy Flamm photograph.

The doors and transom panels are covered with a mauve cut plush. The push plates and lighting fixtures were also designed by Maybeck.

Samuel Goslinsky house, 3233 Pacific Ave., San Francisco, 1909.
Roy Flamm photograph.

An assortment of forms gives this townhouse a unique appearance on an already delightful street. The doors facing the street were moved from the west side of the entrance vestibule when a garage was placed in the basement area.

Another townhouse, built in 1909 for Samuel Goslinsky, is located in the 3200 block of Pacific Avenue. Here, houses built during the decade by Ernest Coxhead, Willis Polk, and Maybeck combine to form the image of the urban street scene that the newcomers had urged as the norm of design for San Francisco. Their range of forms and styles, unified by their shingled exteriors, is fascinating. Maybeck's Goslinsky house, sheathed in shingles and roofed with slates, presents in its exterior details a strange combination of forms which belies the refinement and graciousness of its interiors.

The house is entered from the street through the side of a boxlike vestibule. Its shed roof slopes on a diagonal parallel to the uphill site. Within the entry, a circular staircase rises to the main living areas. From the top of the stair the garden terrace behind the house is viewed along an oblique line extending through the lengths of the living and dining rooms. Maybeck's use of skewed and extended sight lines expands the width of the interior space unexpectedly within the narrow confines of its twenty-five foot frontal dimension. At a later date the doors of the entry were shifted from the side of the vestibule to its front in order to accommodate a garage in the basement. Maybeck's records do not indicate whether or not he was responsible for the change; but the general character of the house remains unaltered.

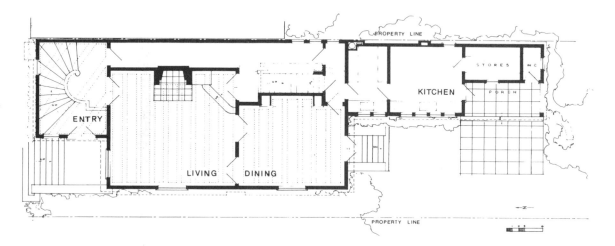

Samuel Goslinsky house, original plan.
Drawn by Alan Williams, Documents Collection, C.E.D.

Samuel Goslinsky house, dining room sideboard.
Roy Flamm photograph.

The mirrored doors of the casework extend the visual space
of the room. There is nothing in the Maybeck documents which
would indicate that the flush lighting panels are part of the
original design.

113

The Senger, Havens, and Roos houses are large and expensive houses, and Maybeck used fine materials and many specially crafted components to complete their design. But the contrasts of costs and scales noted in the first decade of his work continued into the second. Even while he was designing the ornate Roos house, he was giving a small, unadorned school house equal attention.

The project, a small private school for Miss Flora Randolph, was built in 1909 on Berkeley's Belrose Avenue. In later years Maybeck tried without success to obtain a commission for a public school building, and during his efforts he set down his ideas about school design, which are of more than passing interest. In his notes Maybeck advocates "small houses" with separate outdoor spaces for individual classes to be added to as the community grew. These classroom buildings were to be connected by outdoor covered corridors (in California) and heated by radiant heating in their concrete floors. Interestingly, the proposals when read today define recent California school design. Maybeck's lack of success in obtaining commissions from school boards that were looking for a school specialist kept them from erecting the kind of building that was to become standard architectural practice a generation later.

These ideas grew out of his design for the Randolph School. In this building there were no isolated circulation elements, but there was an attempt to give each classroom its own expression and its own garden space. As a private institution serving a limited number of pupils, it must have had a special delight to children as they studied in one of the individual "houses" or made their way through the general assembly to the special purpose areas. The building now serves as a residence and, even thus modified, its ordered jumble of volumes is pleasant. Maybeck used steep, shingle roofs to cover his classrooms and, through standard dormer framing, introduced clerestory windows. The utter simplicity of the shingle walls, roofs without overhangs, and plain board and batten interiors is naive and refreshing.

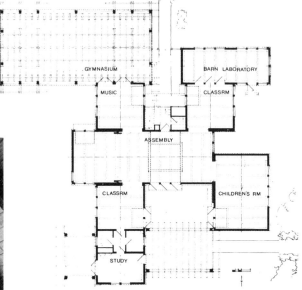

Randolph School, 2700 Belrose Ave., Berkeley, 1909. Documents Collection, C.E.D.

This modest structure allowed for an open plan in which each room had a separate character and garden arrangement. It foreshadowed later practices in California school planning.

Randolph School, interior view furnished as a residence. Roy Flamm photograph.

The school was later adapted as a residence in which its character continued to be pleasant and refreshing.

Many of the Berkeley hillside houses constructed up to this time were later destroyed by fire; but nothing can be more regretted than the loss of the architect's home on Buena Vista Way. Maybeck had purchased a tract of land adjoining that of Andrew Lawson as an investment. He planned to subdivide it and sell lots with preliminary architectural drawings as examples of hillside building. The first structure, his own, was completed in 1909, and the family moved from Berryman Street into a house that must have been the epitome of hillside design. One inadequate photograph is all that has been uncovered, and it can only hint of the adaptation to site, free planning, and straightforward use of materials employed in the design. Unfortunately the drawings of both it and others planned in the Berryman Street studio burned with the new house in 1923. But a description of a portion of it by William Gray Purcell is revealing. Purcell recalls:

B. R. Maybeck house (#2), 2701 Buena Vista Way, Berkeley, 1909. (Destroyed 1923)
Homes and Grounds, May 1916.

The only extant photograph of Maybeck's own home which was destroyed by fire in 1923 and may be considered the epitome of his hillside designs.

That August [1913] evening I walked through the pungent California dusk to Mr. Maybeck's home north of the campus. Beside the broad redwood slab door of this brown shingle house a bay window looked out toward the flower filled front yard, and vine-covered fence. I waited for Mr. Maybeck in an inviting window recess and I began my first experience of a room with a shed-slope ceiling—low where I sat, rising to a considerable height on the far wall, with a very tall fireplace and chimney. To the left, doors and windows looked west and north to the last of the summer sunset sky; to the right of the chimney, a tall opening was carried up to the ceiling beam, and between the jambs at its base some very broad steps led to an adjoining room. . . .

[Maybeck] came through the tall curtained door of his living room, [a] practical figure in movement but softened by beard, comfortable well used jacket, pants shaped to the legs by unfashionable use, and a good welcome smile. . . . The impression was a man in action with a going world, focusing outward on men and works, not a hint of the importance already attained through twenty five years of production of well appreciated buildings.[15]

None of the success noted by Purcell changed the simple life style the Maybeck family had adopted. It was not through necessity but rather by predilection that little emphasis was placed on conventional patterns. Annie, a natural food enthusiast, prepared vegetarian meals and Ben designed clothes for family members. For himself he had devised high-waisted trousers "to keep the shirt tails in," and if a gala event called for a new dress for "Doddy," Ben fashioned one. Even the young son who had been born in Belgium, had not received a name until several years after the family's return to Berkeley. Ben and Annie had decided they would wait for a name until he could participate in its choosing. When he did, he selected Wallen, which was a contraction of the surname of a close family friend—a judge Charles Wallenburg.

The fear of being different did not enter their minds; in fact, Maybeck's romantic individualism promoted idiosyncracy and his gaiety and flair for the dramatic permeated their household activities. Events such as birthdays and holidays, normally festive occasions in any household, were made especially so by elaborate costumes for personal adornment of the celebrant and by colored paper designs which transformed everyday surroundings into romantic images of bygone eras. Wallen, Kerna, Annie, or Ben became the ruler of the day with a gilt paper crown and a retinue of serfs to fulfill every command.

15. William Gray Purcell MSS, "B. R. Maybeck," C.E.D. Docs.

Kerna, Wallen, Annie, and Bernard Maybeck dressed for a family pageant, (no date).
Documents Collection, C.E.D.

By 1910 Maybeck had arrived at the full development of his creative powers. Through the respectable volume of construction he had designed to this time, the nature of the influence of his Beaux-Arts education can be assessed. The dictum of the École was, first, sketch a functional arrangement of rooms required within a reasonable structural envelope— elevations would be beautiful automatically if the plan was good. The drawings of next importance to the Beaux-Arts student were the sections which would proportion the volumes as the plan had related the parts. It is obvious from Maybeck's drawings that architectural sections were more important to him than any elevational studies. His inability, or perhaps lack of concern, to achieve a formally ordered exterior followed naturally from the way he worked. His primary interest was always the inter-relationships of the interior space which he molded and refined without consideration of external appearances.

While more of Maybeck's early designs were based on structural order than his later ones, his attitude towards structural expression fell somewhere between the constructionist theory of Viollet-le-Duc and the architectural accountability demanded by the turn of the century Beaux-Arts theorist, Julien Guadet. Viollet-le-Duc admired the chevet of Notre Dame cathedral for its dynamic expression of the forces of its construction, and he had little praise for its west facade. On the other hand, Guadet saw the entrance elevation as an honest expression of the nature of the structure and the architectural volumes that lay behind it, while he abhorred the chevet, with its flying buttresses and pinnacles, for its unresolved visual effect. Maybeck's concept varied; but his work usually demonstrated a belief in an indication of the nature of, rather than in a direct exhibition of, the structural system. In any case Maybeck used no text book maxims for the execution of his designs. He worked to find the abstract line, the exact color, the adequate symbol that would please the eye and stir the feelings. In his scheme of things, any rule could be broken for the good of the whole.

For Maybeck, Beaux-Arts design was volume design, even to the sacrifice of exterior order, and he did not concentrate his attention on the superficial facades and exaggerated plans that were often characteristic of late Beaux-Arts designs.[16] The significant element unaccounted for by Maybeck's academic training is the way he strived to achieve an architecture expressive of intangible human values. His personal design philosophy, nurtured by German aesthetic theory, and his innate sensitivity to the art in which he worked, were his guides. He once said, "With four sticks of wood you can express any human emotion.[17]

16. See James P. Noffsinger, *Influence of the Ecole des Beaux Arts* (Washington: Catholic University of America Press, 1955).
17. Interview by the author with Walter Steilberg. He stated that this phrase was used by Maybeck in a discussion with Julia Morgan.

First Church of Christ, Scientist, Berkeley,
interior view toward organ loft.
Roy Flamm photograph.

Stencilling in red, green, blue, and gold unites unfinished
concrete with rough wood and metal ties, while identifying the
architect by an emblematic "A."

118

VI

Exponent Of The Sentiment

*Any architectural composition however simple requires
months and even years of thought. This is because a construction must not only express something of the personality of
the composer but must be an exponent of the sentiment of
the era and people among whom he has developed, so that to
one who should see it a thousand years later it would portray
in some measure a phase of life existing at the time of
construction.*

Bernard Maybeck—1903

It is possible that if the First Church of Christ, Scientist, in
Berkeley, had been destroyed by fire, as so many of Maybeck's
works have been, he never would have received the Gold
Medal of the American Institute of Architects. No other building demonstrates so completely his imaginative architectural
genius. His contributions to domestic design are outstanding
and his efforts in architectural education noteworthy; but it is
the Christian Science church, with its masterly handling of
space, structure, color and light, that wins immediate admiration from lay and professional viewers. The church, designed
in 1910 when Maybeck was forty-eight years old, is the visible
statement of his design philosophy at its most fruitful stage.

Maybeck was not a deeply religious man, although his personal philosophy and actions reflected the highest Christian
ideals. He said that his father was an agnostic and encouraged
him to be free in his thinking; but beyond an unswerving belief
in the sanctity of the individual, Maybeck spent little time in
reflection on the supernatural order of the universe. With his
marriage to Annie White, he easily accepted the tenets of her
Unitarian faith.

Maybeck's and Schweinfurth's sympathetic understanding
of the Reverend Worcester's plea for a simple, unadorned
building had contributed to the success of the design of the
Swedenborgian Church in San Francisco. While it is not easy
to sort out their individual contributions, the furniture design
and sketches reflect the character of Maybeck's handiwork.[1]
But had it been Maybeck's own commission, the design would

most likely have been more medieval in mood. His favorite
modern ecclesiastical structure was H. H. Richardson's Trinity
Church.[2] He admired the unified spatial concept achieved by
its barrel vaulting and simple square crossing. The intimate
cloisters and the sensible scale of the original narthex satisfied
his demand for recognition of the individual. Typical church
building with false domes and applied pilasters exemplified
for him "the pretentiousness of Renaissance design and its
emphasis on worldliness."[3] He valued the sincerity of medieval churchwork and felt that direct solutions with modern
materials could create the same integrity achieved by the
medieval structures.

Maybeck's first opportunity to try his own hand at church
design came shortly after he had established his San Francisco office. The project was the Hamilton Church on Waller
Street in the Haight-Ashbury district. Office records indicate
that it could have been completed or under construction at
the time of the San Francisco fire of 1906. While it was in a
section of town not damaged by the holocaust, the fire did
destroy what sketches Maybeck had made for the church, and
there are no documents that reveal the extent of his influence

1. A watercolor by Maybeck of the church interior hangs in the pastor's
   study. A chair from the Rieger house is in C.E.D. Docs. It is the
   same design as those in the church.
2. B. R. Maybeck MSS, "Notes for Principia," C.E.D. Docs.
3. B. R. Maybeck, KPFA Tape, 1953, C.E.D. Docs.

on the existing structure. It seems likely that he did no more than make preliminary sketches for the building. The church as it stands is an undistinguished building consisting of two stories, with parish rooms on the ground level and the church proper above. The detailing suggests that the builder was trying to achieve the quality of an early Renaissance building, but the forms and proportions are not coherent enough to suggest that the attempt was successful, even allowing for the fact that subsequent redecorations have not aided in creating a unified design.

Maybeck's second church, the Unitarian Church of Palo Alto (1906), was executed in a style and materials more sympathetic with his Gothic ideals. This building of redwood shingles and shakes combines a distinctive structural system and architectural massing that is characteristic of his work. Though certainly more individualistic than the Hamilton Church, it too failed to achieve the handsome proportions and refinement of detail associated with the best of his designs.[4]

The framing of the roof of the principal room was carried on six pairs of interior columns. Cantilevered rafters received roof loads and were anchored to the foundation at their wall ends by steel tension rods. The exterior walls were true curtain walls, carrying only the dead loads of the materials of which they were fashioned. The fact that Maybeck carried his load-bearing rafters in continuing lines down and past his columns in a knee brace form partly negated his dynamic framing, and their thrust over the years produced a noticeable bend in the exterior curtain wall. The roof framing was overly complex for the small area it covered and the cramped effect was seen at the entrance where a small porch led to the entry vestibules.

In spite of its deficiencies, the Unitarian Church used some of the elements that made much of Maybeck's work so intriguing. Windows projecting high above the roof of the side aisles provided effective lighting of the interior. A pulpit decorated with glass mosaics and velvet hangings enriched the chancel platform. Handsome cylindrical lanterns furnished light in the nave. The effect of the interior was primitive; its few minor enrichments were inoffensive to a congregation set against the pomp and embellishment of traditional church buildings.

4. The building underwent a series of disfiguring alterations after its sale to another congregation, most of which were erased after its acquisition by the Palo Alto Art Club, but to no avail since the building was recently destroyed.

Unitarian Church, Cowper and Channing Sts., Palo Alto, 1906. (Destroyed)
Documents Collection. C.E.D.

The shingled exterior is softened and given variety by the trellis forms, while the apse was originally finished in a light-colored stucco capped by a crenellated parapet wall.

Unitarian Church, interior view.
Documents Collection, C.E.D.

Wood and plaster are juxtaposed to create an interesting interior.

There is yet another structure connected with church design that exhibits some of the awkward and crude elements that occur in the Unitarian Church of Palo Alto. This is Unity Hall, a building used in connection with the Unitarian Church in Berkeley, to which the Maybecks had belonged since 1892. Although the design of the church has sometimes been attributed to Maybeck, his only work on it was the design of the social hall which adjoined it.[5] The church itself was designed by A. C. Schweinfurth while the Maybecks were in Europe supervising the University Competition. Schweinfurth had worked with Maybeck in A. Page Brown's office on the Swedenborgian Church, and he used similar details and materials for the Berkeley structure.

Maybeck's Unity Hall was an extremely modest structure. Employing trussed rafters with ties exposed above the roof, it was similar to the structure of the Outdoor Art Club. The building had no pretense of being other than a most economical enclosed space for the social functions of the church. It was finished outside with shingles and inside with shingles and board and battens. Its interest lay in the unique, off-center, gable roof that Maybeck used at one end of the hall to create an informal social area around a fireplace in contrast with the large open space used as an auditorium or for church suppers. Unity Hall was built in 1908. Two years later Maybeck was presented with the opportunity of designing the building which is his architectural masterpiece.

5. About 1894 Maybeck remodeled some rooms in a Berkeley commercial building for Unitarian meetings held prior to the construction of the Dana Street church.

Unity Hall, Unitarian church, Bancroft Ave. and Dana St., Berkeley, 1908. (Destroyed)
William S. Ricco photograph.

An extremely modest structure, noteworthy for its off-center gable roof over a portion of the building.

Unity Hall, interior view west.
William S. Ricco photograph.

Wood surfaces which were once with natural finishes had been painted in the last years of the building's use.

First Church of Christ, Scientist, view of west elevation (ca. 1912). Dwight Way and Bowditch St., Berkeley, 1910. Documents Collection. C.E.D.

Maybeck's architectural masterpiece. Before the luxurious growth of wisteria and trees encompassed the structure, colorful plantings in roof flower boxes enriched the design.

Maybeck's own story of how he was selected as the architect for the First Church of Christ, Scientist, Berkeley, reveals many aspects of his attitude as a designer. He related that one day a group of women called on him in his office in San Francisco and stated that they would like to have him design their church. They were familiar with his houses in Berkeley and had decided that he could design the church they were hoping to build. They wanted a simple building, one in keeping with their faith. Maybeck said that he could design such a building and that it would be "the same on the inside as the outside, without sham or hypocrisy," but that he thought they would

not like it.[6] The ladies protested saying that that was just the kind of building they wanted. But Maybeck put them off. Perhaps his experiences with the earlier Hamilton Church and the Unitarian Church had not been to his liking in either design or client relationship. He told them that he would want to use rough materials and concrete as it came from the forms and that they should reconsider.

6. B. R. Maybeck MSS, "Correspondence," C.E.D. Docs.

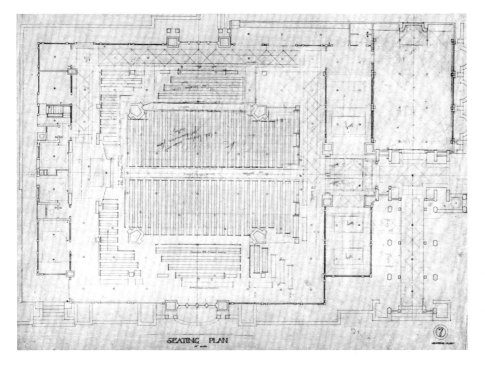

SEATING PLAN

First Church of Christ, Scientist.
Plan, Documents Collection, C.E.D.

Drawings of the church building are from a microfilm made through the courtesy of the Church Board. No original drawings of the building were among those given by Maybeck to the Documents Collection.

Two weeks later the same ladies again called on Maybeck. They stated flatly that they had selected him as their architect.[7] They had even sought spiritual guidance, they added, and were now firmly convinced that he was the only designer they wanted. Maybeck was surprised that they had returned after he had discouraged them, but he was impressed by the sincerity of their feeling and consequently consented to take their commission. He said he felt that he had been hired by a group of people as sincere as he believed people were in the eleventh and twelfth centuries. He therefore tried to imagine himself as a twelfth century designer, imbued with this same sincerity, and he set to work designing as such an individual would but with machine-made two-by-fours and modern technology. It was this quality that Frank Morton Todd was referring to when he said of Maybeck: "In feeling and understanding he steps back twenty centuries as easily as you or I would cross a room."[8]

The church Board of Directors had obtained a corner lot south of the University campus in the heart of an established residential section of the city. It had a slight slope on the hundred foot frontage on Dwight Way, but the site was level in the hundred and fifty foot depth along Bowditch Street. The program called for a church building that could seat seven hundred people, a Sunday school that could be used in conjunction with the church proper, and various service elements. To meet these requirements, Maybeck developed a plan that covered most of the restricted area on which he had to build. He located the Sunday school unit to the front of the property and kept the building as close to the street lot lines as feasible in order to gain some isolation from neighboring properties.

7. Conversations between the author and Maybeck. The "History of the First Church of Christ, Scientist, Berkeley, California" (May 1933), states: "The Plans Committee, after consulting twelve architects, unanimously recommended architect and engineer, Mr. Bernard Maybeck of the firm Maybeck and White. The Board approved their action and authorized the procuring of sketches September 27, 1909."
8. Bernard R. Maybeck, *The Palace of Fine Arts and Lagoon*, p. vii. Introduction by Frank Morton Todd.

A delightful cross-play of axially-centered entrances, a short, major one from Dwight Way to the church and a long, minor one from Bowditch Street to the Sunday school, foreshadows the intricate volume organization within the building. The church is entered from the street through a high-gabled portico. A pair of plain doors opens into a skylighted and low-ceilinged narthex which serves both the church and Sunday school. Double doors lead to the body of the church proper. The floor plan of the room is square, based on a module of ten feet ten inches in each direction. The roof plan is a Greek cross in form with low-pitched gable roofs inscribed in the square of the plan. An intermediate clerestory level lies between the square and the Greek cross. Its walls form bracing panels for the pairs of diagonally-placed Pratt trusses over the central crossing which is forty feet square. A hollow reinforced concrete pier at each corner of the crossing supports the trusses and serves as ductwork for the heating and ventilating system. Forced warm air rising in the piers is distributed by draft diverters through the trusswork of the ceiling. Foul air is taken in at the base of the piers and exhausted through the roof. The six-foot deep panel trusses are built from two-by-six and two-by-twelve stock lumber. Maybeck was aided in their design by his old friend Herman Kower, who had worked with him on the Hearst buildings. Each pair of trusses follows the slope of the valleys of the crossed gable roof until they intersect their transverse number at the center and continue on down to the pier opposite. The entire roof framing is exposed, including the beams, purlins, and sheathing, and rich patterns of structural members thus decorate the ceiling. The walls of the clerestory are of ten-inch board-on-board finish, and the lower exterior walls are a post and beam system framing a glass wall of steel sash.

In 1921, writing of the church, Maybeck said, "Physically the [building] committee wanted color, garden, etc., and they wanted nothing sham. We sensed a need for permanence in religious monument rather as a symbol; therefore, the floor was concrete and on the ground, and the walls are concrete to the seat of the trusses."[9]

9. B. R. Maybeck MSS, "First Church of Christ, Scientist, Berkeley," C.E.D. Docs.

First Church of Christ, Scientist, view west at narthex.
Roy Flamm photograph.

Skylights, translucent windows, and reflections on glass modulate the light in the entrance passageway. The use of industrial steel sash reveals Maybeck's genius and willingness to use modern materials even going contrary to the manufacturer's own opinion of the suitability of the material.

First Church of Christ, Scientist, entrance pergolas and porches.
Roy Flamm photograph.

There is much symbolism in all of Maybeck's work. From the obvious device of the dragon mark of his father's craft to the choice of materials, symbolism of some form exists in most of his work.[10] In the Christian Science church there is a symbolic coordination of ornament and structure. The tracery in the roof truss panels follows the direction of the diagonal tension rods. Metal tie plates are accented with stenciled designs, and hidden structural elements are indicated by ornament on the surface. The gilt of the truss tracery and small accents of primary reds and blues are conscious attempts to suggest the inheritance of early Christian architecture.

The exterior of the church is surfaced with the most common materials. Sheets of cement asbestos board of a light gray color are applied to most of the upper exterior walls. They are fastened with screws placed in small diamond-shaped pieces of the same material, in brick red. The factory steel sash that forms most of the lower wall has been enriched by hammered glass set with leadings bisecting vertically each unit of the standard light. The cast concrete elements are molded in forms derived from, but not copies of, Romanesque details. The roof, now partially covered with Spanish tiles, was originally a standing seam roof of tin clad sheet iron. Trim, trellises, and corbels are of natural redwood darkened with age, and the structural frame and interior boards are rough-sawn Douglas fir. The materials testify to Maybeck's adaptability to the conditions of building in an industrialized economy.

10.   The dragon device was used in Wyntoon, the Faculty Club, Outdoor Art Club, Flagg studio, Owens house, Tufts house (San Rafael), Kennedy studio, and the Chamberlain studio among others.

First Church of Christ, Scientist, longitudinal section.
Documents Collection, C.E.D.

The variety and interplay of volumes and spaces can be seen in the sectional drawing where it is generally only felt as one travels through the structure.

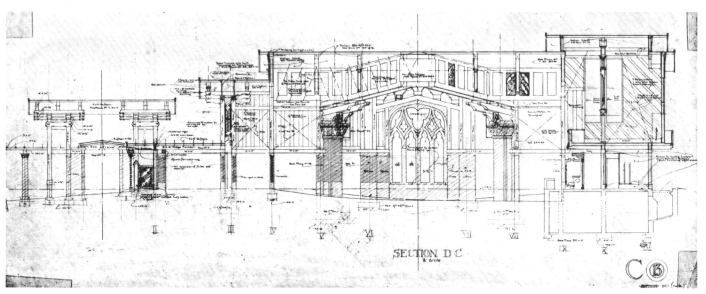

Only the genius and perseverance of the architect made the materials usually associated with factories and utilitarian building appropriate and in harmony with the edifice. In reply to Maybeck's first inquiry as to the cost of providing stock steel factory sash for the church windows, the company's representative wrote that he did not think the product was appropriate for church construction. Maybeck insisted that he knew what he was doing and reiterated his request for a quotation. The bid was finally received and, to Maybeck's great pleasure, was considerably lower than that for any alternative units he might have chosen. The supplier, however, was still dubious and indicated this on the bid form by putting the word "church" in quotation marks.[11]

Maybeck had similar difficulties with the manufacturers of the asbestos panels used to clad the exterior. They were normally applied to roofs or used for insulation and industrial packing, and the company had difficulty in quoting a correct figure until the architect pointed out to them a number of omissions and supplied a detailed list of every piece of asbestos board to be used on the buildings. Such trials, of course, were only the beginning of difficulties to be overcome when he selected materials or methods of construction which differed from traditional practices. Both workmen and clients (represented by a consulting engineer of the Church Board) had to be educated, convinced, or cajoled into accepting his unorthodox treatments.

All fittings, exterior and interior, were executed to designs done by Maybeck. They vary from strap iron exterior lanterns and handsome steeled brass interior luminaires to awkward chandeliers of redwood sticks and bare bulbs used in the Sunday school. The pews of fumed, waxed oak and the red plush cushions and screens used behind the Reader stands are of Maybeck's design and selection. These lecterns of cast

11. B. R. Maybeck MSS, "First Church of Christ, Scientist, Berkeley," C.E.D. Docs.

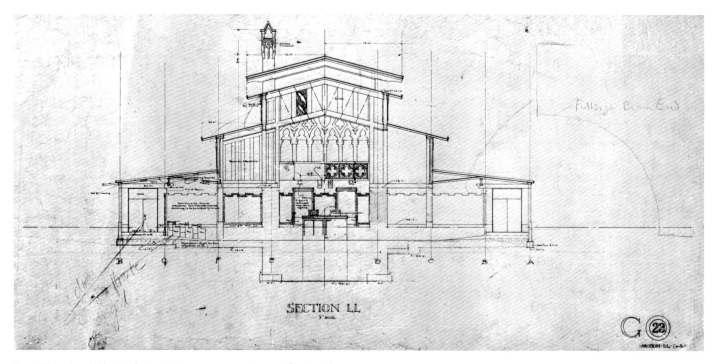

First Church of Christ, Scientist, transverse secton at front aisle.
Documents Collection, C.E.D.

First Church of Christ, Scientist, view southeast from
Reader stands.
Roy Flamm photograph.

The floral patterns of the Reader stands were developed by
Maybeck in response to a construction accident when the paper
coating the forms wrinkled in the process of pouring the
concrete.

First Church of Christ, Scientist, interior view from west aisle.
Roy Flamm photograph.

Basic materials and construction techniques have rarely been
used as effectively and beautifully in the history of architecture.

concrete typified Maybeck's ability to make a creative design out of an adverse circumstance. It was cast in a mold lined with paper to assure smoothness. The paper wrinkled in the process of pouring, and Maybeck utilized the creases formed in the resulting block as the basis of floral pattern. His designing did not stop with the furnishings of the church. He also provided a landscape plan. Some of the wisteria vines now on the church are from the original planting. However, the carmine bouganvillea, pink geranium, blue hydrangea, and lavendar verbena indicated on his drawings are no longer in evidence.[12]

Much has been made of Maybeck's use in the church of sliding doors to accommodate overflow crowds, of the industrial steel sash in the exterior curtain walls, and of its asbestos siding. But these features are not the true measure of his architectural accomplishment. It was his mastery of the architectural elements of light, space, proportion, and scale that created a building of lasting significance. His church makes man its measure and reflects the humanistic qualities of the religion it shelters. Maybeck felt that members of the congregation "were in direct touch with an omniscient power in everything they did"—perhaps through a kind of partnership. He said:

> We tried to fit the clothes to the man. The form of the building was such that the seating was arranged so that everyone, as far as possible, could see the one who rises to give his experience, which seems to us a vital part of their church work.... Summing it up, to build a church edifice can be done by being strictly honest, i.e., make no forms other than those needed for the construction and furnishings, make no ornaments and no color, except those needed and of the form suggested by the need. Avoid all hiding of unpleasant forms. Do not borrow from history, but use form and color as you do words and music.[13]

Maybeck's color scheme for the church has been well preserved. Starting with the natural wood brown of the truss members and tin gray of the natural concrete piers, the gray, pink, and blue of the roof sheathing boards and walls are accented by gilt on the tracery and by rich red, blue, black, and green in the depths of modeled ornament and flat stencil work. At one time the organ loft was screened by a blue net fabric on which the women of the congregation fashioned gilt stars. Maybeck planned this activity to make them feel that they had actively contributed to the building of the church. The organ loft and its curtain of stars were lit by clerestory windows glazed with art glass.

Maybeck also employed both natural and artificial light to enrich the structure. Windows in front of the organ screen were to be glazed with yellow, amber, and red and those behind with green, purple, and ultramarine blue. Maybeck simplified his original color scheme and used warm pinks in the glass in front and blues in the window at the rear of the screen. Great care went into the selection of the glass to be used in the sash which forms a continuous glazed wall around the perimeter of the church room. His choice was a glass imported from Belgium that had a shimmering, translucent quality. For artificial lighting he chose prismatic glass reflector units and designed housings to enclose them. In addition to the down lights for the pews and the general illumination of the large hanging fixtures which cast their glow towards the ceilings, concealed lights of red and blue accent various portions of the structure.

12. The furnishings and garden were finished in 1912. After completion, the Board of Directors always sought Maybeck's approval of any change proposed for the church or gardens.
13. B. R. Maybeck MSS, "Correspondence," C.E.D. Docs.

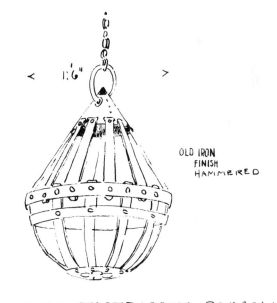

OLD IRON
FINISH
HAMMERED

MAIN ENTRANCE PERGOLA,

First Church of Christ, Scientist, sketch for entrance lantern. Documents Collection, C.E.D.

Throughout the construction phase of his designs, Maybeck was always at work selecting the proper material at hand. His activity has led to stories that each of his designs was handmade, created on the site in a sort of medieval masterbuilder tradition. Nothing could be further from the truth. His presence on the site was to assure the most effective use of the material on hand. Conceptually his designs were complete before any work was undertaken. Each board and its size, each material and its finish, and even the color of all or part of each is shown on the drawings.

During the busiest years of his practice Maybeck employed the device of letting bids for construction by segregated contracts. He thus became acquainted with a number of specialty contractors who knew the kind of work he expected. Many of those who participated in the building of the Christian Science church were men with whom Maybeck had had repeated building experience, so he was confident of their abilities. William Boldt was the general carpentry contractor, Christian Schneckenburger the painting contractor, and Hoff and Hoff of San Francisco the architectural modelers.[14] Maybeck's function as a semi-general contractor gave him a direct control which he used to full advantage. His unbelievable energy and enthusiasm turned the tide against all obstacles. His lack of preconceived architectural solutions to the problems he faced coupled with his complete domination of every detail of the basic structure, mechanical systems, and furnishings of the church helped create a building noteworthy in the history of American architecture.

In 1928, in association with Henry Gutterson, Maybeck added a new Sunday school to the church on land adjoining to the east. The original school room was turned into a lounge area and was extended to house the church office. The addition was done in sympathy with the original design; but the intervening years had taken their toll. Maybeck's design and Gutterson's execution of the Sunday school building did not achieve the same mastery and delight in detail and form as did Maybeck's earlier structure.

14. B. R. Maybeck MSS, "First Church of Christ, Scientist, Berkeley," C.E.D. Docs.

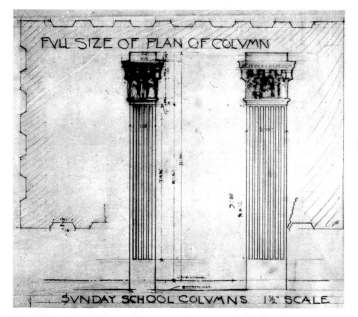

First Church of Christ, Scientist, drawing of old Sunday school columns.
Documents Collection, C.E.D.

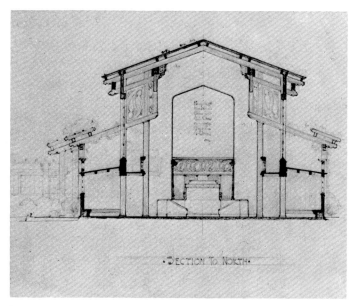

Drawing in charcoal and pastel (unsigned), section of Sunday school.
Documents Collection, C.E.D.

Sunday school, First Church of Christ, Scientist, Berkeley,
Bernard Maybeck and Henry Gutterson, Architects, 1928.
William S. Ricco photograph.

In 1928, in association with Henry Gutterson, Maybeck added
a Sunday school building to the east of the church. Although
doen in sympathy with the original structure, and very pleasing
in itself, it lacks the masterful quality of the church.

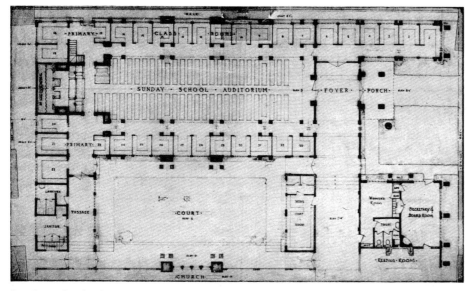

Sunday school, plan.
Documents Collection, C.E.D.

The addition of the Sunday school allowed for the development of a sheltered and peaceful central court between it and the existing church.

The Christian Science church brought no immediate fame to Maybeck. Indeed, its exterior appearance, following all the changes of its interior form, plus the strange "wellheads" set diagonally over the exposed portions of the roof trusses and foul-air vents, produced a less ordered and familiar profile than the community expected in ecclesiastical architecture. It took the aging of several years and the maturing of the heavy planting of wisteria along the trellises before the building fit comfortably into the Berkeley landscape.

After the completion of the church, Maybeck's practice fell into the general slump that was affecting building in the entire region. In contrast to the busy years following the 1906 fire, Maybeck and White found themselves with few commissions for buildings. One ambitious project for a residential divinity school for the Unitarian Church of Berkeley was carried through complete preliminaries and estimates of construction costs in 1912, but fell victim to the economic tide. The preliminary drawings show a building suggestive of Spanish baroque details. However, as with all of Maybeck's work, his personal style is more in evidence than any historical mode.

Style, to Maybeck, was the unique quality of a work of art achieved by proceeding from the basic nature of the materials of construction. The arrangement and connection of each building element should be subordinated to the comprehensive scheme of the design. Working in this way, he wandered freely among historic details seeking principles of design. Often visitors to the First Church of Christ, Scientist, asked him to name its style of architecture. Maybeck always answered "Modern."[15] He was fully conscious that those with a limited knowledge of architectural history would see Gothic detail, Romanesque forms and modern materials. However, the rational structural principle of bracing the central piers by the clerestory walls is more Gothic than the cusps and trefoils of the window tracery. The introduction of human scale and proportioning of the structure is more Romanesque than the detail of the column capitals. The total application of a modular skeletal frame and its exploitation to achieve changing and combining spatial units is more Modern than the obvious adaptation of industrial steel sash. These are the universal architectural principles Maybeck would have had understood when he called his work "Modern."

15. B. R. Maybeck, KPFA Tape 1953, C.E.D. Docs.

Bernard Maybeck, wash drawing of Unitarian Divinity School,
Berkeley, 1912.
Documents Collection, C.E.D.

This ambitious project was carried through all the preliminaries,
but was a casualty to a general building slump that affected
the region at the time.

Palace of Fine Arts, view from lagoon through the rotunda to the peristyle and gallery wall.
Documents Collection, C.E.D.

The changing vistas and grand scale of the Palace evoked favorable criticism from most of the contemporary journalists reporting on the Fair, and has enthralled visitors for 60 years.

VII

Expression Of Human Experience

In discussing plans for a World's Fair it is necessary to assume that the hearers admit that there are mental processes that are not expressed in language. The first example that comes to our mind is the process of understanding music. The stone and wood construction bears the same relation to architecture as the piano does to the music played upon it. Architecture and music are conveyors of expression of human experience.
Bernard Maybeck—1915

Prior to the San Francisco earthquake and fire, the city's business community had been planning an international exhibition to celebrate the opening of the Panama Canal route to the Pacific Ocean. The slump following the initial spurt of rebuilding after the fire renewed the efforts of the Fair's promotional committee to get construction underway, a move which was felt would boost the economy. By spring 1911, the group had obtained support of the Federal Government and immediately began searching for an appropriate site. Many places were considered—from Golden Gate Park on the west edge of the city to the Embarcadero on the east. But perhaps the most original was the one suggested by Maybeck. The San Francisco *Call Bulletin* of February, 1911 reported that Maybeck had proposed that the Fair should have its midway located in the center of the city and its major exhibition palaces distributed throughout various districts. In addition to providing useful large structures for community gatherings after the Fair, his scheme, he said, would "bring World's Fair visitors in touch with the human side of San Francisco rather than...give them a superficial view; [and it] would interweave the life of the city itself with the greatest exposition in the history of the world, [to give] every one a knowledge of [its] warm human side."[1]

Maybeck's public comment on the Fair's location was only one of many given to its directors, but they did not seek his advice. Instead, the president of the Board, Charles C. Moore, asked the San Francisco Chapter of the American Institute of Architects for a list of ten men who might be considered as members for the initial advisory group. The architects responded and the Board of Directors named William Curlett, John Galen Howard, Albert Pissis, Clarence Ward, and Willis Polk as the Advisory Committee of the Panama-Pacific International Exposition. By 1906, Polk, on his own and through his work for the D. H. Burnham organization, had become an architect of prominence in San Francisco.[2] He had designed several projects for William H. Crocker, one of the financial backers of the Fair, and it was not surprising to seek Polk selected to serve with the architectural planning group.

The initial planning of the Fair went ahead without Maybeck's participation. Of course, it was unlikely that he would have been chosen for the committee. Although he knew many of the influential backers of the Fair through his membership in the Bohemian Club, Maybeck did not belong to any of the professional organizations in the city. Unlike Polk, he, had few aggressive business instincts. His preference for the simple life had kept him from pressing the advantages of publicity he had gained while at the University. And when the work slowed in his office upon completion of the drawings of the Christian Science Church, he tried once again to expand his practice by entering competitions.

1. *San Francisco Call Bulletin* (February 22, 1911).
2. Cf. Charles C. Moore, *Daniel H. Burnham*, 2 vols. (Boston: Houghton Mifflin, 1921), which describes Burnham's plan for San Francisco as well as Polk's and Bennett's participation.

Bernard Maybeck at the height of his career (ca. 1910).
Documents Collection, C.E.D.

The competition for the design of the Federal City of Canberra (1910-11), which catapulted its winner, Walter Burley Griffin, into international recognition as well as into the political turmoil of planning policy in Australia, was the first that he tried. The program called for a plan for a city of one hundred thousand inhabitants, designed to be suitable as the cultural and political center of the nation. The selected site, bisected by the meandering Molonglo River, was a narrow plain surrounded by hills of moderate elevation. More distant mountains rose to an average height of four thousand feet. Although Maybeck's index of drawings submitted listed all those required by the rules of the competition, only one drawing and a written evaluation of the design survive to define his scheme.[3]

Maybeck's plan for Canberra contained elements of nineteenth-century city layout—broad tree-lined avenues intersected in circuses and *pleins* enhanced by important architectural constructions or views of the distant mountain peaks. Irregular parcels, developed throughout the design at the crosspoints of angled arterials, were retained for community buildings and public open spaces. The scheme was not based on a geometric order as found in Washington, D.C. or Griffin's winning design. Instead it featured curving and contoured avenues leading to garden city residential blocks adapted to the surrounding hills. Maybeck's plan included other progressive ideas of the City Beautiful. In its commercial center, service and public traffic were vertically separated. The Molonglo River, which divided the commercial and governmental sections, formed a green belt where sport and recreation facilities were placed to give life to the city center.

Maybeck's comments on both his entry for Canberra and the placement of the Fair, reveal that he was not anti-urban. His emphasis of the natural landscape and gardens in residential work tends to obscure his warm appreciation of urban life and form. He admired Paris for its broad, tree-lined boulevards which afforded views or led to handsome landmarks. He would have been pleased if something similar had developed in San Francisco. But his concern was for more than the visual order of the city. He relished the pageant of action on busy streets and in public squares and thought it could be enhanced by structures and planting. For Maybeck the pageant of people was an integral part of architectural places.

3. B. R. Maybeck MSS, "Canberra Competition," C.E.D. Docs.

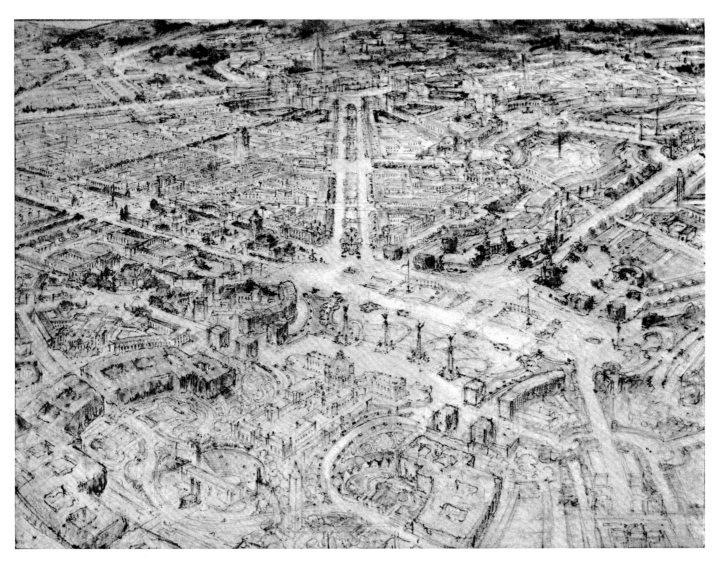

Competition Drawing, Federal City, Canberra, Australia, 1911.
Documents Collection, C.E.D. (original 9″ x 12″)

Maybeck's plan for the city featured broad, tree-lined boulevards,
contoured avenues, public open spaces and other ideas of the
City Beautiful. It was a plan that adapted to the location rather
than imposing its own order upon the landscape.

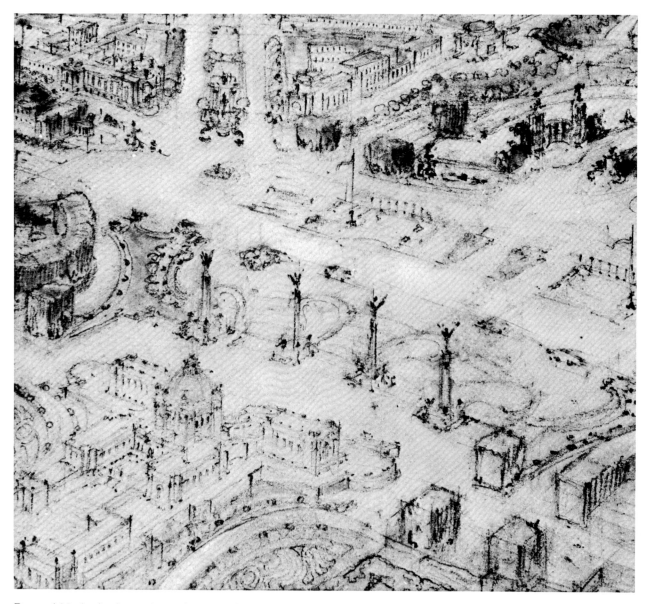

Bernard Maybeck, charcoal pencil on manila tracing paper,
detail enlarged four times.
Documents Collection, C.E.D.

An enlargement of the small original drawing reveals Maybeck's
skill as an artist and draftsman. Incredible detailing is evident
upon magnification.

Late in the year 1911, increasing publicity about San Francisco's international exposition prompted the city fathers to seek a design for a new city hall which was to be occupied by the Fair's opening day. Maybeck entered the competition. Although he did not win or even place, he at least had the satisfaction of seeing two of his students from the Berryman Street studio, John Bakewell and Arthur Brown, Jr., walk away with top honors.[4] Twenty of the twenty-two published entries had a tower or a dome as a dominant theme. Maybeck's design had neither. His City Hall project proved to be no exception to his Beaux-Arts concept of design, which differed—as usual—from that of the turn-of-the-century École graduates.

Maybeck's scheme started with the placement of a circular council chamber in the center of the building with the law library over it and the Recorder's office under it. All the rooms received daylight from two interior courts formed by the distribution of other required departments in a rectangle around the perimeter of the city block site. Major service agencies, each located at a corner of the building, had elliptically-shaped public rooms with entrances from the major and minor streets of the site. The Justice Courts were located on the fourth or top story so that each could contain skylights and be designed with volumes of varying shapes. The Superior Courts, placed on the third floor, connected to an open loggia designed as a part of the principal facade.

4. John Bakewell, Jr., "The San Francisco City Hall Competition," *Architect and Engineer*, 29, (July, 1912), pp. 46-53.

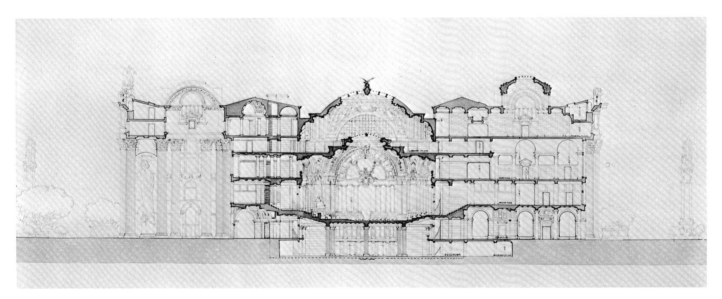

Competition Drawing, section, City Hall, San Francisco, (1912). Documents Collection, C.E.D.

Maybeck's competition entry for the San Francisco City Hall did not win nor place, but it did confirm his independence as a designer, being one of only two published entries not based upon a large classical central dome as a dominant feature.

Although the combination of circular, elliptical, and rectangular forms may seem chaotic and forced, the plan worked reasonably well. In fact, it provided more functional space than the winning design. But Maybeck's submission differed significantly from Bakewell and Brown's entry in the assembly of the parts and their composition into elevations. Bakewell and Brown had one huge circulation space rising high in the center of their building. It was covered by a dome supported on a windowed drum. Their elevations followed text-book rules of composition—balancing the dominant central columned and pedimented pavilion with minor (but substantial) end bays. Its strong, rusticated base, carrying a two-storied columnar facade capped by an attic story, was a popular pattern used by Beaux-Arts architects who followed Renaissance traditions. Maybeck's design was in a free classical style; its details were equally derivative. But its bold composition of solids and voids, without dependence on massive towers or domes suggests baroque antecedents and also confirms his total independence from fashionable architectural idioms.

Bernard Maybeck, India ink wash drawing, elevation, City Hall. Documents Collection, C.E.D.

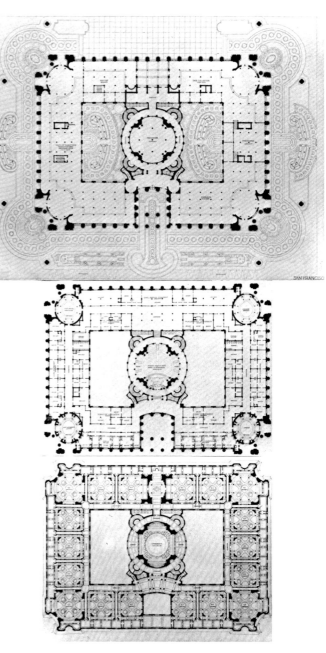

City Hall, ground floor plan.
Documents Collection, C.E.D.

City Hall, third floor plan.
Documents Collection, C.E.D.

City Hall, Superior Courts floor plan.
Documents Collection, C.E.D.

Maybeck's plan drawings are beautiful drawings in themselves incidental to their room arrangements and development of functional spaces.

The City Hall drawings had been judged in the spring of 1912, and by then the amount of work in Maybeck's office had fallen to a new low. His entry in the competition for the design of a Courthouse in Dayton, Nevada, had also failed to win a prize. In the past twelve months only a half-dozen projects had come into the office, and the few that continued beyond the preliminary design stage were for inexpensive houses and minor remodeling work for the Oakland Playground Commission. So, reluctantly, but out of necessity, Maybeck secured employment as a draftsman in the office of his old friend, Willis Polk, where planning for the Fair was already underway.

In the meantime, the architectural Advisory Committee of The Fair had undergone some significant changes—ones that set the stage for events that altered the basic nature of Maybeck's professional practice. In the summer of 1911 the Grounds Committee, led by William Crocker, had recommended that the Advisory Committee of five men be made the permanent architectural Executive Council and that Willis Polk act as its chairman. The Board of Directors concurred; but shortly thereafter the three conservative members—Curlett, Howard and Pissis—resigned, leaving Polk in full command. Within a month Polk had formed a new council of three members who were to appoint the architects of the exhibition halls.[5] He hired Edward H. Bennett of the D. H. Burnham organization to begin the development of block plans for the selected site lying between Fort Mason and the San Francisco Presidio.

By the beginning of 1912 the architects for the full commission had been named: Thomas Hastings, Henry Bacon, and the firm of McKim, Mead and White, all of New York; George W. Kelham, Louis C. Mullgardt, Arthur Brown, Jr., of San Francisco; and Robert D. Farquhar of Los Angeles. Now the Architectural Commission had as its members not only Willis Polk and Thomas Hastings, who were friends of Maybeck, but also Edward Bennett and Arthur Brown, Jr., his former students. Maybeck's records do not indicate exactly when he gained employment on Polk's staff, but he was instrumental in keeping part of the site—water covered one-third of it—from being filled, thus forming the lagoon which became a significant part of the Fair's plan. While Edward Bennett is credited with the creative concept that called for courts rather than buildings to be designed by the architects, it seems likely that Maybeck had some influence on his former student in this

decision. His own fascination with negative spaces would support such a speculation. In any case it was a scheme that he later was able to exploit and dramatize.

Polk, as Chairman of the Commission, had been given the most important and expensive building to be constructed on the site. Unlike the other structures which were to be built of wood, the Palace of Fine Arts was to be constructed in steel to provide fire protection for its valuable contents. For the second meeting of the Architectural Commission in August of 1912, each architect had been asked to present preliminary sketches. Polk had decided to have an office competition to select the design for the Fine Arts building. When all drawings were done, a unanimous decision of his office staff led to the selection of Maybeck's charcoal sketch as the preliminary design to be presented to the Commission. Henry Bacon, in particular, was enormously impressed by the sketch.[6] When he and others began congratulating Polk on his brilliant composition, Polk revealed the author of the design and, in a magnanimous gesture, proposed Maybeck in place of himself as architect for the structure. In one stroke Maybeck's status was changed from that of a minor draftsman working on Fair buildings to the architect of the principal structure.

5. The three members were Willis J. Polk, Clarence Ward, and William Faville.
6. B. R. Maybeck, KPFA Tape 1953, C.E.D. Docs.

Bernard Maybeck, charcoal drawing, sketch for the Palace of Fine Arts executed for Willis Polk, 1913.
Photograph courtesy of Hans Gerson.

The preliminary design sketch that so impressed Henry Bacon that it changed Maybeck's status from a minor draftsman to the architect of the Fair's principal structure and his own most famous and popular work.

Palace of Fine Arts, Panama-Pacific International Exposition, San Francisco, 1913, plan.
Documents Collection, C.E.D.

Even though this plan is from the final set of drawings, Maybeck was able during construction to eliminate the approach paths shown crossing the lagoon which had been added to the design over his objections.

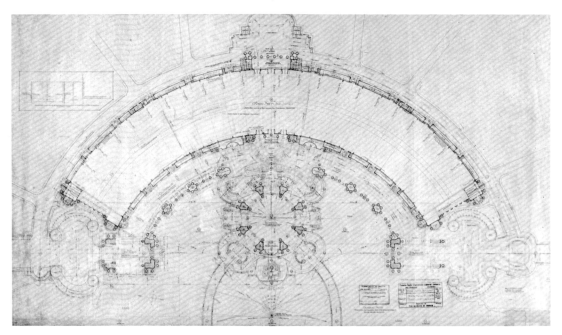

142

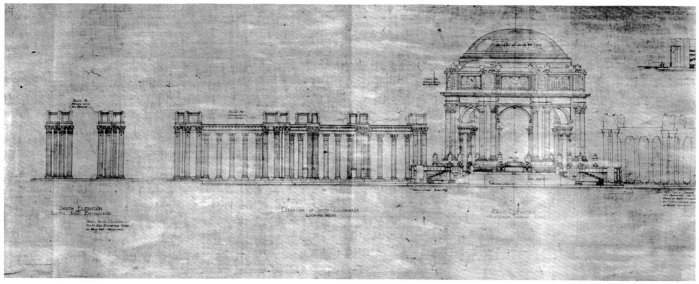

Palace of Fine Arts, elevation.
Documents Collection, C.E.D.

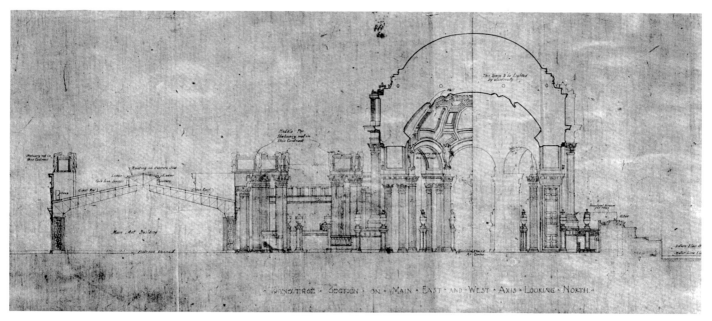

Palace of Fine Arts, section.
Documents Collection, C.E.D.

143

The Fine Arts Palace is the best known, most photographed, and most well documented of Maybeck's buildings. in *The Story of the Exposition*, Frank Morton Todd gives complete technical and physical descriptions of the structure, but when attempting to describe the character of the building in his volumes, he hesitantly states:

> Nowhere in America had such a thing been built before, nothing in American architecture had ever approached it. These are strong statements. We base them not merely on our own appraisal but on the way it affected qualified art critics, and visitors in general....
>
> The theme itself we might attempt to state as the mortality of grandeur and to describe as having some affinity with our eternal sorrows over the vanity of human wishes....
>
> Some such feeling as this, though vague, must have come to every responsive intelligence that looked across the Fine Arts Lagoon and the Palace itself. It represented the beauty and grandeur of the past. A cloister enclosing nothing, a colonnade without a roof, stairs that ended nowhere, a fane with a lonely votary kneeling at a dying flame, fluted shafts that rose, half hid in vines, from the lush growth of an old swamp,...all these things were in the picture.[7]

It was evident that Maybeck had succeeded in setting a mood. It was also evident that he had achieved his goal of creating a beautiful building. But all the words and the praise heaped on the building fail to explain what it was about the architectural forms that contributed to its universal appeal. Even when Maybeck wrote about the Palace, not one word refers to the building itself, or even to any of its parts. All of his explanation is devoted to the mood appropriate for an art gallery—which was "a sad and serious matter"—and this is done through repeated allusions to the haunting character of remnants of past civilizations and natural landscape forms. In his small booklet, *The Palace of Fine Arts and Lagoon*, he writes: "I find that the keynote of a Fine Arts Palace should be that of sadness, modified by the feeling that beauty has a soothing influence."

7. Frank Morton Todd, *The Story of the Exposition*, vol. 2 (New York: G. P. Putnam's Sons, 1921), pp. 315-17.

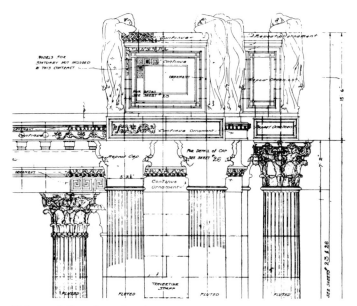

Palace of Fine Arts, details.
Documents Collection, C.E.D.

On the corona of the peristyle and on the architrave supporting the planting boxes Maybeck's signatory "A" is used as ornamentation.

B. R. Maybeck, book cover, *Palace of Fine Arts and Lagoon*, 1915.

Maybeck designed the embossed cover for his own booklet describing the Palace of Fine Arts.

Palace of Fine Arts, view from rotunda to peristyle.
Roy Flamm photograph.

"Nowhere in America had such a thing been built before,
nothing in American architecture had ever approached it." The
academic architect could criticize the details and proportions,
but the Palace of Fine Arts has captured the hearts of millions.

You examine a historic form and see whether the effect it produced on your mind matches the feeling you are trying to portray—a modified sadness or a sentiment in a minor key.

An old Roman ruin, away from civilization, which two thousand years before was the center of action and full of life, and now is partly overgrown with bushes and trees—such ruins give the mind a sense of sadness.... Great examples of melancholy in architecture and gardening may be seen in the engravings of Piranesi, who lived a century ago, and whose remarkable work conveys the sad, minor note of old Roman ruins covered with bushes and trees. There seems to be no other works of the builder, neither Gothic, nor Moorish, nor Egyptian, that give us just this note of vanished grandeur.

This was a feeling "similar to the sentiment expressed in the statue of the muse finding the head of Orpheus—its beauty tempers the sadness of it."[8]

8. Bernard R. Maybeck, *Palace of Fine Arts and Lagoon* (San Francisco: Paul Elder and Company, 1915), pp. 9-11.

"Foggy Night," from the *Palace of Fine Arts and Lagoon*, 1915.

One of two gravure-printed photographs used to illustrate Maybeck's excellent little book.

Palace of Fine Arts, view through rotunda. Roy Flamm photograph.

Palace of Fine Arts, coffered
ceiling of rotunda dome.
Roy Flamm photograph.

Maybeck's design corrections
for visual distortion may be
seen in the receding planes
of the coffers of the ceiling.

Palace of Fine Arts, sculptured planting boxes of the peristyle. Documents Collection, C.E.D.

Although of monumental proportions, the detailing of the structure and its landscape design afforded vistas that provided moments of peace and quiet contemplation.

Perhaps the popular acceptance of the Palace of Fine Arts can partially be attributed to the temper of the times. The Exposition opened at a time when the nations of Europe were at war. The transition from a state of peace to war had been abrupt. Daily reports of devastation, slaughter, and suffering dampened the spirits of even the most optimistic. Instead of celebrating the achievement of man by an international exhibition, it seemed a time to mourn the turning of productive agencies into forces of destruction and degradation of human life. The mood almost caused the failure of the amusement zone of the Fair, where frivolous games of darts and pitch-penny drew few takers; but it insured the success of the Palace of Fine Arts. The note of melancholy, akin to sorrow, which Maybeck attributed to great art, matched the spirit of the times while also soothing it:

> You would recall the days when your mother pressed you to her bosom and your final sob was hushed by a protecting spirit hovering over you, warm and large. You have there the point of transition from sadness to content, which comes pretty near to the total impression of the Fine Arts Palace and lake.[9]

No matter what subjective evaluation is made of Maybeck's design, objective measurement of its strong composition of negative space is of great significance. Maybeck had consciously manipulated the spaces for scenic and dramatic effects. One writer noted that no matter where you stood around the structure, each position gave a different grouping of columns, dome and wall, a different setting of trees and water.[10] The ever-changing vistas seen by delighted visitors verified the previous reports of unparalleled beauty.

The visitor would arrive at the end of the main axis of the Fair and step into a space dominated by the great rotunda and its reflection in the quiet lagoon. To gain a closer view he was forced to turn and proceed around the lake to one of the two entrance pavilions. Following an elliptical path, he arrived at a rectangular grouping of paired Corinthian columns through which the great dome was seen off-axis, suggesting the route to be taken. The way led between the semi-circular peristyle and the curving wall of the gallery. The colonnade and its architrave swept in a strong line under and apparently through groups of four stately columns supporting nothing more than what many writers have described as caskets or great boxes. As the visitor neared his goal, the peristyle suddenly terminated, revealing views into and through the rotunda to the great palaces he had left a thousand steps ago. The experience of moving within and seeing through the spaces of the Palace of Fine Arts enthralled the visitor, whether or not its architectural details delighted him.

If The Fine Arts Palace had a wide popular appeal, the admiration of architects was far less universal. It is well summed up in John D. Berry's criticism of the Fair buildings, published in the *Transactions* of the Commonwealth Club of August, 1915:

> It was good planning that placed the Palace of Fine Arts at one end of what the architects called the main axis of the Exposition. And Bernard R. Maybeck, the San Francisco architect who made the design, had a happy inspiration when he lifted it up from the surrounding flatness and made it seem to stand on an eminence where it would dominate.
>
> The Rotunda is a free use of the Roman classic style and remotely resembles the Pantheon in Rome. The colonnade behind is Roman, too. But the treatment with its refinement of detail is Greek. The architects say that Maybeck has broken all the rules: but they acknowledge that he is justified by his success. He has done something unique, of astonishing beauty. In his use of the lagoon he has been very successful and in the planting he has had fine cooperation from McLaren.[11]

Behind these words lies the implied criticism of many architects that Maybeck did not know his architectural orders. He used Corinthian columns only eight diameters high, and they knew from Vignola that ten diameters was the correct proportion. His frieze, adapted from the Temple of the Sun, varied greatly from d'Espouy.[12] Moreover, he used cornice molds of a Greek proportion on the otherwise Roman entablature. From the uppermost cornice, which Maybeck decorated with the motif of his flowing "A" and anthemions, to the insubstantial bases of the great columns, there were many details the academic architect could criticize. Perhaps even some pique was felt at the fact that Maybeck had connived with his friend McLaren to drop several truckloads of large trees destined for other areas into the muck surrounding the lagoon, much to the consternation of the supervisor of construction.[13] When he came to have them removed to their assigned destinations, the trees had sunk far enough into the mire to make it impossible.

9. *Ibid.* p. 12.
10. Ben Macomber, *The Jewel City* (San Francisco: John H. Williams, 1915), p. 104.
11. Commonwealth Club, *Transactions*, 10, (August, 1915), p. 386.
12. Hector d'Espouy, *Fragments d'Architecture* (Paris: 1905).
13. H.D.H. Connick was Director of Works, and J. McLaren was Landscape Engineer of the Exposition.

Maybeck is rightfully remembered as a mild mannered, modest man; but when it came to a design problem he was determined and resolute in seeing that his ideas prevailed. Contractors and craftsmen who worked with him attest to this fact.[14] He demanded perfection and, at the same time, admitted that it was impossible to achieve. In the Palace of Fine Arts he corrected for optical distortion by skewing each receding plane of the coffers of the rotunda dome to give them equal visual exposures. His ideal shape for the gallery plan was made of elliptical curves, but he modified it to arcs of a circle to make its construction more rational and economical for building with repetitive, radially placed, steel bents. The compromises demanded by architecture inevitably meant a failure to attain the perfection he sought. But he cherished the seeking as a reward of being human.

While Maybeck believed in absolute design values, he never thought mechanical ordering of shapes could create beauty. The basis for his dislike of Renaissance design lay in its dependence upon the diameter of a column as the module to generate acceptable proportions. He felt that each civilization reflected its own spirit in the harmony of lines and the correspondence of forms in its buildings. He believed firmly that the history of architecture could teach him principles of design. His view included vernacular building as well as formal structures. He developed an understanding of architecture as an expression of the human spirit, and he was uninterested in the study of archeological detail or the development of proper "good taste" in historic styles. History was alive for him, and in his studies he had deduced that new materials or architectural shapes, no matter how revolutionary, evoked responses growing out of man's common psychological reactions to color and form, modified by the particular values of a national culture.

The Palace of Fine Arts was as much a landscape composition as it was an architectural one. The great trees, the clipped and flowering shrubs, the high boxes of the colonnade intended to be planted with trailing vines, even the reflections in the lagoon, were calculated to soften the outlines of sharp architectural edges. So too, the great curving wall of the gallery had its crowning cornice stippled by the shadows from a feathery trellis and its surface modulated by the shrubs growing in its high planting ledge. What Maybeck sought was a flawless balance of line, form, light, and color which only time can create—a perfect harmony between nature and architecture.

Bernard Maybeck, charcoal and colored chalk drawing (30"x66"), study for column capital.
Documents Collection, C.E.D.

Even Maybeck's preliminary sketches evoke a feeling complementary to that presented by the actual structure.

14. In spite of the comment, contractors N. Boldt, A. H. Broad, and others did much work for Maybeck.

Palace of Fine Arts, Mesembryanthemum hedges.
Documents Collection, C.E.D.

Maybeck worked with landscape materials as well as with building forms to achieve his architectural effects. This early photograph reveals the sculptured hedges of the original planting.

Palace of Fine Arts, gallery structure.
Documents Collection, C.E.D.

Within this structural shell, the exhibition rooms for paintings were constructed with translucent ceilings to utilize the natural illumination provided by the skylights.

The Palace of Fine Arts established Maybeck's ability as a designer to the San Francisco populace. To an eye not prejudiced by Vignola or d'Espouy, it seemed not much different in detail from the buildings of McKim, Mead and White; Carrère and Hastings; or Henry Bacon, the well-known New York architects. Yet the Palace was more appealing than their work. Even before the closing day of the exposition, a plan to save the Palace of Fine Arts and the Marina took shape. October 16, 1915 was designated as Preservation Day, and excess gate receipts, amounting to $18,000, were collected to form a preservation league. A prime thorn in the side of the preservationists was the question posed by "practical men" who wanted to know what end the use of the structure would serve. John Bakewell answered this question as well as anyone:

> Whether there is any practical use to which the Fine Arts Palace, as at present arranged, could be put is outside the question. The portions of the building which most strike the imagination are the central rotunda and the flanking colonnade, or the very parts which even now have no very practical use, but which with the lagoon and landscape about them have an added touch of romance that we had thought only time and nature could bring. The building itself, that is the roofed portion of the building, can be rearranged or even rebuilt to suit the purpose for which it may be found advisable to use it.[15]

The committee formed to preserve the buildings of the Fair failed in its efforts. It was the commercial interest in the residential development of the fairgrounds that prevailed. But, by mere chance, the Palace of Fine Arts, located on ground leased from the U.S. Military Reservation of the San Francisco Presidio, survived long after the destruction of the palaces around it. For more than two generations its plaster ornament and landscaped grounds enchanted viewers as they did during the Fair. After almost forty-five years of disintegration and decay, a sense of civic pride, the ingrained nostalgia of San Franciscans, and an increased recognition of Maybeck as an imaginative practitioner of architecture renewed efforts for its conservation. Many architects had doubts about rebuilding in permanent materials a structure of lath and plaster that was designed for an instant in time, a consciously created fantasy that was part of the illusionary architecture of a world's fair.

15. John Bakewell, Commonwealth Club, *Transactions*, 10, (August, 1915), p. 375.

But the work of concerned preservationists raised enough money from private and government sources to assure its reconstruction.[16] And, beginning in 1962, over six million dollars was expended to build in steel and concrete a modified version of Maybeck's ephemeral creation.

During the period when funds were being gathered for restoration, Maybeck had his own ideas concerning the fate of the Palace of Fine Arts. They ranged from demolishing it in order to create an active community center, to heavily planting its site with redwoods in order that children of the future might find bits of ornament and sculpture of a wondrous ruin of a previous generation among the trees.[17]

16. Kenneth H. Cardwell, "Bernard Maybeck: San Francisco Genius," *Northern California Chapter, A.I.A. Bulletin*, 22, (April, 1960), pp. 22-25.
17. Conversations between Maybeck and the author. In addition to the two proposals related, he urged friends to investigate the possibility of preservation by "industrial cocooning," a process used to preserve surplus ships from World War II.

Maybeck's schemes, spread from the practical proposal to the romantic dream, differ no more than the other buildings he designed for the Fair. Barns, grandstand and racetrack, a small auditorium and office building, all fell to the lot of Maybeck. Frank Morton Todd commented on these structures:

> With wonderful adaptability, B. R. Maybeck, designer of the Palace of Fine Arts, turned to planning barns, with the result that instead of looking like some bald array of sheds and byres the whole Live Stock Section had a light, spacious and festive air that was very charming; and utility was consulted in every detail. The barns were made interesting with broad, overhanging eaves that cast cool shadows on the walls, and they were gay with hundreds of slender, painted flagpoles like Venetian masts. It is not likely that live stock was ever exhibited in any handsomer quarters, and the congress hall and office pavilion was pleasant and inviting. This building was equipped with moving picture facilities, and would seat 500 people.[18]

18. F. M. Todd, *The Story of the Exposition* 4, p. 339.

Palace of Fine Arts, gallery wall and wooden trellis.
Documents Collection, C.E.D.

Even in decay, the structure retained its wondrous grandeur and feeling. When this photograph was taken the advanced deterioration of the nephelinic plaster was well underway.

Livestock Pavilion, Panama-Pacific International Exposition, San Francisco, 1914.
Documents Collection, C.E.D.

Totally different in character from the Palace of Fine Arts, Maybeck's Livestock Pavilion has a festive air while being spacious and functionally planned.

In addition to his festive barns and his pensive gallery, Maybeck designed a whimsical club building for the Lumbermen's Association, which reveals an aspect of his personality that has received little comment.[19] He had a well-developed sense of humor, and his House of Hoo-Hoo generated the spirit of rough fun usually associated with lumbermen at play. The building gave the impression that it might have been made in a forested area by felling a number of sturdy trees, and using their branches and boughs to provide a shelter between the remaining stumps. Its rustic character, created by the vigorous strokes of a skillful designer, could not be associated with mountain cabins or summer houses. Sham redwood tree trunks, sixteen feet in diameter and forty feet high, placed at the corners of the building, set the scale of the structure. Its exhibition columns formed of unbarked pines, cedars, and firs supported log flower boxes containing trailing vines in parody of the ones planned for the Fine Arts Palace. A terrace on the south with a log and sapling trellis formed a forecourt and, planted with specimen trees and stumps, it extended the feeling that this was a structure hewn out of the forest by some mythical northwoodsman.

19. "Lumbermen's Building," *The Western Architect*, 21, (Sept. 1915), p. 25.

"House of Hoo-Hoo," Pacific Lumbermen's Association, Panama-Pacific International Exposition.
Pacific Coast Architect, July 1915.

Maybeck's joyful structure expresses a sense of playful activity while evoking the monumental, sturdy aspect of the forests and lumbermen.

Besides providing for hospitality, the building exhibited all marketable species of western woods in their natural and finished forms. Slabs of fir, redwood, and pine paneled the walls and formed the balcony rail at one end of the room. Fanciful furniture designed by Maybeck in contrasting colored woods added to the total spirit of the structure. The ceiling, of eight-inch rough fir boards, spaced by dressed two-by-fours, was constructed on purlins hung from the lower chord of four broken-chord trusses which spanned the room. Pairs of trusses, projecting above the main roof of shingles were roofed with courses of hand-split shakes, terminating on three-inch saplings. At the conclusion of the Fair, the building was placed on a barge and floated down the Bay where it was rebuilt, shorn of its make-believe forest setting, in the Peninsula area south of San Francisco.[20] A few years later it was destroyed by fire.

20. Late in life Maybeck made sketches of improvements for San Francisco by linking the bridges with a freeway system. He included the idea of preserving worthwhile buildings in the clearance path by removing them on barges to outlying areas.

"House of Hoo-Hoo," interior view.
Pacific Coast Architect, July 1915.

The interior was finished in various woods that displayed the Association's products while enhancing the light and free spirit of the design.

Maybeck's reputation grew as a result of his designs for the Fair, and so did his practice. The year 1915 marked the end of his dependence on small residential structures. He continued to design the modest house; it was what delighted him most. But with an increase in budgets and scope of commissioned work, Maybeck found himself less able to give the full personal attention to each structure that he had given previously. More and more work was delegated to an expanding office staff.[21] Eventually, in the last decade of his practice, expeditious arrangements were made with other architectural offices for drafting labor which led to the complete separation of the roles of the artist, architect, and artisan Maybeck had so successfully combined in his early years as an independent, self-sufficient practitioner.

Success even produced a change in Maybeck's modest habits; but not for long. Late in the autumn of 1915 he decided to live up to the image of the celebrated architect of the Palace of Fine Arts by purchasing a new hat. On the first day of its wearing he was pleased to note that as people passed him on Market Street on his way to the office they turned and smiled.

He was warmed by the acknowledgment of his status and began to glow with pride, which he justified by the universal acclaim his design had received. His mood lasted until he faced his office staff, who asked what was the nature of the celebration that he should be wearing such an unusual head adornment. Upon removing his hat, he was chagrined to find that the warm smiles had not been caused by recognition but by amusement—the supporting cardboard band of the new hat had come free of its box and ringed the headpiece in a crowning halo.

21. Maybeck's office never became large. Office records beginning in 1922 show no more than 12 draftsmen, not including the Whites. Prior to that date no more than 3 or 4 casual employees are noted in the records. The principal draftsmen and the initial dates of their employment include: John White 1898, Mark White 1902, Chester Chapman 1903, George Howard 1904, Charles Lundgren 1915, Mark Manning 1923.

R. H. Mathewson house, Berkeley.
K. H. Cardwell photograph.

VIII

The House Is A Shell

The house after all is only the shell and the real interest must come from those who are to live in it. If this is done carefully and with earnestness it will give the inmates a sense of satisfaction and rest and will have the same power over the mind as music or poetry or any healthy activity in any kind of human experience.

Bernard Maybeck—1908

The influence of the simple homes of Berkeley on many of the suburban houses built following the earthquake and fire created in the San Francisco Bay region a domestic form of architecture which critics later denoted as a style. Lewis Mumford defined it as a "native and humane form of modernism . . . a free yet unobtrusive expression of the terrain, the climate, and the way of life on the Coast," and saw in the work of a later generation, including William W. Wurster, Gardner Dailey, and John Ekin Dinwiddie, the continuity of principles of architectural expression initiated by Maybeck and his contemporaries.[1]

The new moderns all paid homage to Maybeck, but rebelled as he did at the appelation "style" with its connotation of crystallized form and repeated detail. Instead, they referred to his original and unpretentious design, to his logical and economical construction, and to his knowing response to his clients' informal and liberal attitudes, as often as they referred to the more obvious characteristics of his houses— informal planning, wooden framing, and adaptation to site and climate.[2] Maybeck's importance to the regional expression of the following generation was not his use of shingle walls and wide overhangs but rather his use of simple materials and carpentry techniques in diverse structural and spatial arrangements responsive to human nature. His starting point was man's relation to a building, even in his non-residential structures.

It would be an error to suppose that Maybeck, alone, was responsible for the widespread development of the weathered shingle house. Coxhead and Polk had been building such structures in the region since 1890. John Galen Howard, who had worked with the shingle tradition of the Atlantic seaboard, and William Charles Hays, his able assistant, easily adopted the local patterns and produced fine residential designs.[3] But perhaps more visually significant, shingled exteriors and broad and beamed eaves became the style of the anonymous carpenter builders who produced houses, five and ten at a time, that line the streets of Berkeley and the communities ringing the San Francisco Bay.

The Bay region architecture Mumford noted was not based on the details of the crumbling examples of California's Spanish colonial past. Indeed, most of the buildings of that period had disappeared by the turn of the century, but the relevance of climate and native materials to the development of the forthright forms of the indigenous architecture did not go unnoticed. Unique to the region was the extent to which an informal way of life had produced a freedom in architectural expression which was later praised as modern and humane.

1. Lewis Mumford, "Skyline," *New Yorker* (October 11, 1947), pp. 94-99.

2. "Is There a Bay Area Style?" *Architectural Record*, 105, (May 1949), pp. 92-97.
3. A good example of informal composition in redwood and shingles is the Warren Gregory house, 1459 Greenwood Terrace, Berkeley, by J. G. Howard with additions by W. C. Hays.

Perhaps dependence upon neighbors in a new land where everyone was a stranger made it easier to break with the traditional patterns and manners of solid and staid eastern communities. Trim and spare detailing gave the Bay area architecture its greatest cognate relation with the International style and the Modern movement. And, still greatly unheralded, its economy in construction achieved by economy in design made a strong contribution to its regional character.

Maybeck acknowledged in his building art that climates and conditions varied from place to place and that ideals of life were diverse. Hillside sites called for forms differing from those built on flat lands. In northern California, a region of trees, wood became the natural material with which to build. And where sunshine abounded but the weather was cool, as in Berkeley, windows multiplied to let in the warmth. Houses built in other climates would develop in other ways. Maybeck was interested in modern materials and processes, but he felt standardization of the kind of life people live was neither desirable nor possible. His desire to solve the problem of creating a frame for human life in the best and most expressive way possible meant that his solutions would vary as did his clients' styles of living, even if the locale of their houses did not.

Two examples of Maybeck's work, in areas over two hundred miles away from San Francisco Bay give physical form to his belief in the influence of climate and place. They were designed for construction, one to the north and one to the south, in the hot Sacramento-San Joaquin Valley of California. The Dudley Saeltzer house (1907) in Redding is a hillside house adapted to the climate by the addition of a deep eastern porch to serve as a cool retreat from the intense heat of the western sun. For its construction Maybeck chose a local Oregon cedar which was much less expensive in this inland town than the redwood of the coastal regions. On the Chester Rowell house (1909) in Fresno, also built in wood, Maybeck proposed to use as a cooling device an ingenious double roof which created a ventilated air space over all the structure, but building costs led to a final solution of traditional construction. Neither of these houses alone—even with materials and details shaped by climatic influences—would Maybeck have called a regional expression. But each, he believed, when viewed with many others also responding to unique local conditions would reveal a regional quality just as do the houses built on the sunny but cool slopes surrounding the San Francisco Bay.

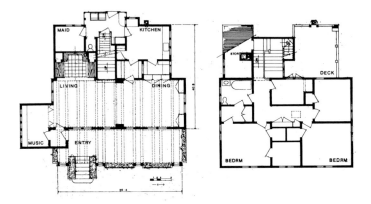

Dudley Saeltzer house, Redding, California, 1907, plan. Documents Collection, C.E.D.

Maybeck designed a deep, sheltered eastern porch to provide a cool retreat from the hot western sun of the Sacramento–San Joaquin valley.

Dudley Saeltzer house, north and east elevations. Documents Collection, C.E.D.

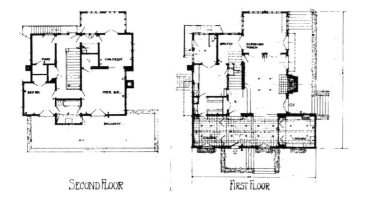

SECOND FLOOR   FIRST FLOOR

Chester N. Rowell house, Mildreda and Forthcamp Sts., Fresno, California, 1909. (Destroyed)
Plan, Documents Collection, C.E.D.

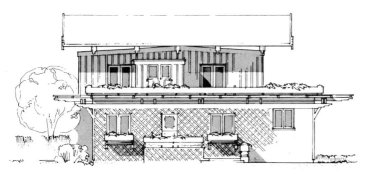

Chester N. Rowell house, elevation of original scheme.
Documents Collection, C.E.D.

As an answer to the hot dry climate of the area, the original design of the house featured a unique "double" roof which provided ventilated air space over the structure.

No architect of his generation was more successful than Maybeck in the design of distinctive inexpensive structures. Clients with limited budgets sought him out, for they felt they got the most "architecture" through his efforts for what they had to spend. While he could be lavish in decorative effects, he could also produce rich patterns with the very bones of the structure, not wasting a board or a nail in applied ornament or finish. Both his gymnasium design (1910) for the San Francisco Settlement Association and the second house (1912) built in Berkeley for Isaac Flagg are vivid illustrations of his ability to create distinctive buildings with a limited expenditure of money and material.[4]

Located in an extremely poor neighborhood of mixed residential and industrial uses, the San Francisco Settlement Association operated in a converted residence. Maybeck had been hired to design a building for community meetings, which could also serve as a gymnasium for the Boys' Club. The space proposed for the building was limited, but, for about one dollar a square foot, he constructed a gymnasium of forty-five by sixty feet, innovative in its structure and handsome in its utilitarian expression.

4. In 1906 Maybeck had designed a settlement house for a predecessor of the Association. The only extant record of the building is found in Telegraph Hill Neighborhood Association, *Fourth Annual Report* (January 1907), p. 1.

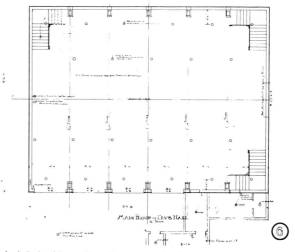

Boys' club building, San Francisco Settlement Association, 2520 Folsom St., San Francisco, 1910. (Destroyed)
Plan, Documents Collection, C.E.D.

Drawing on the experience with Hearst Hall, Maybeck employed a newly modified form of his laminated wood arches to span the width of the building.[5] The arches, which rose to a height of twenty feet, were built of rough one-by-twelve pine boards, bent to a radius of thirty-five feet. Each half-arch was four inches thick at its foot, increased to a total depth of sixteen inches at its third point, and decreased to four inches again near the ridge of the building where it was fastened to its opposite half-arch with a steel plate. The increase in thickness was accomplished by adding, in pairs, inch-thick boards to the central four of the arch's core. Laminations and curves were formed by nailing during assembly on the floor and were later made permanent by bolting when erection and loading of the arches had taken place.

Beams were placed on five arches to carry a wide skylight over the ridge and the balconies on each side of the room. The skylight, the painted standing-seam metal roof, and the walls of redwood shingles formed the exterior skin of the structure. Above the balcony level, the shingles were double-coursed, laid with a ten-inch exposure, while the lower portion of the wall was treated with single six-inch courses. Conventional pine sash and doors of stock dimensions were used throughout the building. The interior was enriched by leaving the diagonal sheathings of the wall and roof exposed and by staining every third board green before laying.

To accept Maybeck's simple and direct material and structural treatments as artless solutions would be to overlook his conscious effort to make the most out of the least. Covering a wall with shingles laid in double courses takes no more material or labor than setting them in narrow single ones. Yet, by employing both methods Maybeck varied textures, accented lines, and established pattern areas at will. He could have spanned the small room with carpenter trusses instead of arches but he probably would not have saved material and he certainly would not have achieved the same graceful lines or an uninterrupted light source. And the small effort he expended on the exposed interior surfaces gave him a simple means to select rhythms and patterns on a scale appropriate for the structure. Maybeck, combining his skills as an artisan with his knowledge as an architect, turned an ordinary building into architecture.

5. H. Kower, who had done the engineering on Hearst Hall, also worked for Maybeck on this structure.

Boys' club building, laminated arches of the interior.
William S. Ricco photograph.

Leaving the exterior sheathing exposed for the interior finish was economical and attractive when done by Maybeck. Prior to its destruction, the gymnasium was used as a storage space for a little theater group.

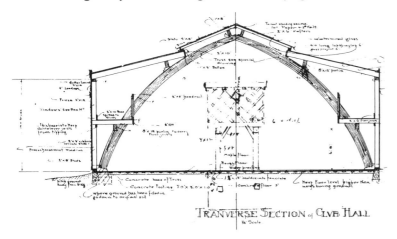

TRANVERSE SECTION of CLUB HALL
¼ Scale

Boys' club building, section.
Documents Collection, C.E.D.

Maybeck used laminated arches for the structural basis of his handsome but very economical utilitarian building.

In 1912 Maybeck built a third structure on the Flagg property in Berkeley. He used stock doors and windows and the post and beam framing found in the early Hall and Boke houses in a method which was his solution to the problems of modular and exposed structural design. The house, the last all-wood residence that Maybeck designed, was constructed for about two dollars a square foot. Redwood shortly became too expensive to use for general construction and he began to restrict its use to interior finishes for the principal living areas. The design, the ultimate development of Maybeck's Gothic house, provides cross ventilation for every room, a flue for individual heaters in each habitable space, and a concealed system of wiring for lighting fixtures and switches in a frame in which all studs, joists, and rafters are exposed. It is a disciplined achievement, a remarkable architectural solution.

Although the house was built for a newly wedded daughter of Professor Flagg, it was sold in a few years to A. W. Ransome whose family occupied it for a generation. The house, vertical in character, is built on a high basement in order to give the first floor a view—the principal visual axis of the living rooms, if extended, would pass through the center of the Golden Gate of San Francisco Bay. Its almost three-story height is softened only by the rake of the eaves and the flare of the walls over the foundation as they near the grade. Balconies, carried on beams or joists which are extensions of the interior framing, and wide eaves enliven the profile of the building.

The plan of the Ransome house, as it is known locally, is freely organized, centering around the stairway to the second-floor rooms.[6] Strong, oblique axes organize the interior spaces and add a subdued note of contrast to the strong rectilinear framing patterns. The various rooms make an irregular plan form as they thrust from the central area and, in contrast with the earlier Gothic houses which had articulated pavilions with individual roofs, the entire house is covered by a large gable. The second-floor study has a low plate line as a result of the simplified framing; but its restricted volume is made both usable and intriguing by the introduction of a large dormer opening onto a balcony through paired French doors.

6. Although little is known about Maybeck's library due to the destruction caused by three major fires, an interesting comparison can be made between the Ransome house and "Rural Home No. 4" in John Bullock, *The American Cottage Builder* (New York: Stringer and Townsend, 1854), p. 223.

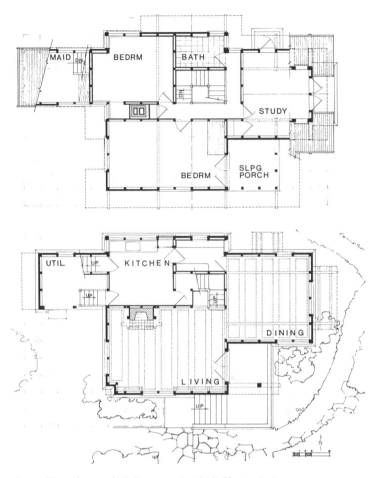

Isaac Flagg house (#2 Ransome), 1210 Shattuck Ave., Berkeley, 1912.
Plan drawn by Alan Williams, Documents Collection, C.E.D.

The freely organized plan featured cross-ventilation for every room and strong, oblique axes which organized the interior spaces and provided a contrast to the rectilinear framing patterns.

The module Maybeck employed for design and construction derives from the combined widths of one ten-inch and two twelve-inch boards. These are applied vertically as sheathing to the exterior of four-by-four studs. The assembly gives an equal exposure of the boards on the interior. The module selected also works well with stock dimensioned doors and windows which close, without frames, against the exposed studs. The exterior is covered with redwood shingles applied over a layer of stripping and insulation. Except for the metal flashing of the heavy redwood sills which dado into the structural frame, the shingle skin forms the weather seal around the openings. The studs, plates, blocking, posts, and sheathing boards, all of redwood, are worked as a pattern in the design of the interior finish. Even the heading of the second-floor joists is treated as an overmantle for the fireplace. Although the timbering may be heavy for contemporary tastes, the design of the house has a consistently small scale and it demonstrates a wide diversity of forms, and variations in patterns, within the limits of a strictly modular system.

Isaac Flagg house (#2), view of fireplace framing.
William S. Ricco photograph.

Simple, strong wood treatments throughout the interior lends a unified richness to the structure while providing a comfortable atmosphere in which to live.

Isaac Flagg house (#2), front elevation.
Documents Collection, C.E.D.

The last of Maybeck's all-redwood houses, it is also one of his best—a high point of his Gothic design.

In spite of Maybeck's general success with limited budget construction, there were projects like the C. C. Boynton house (1911) which rushed headlong into financial disaster, propelled by the enthusiasm of both the client and the architect. A revealing story of its design and of the nature of the hillside community is told by Florence Treadwell Boynton who first met the Maybecks through her lectures on open-air schools and the dance and music of Isadora Duncan. In a paper written in 1958 to memorialize the work of Maybeck, she tells of forming a number of study circles at the urging of the individualists of the north Berkeley hillside; one on architecture, led by Mr. Maybeck; one on posture, poise, motion, grace, and dance; one on garments suitable for the same; one on simple and uncooked foods; and one on the garden. Through these activities she became interested in living in Berkeley, purchased a portion of the Maybeck land on Buena Vista Way, and, with her husband and six children, began an experiment in living close to nature. "Mr. Maybeck" she writes:

> built us a model camp above the present homesite, consisting of two pergolas, one for living and sleeping, ... having a canvas roof which rolled back ... to allow us to sleep under the stars.... The second pergola, a little farther to the north ... consisted of a dining room and kitchen.... This pergola was surrounded by glass windows, screened.... The kitchen had a cook stove and sink without running water. The water flowed down from a spring up the hill to the back door. The garbage was buried; the toilet was beyond the eucalyptus trees. These pergolas were nestled into the hill in the typical Maybeck fashion in seclusion from any others.[7]

The Boyntons lived in the temporary camp dwelling that Maybeck designed while he and Mrs. Boynton developed the preliminary drawings of the ideal home in which to raise the family steeped in the culture of Greek art, dance, and philosophy. The house was to be open to the breezes with only its most private compartments contained by conventional walls. It took the form of an exedra of Corinthian columns set on a radiantly-heated concrete platform constructed over hollow tiles carrying hot air, permitting family members, clad in *stola* and *pallium*, to recline comfortably on cushions placed on its stepped recesses or to dance freely on the broad expanse between the columns that overlooked the city and the Golden Gate. In her story, Mrs. Boynton reveals that when she first told Maybeck that she wanted "an atrium in the center of the house from which all the activities of the home would radiate" he explained that

the atrium would not have to be enclosed on all four sides, but that one side could remain open and the atrium would be without draft or breeze. It would be a "pocket of air" into which no more air could enter. The open side would preferably be to the southwest in order to be benefitted by all possible sunshine.[8]

Unfortunately Maybeck did not have the opportunity to execute the design. His enthusiasm for Mrs. Boynton's ideas outran her husband's unstated budget. Other disagreements arose between Mr. Boynton, a lawyer, and Annie Maybeck, the shrewd developer of the Buena Vista properties. Conflict over the terms of the sale, dedicated rights of way, and public access to other Maybeck parcels ground all action to a halt, and Maybeck's design passed to A. Randolph Monro, a young draftsman in John Galen Howard's office. He completed the project as an independent commission.[9]

When Monro took over the project, thirty classic columns had already been erected, and he designed the open pavilion and compartments which Berkeley residents have long known as the "Temple of the Wings." The name, Mrs. Boynton relates, was derived from the roof which took the shape of a "pair of wings sheltering our nest."[10] Without trying to assay the proportionate contribution of architect, owner, and draftsman to the design of the Boynton residence, it reveals the extremes of architectural expression which Maybeck believed could exist in a community development harmonized by judicious siting within the landscape. Contrasting in color and form with the Boyntons' Grecian temple, Maybeck's own brown shingled house with projecting eaves and recessed porches and Lawson's concrete one with ornamental tiles and sgraffito were only a few hundred feet away. Maybeck reasoned that if each house was individually beautiful in the landscape, then collectively their diversity enriched the community.

7. B. R. Maybeck MSS, "F. T. Boynton," C.E.D. Docs.
8. *Ibid.*
9. Interview by the author with Mrs. R. Monro.
10. B. R. Maybeck MSS, "F. T. Boynton," C.E.D. Docs.

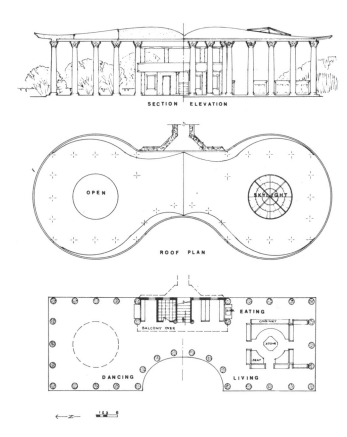

SECTION ELEVATION

OPEN   SKYLIGHT

ROOF PLAN

EATING

BALCONY OVER   CABINET

STOVE

SEAT

DANCING   LIVING

←—N—

Charles C. Boynton house, "Temple of the Wings," 2800 Buena Vista Way, Berkeley, 1912, A. Randolph Monro, Architect. Documents Collection, C.E.D.

This unique design was begun by Maybeck to provide the "ideal" home for a family steeped in Greek culture. Financial problems and other disagreements caused Maybeck to withdraw from the project which was completed by Randolph Monro; but it serves as another example of Maybeck's architectural adaptability, talent and enthusiasm.

Charles C. Boynton house, original columns in rebuilt house of 1924.
K. H. Cardwell photograph.

164

Maybeck's second decade of practice climaxed brilliantly in 1910 with the construction of the Christian Science Church; but in the following two years his commissions dwindled rapidly. Aside from the Boynton temporary shelter, Maybeck built only two houses during the year 1911. His lack of success in the competitions as well as the loss of the Boynton commission and one for the Pacific Unitarian Church and School, made 1912 no better. It was the slowing of his practice that had led him to seek work at the Fair. His appointment as the architect of the Palace of Fine Arts assured that soon after the start of his third decade of practice, his office was as busy as it ever had been. His commission for the Lumbermen's Association at the Fair led to work for a company town in Brookings, Oregon. And, with an improvement in the economy, the number of residential commissions for his Berkeley neighbors increased.

Most of Maybeck's work designed prior to the construction of the Christian Science church can be roughly categorized as medieval or classical by noting its predominating lines and details. But the fusion of idea and form, modeled volume and structural order, handcrafted and machined materials, which had been so brilliantly achieved in the church, are repeated to a degree in all later residential designs. This blending makes any classification very arbitrary. The houses become neither medieval nor classical, but they do reveal a strong individualistic order—sometimes emphasizing economy, the terrain, or structure, but more frequently portraying a way of life. Maybeck expressed this in an interview: "The thing to do is to make the home fit the family.... I never plan a home for a man until I have asked him a lot of questions. 'What sort of woman is your wife? What kind of clothes do you both wear? What do you most like to read? Do you enjoy music?' "[11]

One of the first designs of the new decade, the Guy H. Chick house (1914), is the ultimate statement of the chalet in its most sophisticated form.[12] The low-pitched gable roof derives from the earlier chalet types; but Maybeck's integration of the house and its garden is not found in vernacular Swiss structures and his personal interpretation of details obscures prototypical forms. The house is two-storied; portions of its upper-story are covered by vertical redwood boards and specially molded battens, the remaining surfaces are clad in gray-green stained shingles or natural sand-finished plaster. Strong cubical projections from the main block accent the corners and function as closets for the upstairs bedrooms. Its

Guy Hyde Chick house, entrance pergola.
Roy Flamm photograph.

The many trellises softened the exterior of the house while also effectively joining it with its luxuriant setting.

broad eaves are patterned by doubling and tripling framing members, and feather into trelliage which, with the design of the Christian Science church, had become a characteristic detail of Maybeck's work. All the trellises—at the eaves, at the entrance, and the handsomely arranged one around the exterior shoulders of the concrete fireplace—blur the silhouette of the house to blend it with its verdant setting.

11. Bernard Maybeck interviewed by Mark Quest, 1927.
12. The house has been remodeled and published in *House Beautiful*, 104, (May 1962), pp. 150-57.

Guy Hyde Chick house, 7133 Chabot Road, Berkeley, 1914,
view from the garden.
Stone and Stecatti photograph.

Maybeck's chalet design in its most sophisticated form.

Located in Berkeley's Chabot canyon, the Chick house is sited on a large piece of gently sloping land covered by a superb growth of California Live Oaks. Over the years the garden grove has been supplemented with plantings of azaleas and rhododendrons. Walks and terraces create a transition space between the house and garden and, by providing large sliding glass doors, Maybeck made it easy for the occupants to move from one into the other. Although the Chick house makes excellent use of its garden spaces by extended vistas, it does not fit Maybeck's early definition of architecture as "landscape gardening around a few rooms."[13] The house is not a casual arrangement of a few rooms; but, more importantly, it displays fully, as the Senger house had only hinted, the design of interior and exterior spaces as correlative units rather than adjunctive ones. Renaissance design and Beaux-Arts training have produced many superb examples of gardens complementing building forms, but the scale and the sensitivity of Maybeck's design often had a greater affinity with Japanese work which combines natural and constructed environments into one inseparable design.

The Chick house has a central hall plan similar to the Flagg chalet; but it is more formal in its organization. The house is entered from beneath a circular pergola through glass doors into an entry hall which bisects the building. Distant views of the surrounding gardens are visible through glass doors or windows of adjoining rooms. The interiors, when seen in photographs, appear more conventional than others that Maybeck designed; but the rooms are finely proportioned and confidently accented with solids and voids to give a sense of unity and flowing volume. The walls of the living room are covered with a dull gold velvet, matching the highlights of the redwood trim. Rough beams carrying the second-story rooms are boxed with finished lumber, and, near the plastered ceiling, a molded wood cornice forms a trough for indirect lighting. The finish used for most rooms is a plaster surface trimmed with natural redwood; however, in the large upstairs space designated as the boys' room, board and batten walls and exposed beams and rafters were Maybeck's selection for rough-and-tumble action.

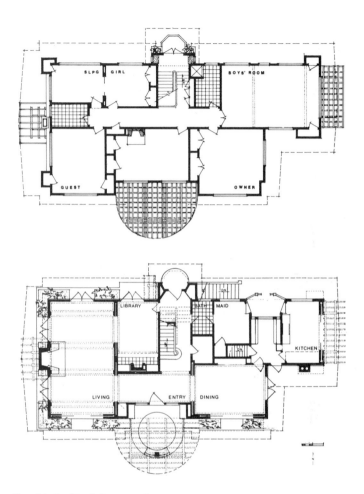

Guy Hyde Chick house, plan.
Documents Collection, C.E.D.

13. *Hillside Club Bulletin* (1906-07).

Guy Hyde Chick house, view from living room toward entrance.
Stone and Stecatti photograph.

The elegantly proportioned and finished interior featured large windows and glazed doors providing vistas into the gardens— again gracefully blending the interior with the surroundings.

Guy Hyde Chick house, second floor boys' room.
Stone and Stecatti photograph.

Natural wood surfaces and exposed structural members were used by Maybeck as the finish for a happy, sturdy room for the family's young boys.

Alma S. Kennedy studio, 1537 Euclid Ave., Berkeley, 1914. (Destroyed 1923)
Photograph of original structure courtesy of A. S. Kennedy.

Gothic features and a two-story height emphasize verticality, but this was balanced by the low-pitched roof and horizontal lines of the structure.

The Alma Schmidt Kennedy studio (1914) for voice and concert performances combines Gothic ornament with classical lines and adds to the diverse forms that Maybeck had built on the Buena Vista hillside. On a corner lot, difficult to build on because of its limited size and steep slope, Maybeck joined a high studio room to a two-storied living unit under a cross-gable roof. An enticing walled walk from the principal street curves its way around the corner of the building to arrive at the entrance vestibule of the living unit a half-story below the studio level. The gabled end of the concert room dominates the composition—its beamed overhangs are cut back to the wall surface near the ridge point, accenting a large window. A lancet window, a deck railed with cusped roundels, and half-timbering reinforce the Gothic imagery and suggest verticality, but low-pitched roofs and horizontal lines balance the composition.

Stucco in tones of terra cotta, umber and warm gray, and painted wood in blues, greens, and carmine combine with a red tile roof in a color scheme more harmonious than its description. The studio was heavily damaged by fire in 1923 but it was reconstructed in nearly the same form with the exception of the roof which originally was shingled and had overhangs ending in lacy trelliage. The interior of the studio is furnished in natural redwood and simply detailed built-in casework. The plan is functionally arranged to take advantage of the split levels by using the dining and bedroom spaces of the living unit for overflow audience seating during public recitals.

When the studio was rebuilt in 1923, a second living unit, detailed in the same style as the first, was added at the eastern edge of the property and connected to the original building by an engaging bridged passage. In rebuilding, Maybeck also solved an environmental problem common to the Berkeley hillside sites. Both the view and the strong afternoon sun are to the west, and, if a designer provides for the view by a large window, the resulting heat and glare can make a house untenantable. Maybeck's solution for the large Kennedy studio window is effective and richly decorative. A pair of dark blue canvas hangings set in the recesses on the outside of the building can be closed from the inside to stave off the heat of the sun, and when they cover the window their rich color contrasts with the warm tones of the exterior.

Alma S. Kennedy studio.
Plan, Documents Collection, C.E.D.

The functional plan took advantage of the split level to provide additional seating in the dining and bedroom spaces. After the Berkeley fire the house was rebuilt with additions and a tile roof.

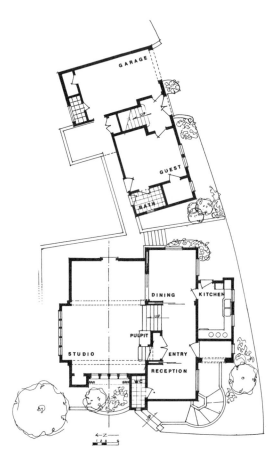

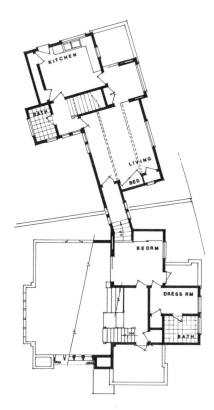

To Maybeck beauty was an essential element of house construction, and he was determined that it should not be eliminated by the increasing cost of building. In the R. H. Mathewson design (1915) also on Buena Vista Way in Berkeley, Maybeck illustrated in simple carpentry construction the blending of structure, color, and pattern into a crisp architectural form in which he reduced costs by reducing sizes.[14] Just as in the 1902 Boke house in which he had manipulated the plan to increase the sense of spaciousness, so again he turned to the plan to accomplish his purposes. The house has no dining room nor even a nook pretending to be one; in addition, all of its essential service elements are minimized, sacrificing secondary areas in order to create a large, handsome living space.

Built on a corner site, the house has a one-story living room and a two-story service wing skillfully contained under a dog-leg gable roof which slopes off into minor gables over projecting forms of the plan. The living room is spanned longitudinally by two built-up beams which eliminate the necessity of horizontal ties for transverse framing members and end wall supports. A small shed roof over the large north window runs counter to the pitch of the main gable and becomes a visual statement of the resourceful and imaginative framing of the interior volume. The walls of the house are gray stucco, while their upper reaches are covered with boards and battens stained gray-green. Windows divided into small square lights by thick blue-green muntins—suggesting a grille set between the sill and the projecting eaves—fill the gable ends.

Maybeck had used the theme of glazed gable walls with great success in the Christian Science church, and in the Mathewson house it was made possible by the longitudinal framing that was natural but contrary to normal practice. A windowed gable with sheltering eaves is, perhaps, the single detail of Maybeck's work most repeated by later moderns, and it is one so distinctive in form that it suggests a regional style as strongly as do the horizontal lines of windows and extended overhangs used by the architects of the Prairie School.[15]

14. At the time of the Berkeley fire in 1923, Maybeck responded to a request from E. R. Sturm, Glendale, California for a small cottage with a design practically duplicating that of the Mathewson house.
15. Cf. Jean M. Bangs, "Bernard Ralph Maybeck, Architect: Comes Into His Own," *Architectural Record*, 103, (January 1948), pp. 72-79.

R. H. Mathewson house, La Loma Ave. and Buena Vista Way, Berkeley, 1915.
Documents Collection, C.E.D.

Simple construction combined with excellent design was Maybeck's answer to the problem of building a beautiful home at a modest price.

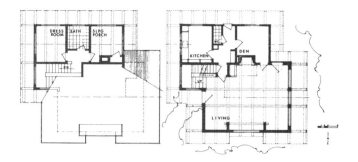

R. H. Mathewson house, plan.
Documents Collection, C.E.D.

Maybeck provided a sense of spaciousness to the modest dimensions by eliminating secondary service areas to create a large living space.

A change in the consistent good quality of Maybeck's work started in 1914 when demands on his time to finish the Fair buildings forced him to hire draftsmen to complete his own projects. He seemed to be unable to direct men other than Mark and John White whom he had trained to develop his sketches into strong, integrated designs. Perhaps his failure was due to the way he worked—his preliminaries set a broad framework which he strengthened and refined as the detail drawings developed. Unless he directed the design and construction through to completion, including supervision on the job site, the resulting houses were not always successful. One house built in 1915 in north Berkeley for C. W. Whitney failed to resolve Maybeck's conception of a building angled to conform to a difficult terrain.

Built on a steep downslope fronting on Keith Avenue, the Whitney house consists of two rectangular blocks angled and merged to fit the shoulder of the hillside. One block contains the entry and parents' rooms, the other combines a two-storied living room, surrounded by a gallery with an open loft space for the children over the dining room and kitchen. A large, rough concrete fireplace, stained black and freely ornamented with abstract swirls of ultramarine and gold, is set against the north wall of the living room facing the dark void of the loft space. The design starts to develop a theme of angled spaces with projecting bays and recessed decks to repeat the re-entrant form to the building mass; but the conflict of the modular patterning with the neo-baroque exuberance of detail and decoration combined with discordant angular lines, creates a design lacking in coherence and the refinement of form and pattern expected of Maybeck.

C. W. Whitney house, 1110 Keith Ave., Berkeley, 1915.
K. H. Cardwell photograph.

Exuberant detailing combined with angular planning to produce an erratic design when Maybeck was forced by the press of other work to hire new draftsmen to complete his projects and devote less time than usual to supervision of the design.

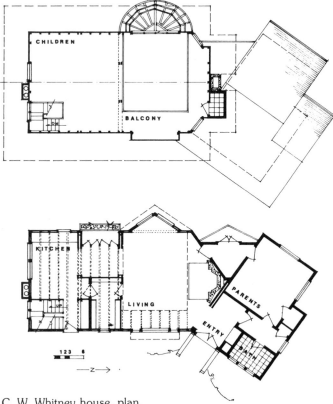

C. W. Whitney house, plan.
Documents Collection, C.E.D.

Even in the 1915 house for Thomas F. Hunt where materials and form are used with restrained elegance, Maybeck's performance is erratic.[16] The Dutch colonial overtones of the house can perhaps be attributed to the fact that Professor Hunt and his family were recent arrivals from the Atlantic Coast. (It is not recorded whether the owners prevailed on Maybeck for a Colonial design or whether Maybeck used a gambrel roof and white trim to express their eastern background.) Certainly the results bolster the criticism of the academic architect that Maybeck was at best casual in his use of historical styles. The house was set close to the street to reserve the rear of the site for a tennis court. Its facade is symmetrically composed in contrast with the plan. The entrance portico is tightly fitted between the two shingled blocks railed with classic balusters. Its pediment and wood painted cornice are penetrated by an arched recess, which appears too large for the portico and too small for a welcoming entrance.

The interior walls of the Hunt house are finished with alternating boards of redwood and ponderosa pine, separated by a narrow strip of wood stained deep blue. A Greek fret of the same blue is stenciled on the boards and a silver design accents the strips. Base and cornice moldings of the walls are enamelled white. French doors separate the entry, living room, study and, in the dining room where china closets are covered by similar units, the doors are glazed with mirrors. A fireplace with hobs is finished in a special concrete made with a white marble sand, and its wood mantel, also painted white, is supported on classic *mutules*. The stairway has an open stringer, and its railing of turned spindles ends in a swirl caging the newel post. Even though the individual balusters and newel post are strangely proportioned, the verve with which the design of the stairway is executed is admirable.

16. The house has been relocated and remodeled.

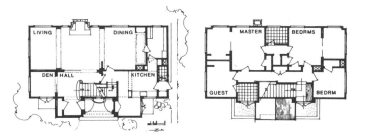

Thomas F. Hunt house, plan.
Documents Collection, C.E.D.

Thomas F. Hunt house, view of fireplace.
William S. Ricco photograph.

Thomas F. Hunt house, 1800 Spruce St., Berkeley, 1915.
William S. Ricco photograph.

The Hunt house with its Dutch Colonial features did not achieve the grace of proportioning of most of Maybeck's houses.

173

S. Erlanger house, 270 Castenada, Forest Hills, San Francisco, 1916.
Documents Collection, C.E.D.

The owners wanted a house based on a medieval English manor, Samlesbury Hall, but Maybeck's creativity transformed the structure into a design of his own featuring a three-storied, shingled residence with rooms, bays, decks and dormers piled in almost casual, but charming, abandon.

As a result of Maybeck's buildings at the Fair and the recognition that followed, 1916 saw the start of construction of a series of houses whose scale and budgets Maybeck had not known since his work on the Roos house in San Francisco. Clients impressed by the popularity of the Palace of Fine Arts turned to Maybeck as an artist worthy of patronage. One of the first commissions of 1916 was for the S. H. Erlanger house in Forest Hills, San Francisco. The owners had selected as a prototype an English medieval manor, Samlesbury Hall, in Lancashire, but Maybeck's creative interpretation of English Gothic dissolved into details and proportions peculiar to him. In his design, Maybeck piles room on room in casual abandon to form three stories burgeoning with polygonal bays, protruding dormers, and open decks. It is a large, shingled house with steep, gabled roofs. While its overall form discourages classification, its articulated living room pavilion, tall, trussed and raftered, echoes Maybeck's Gothic designs.

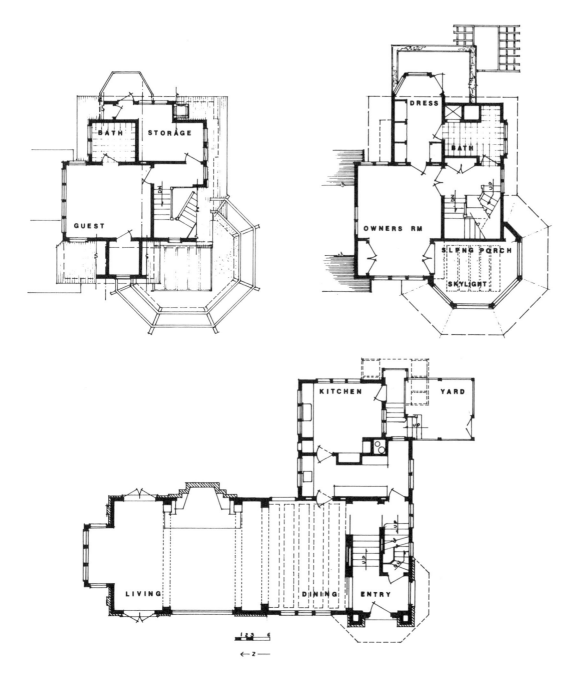

S. Erlanger house, plan.
Documents Collection, C.E.D.

B. D. Marx Greene house, 7240 Chabot Road, Berkeley, 1916. (Destroyed)
Stone and Stecatti photograph.

The Greene house blended with the landscape even before being enveloped by the vegetation.

B. D. Marx Greene house, plan.
Documents Collection, C.E.D.

The open plan with its porches and terraces related well to the surrounding gardens.

The second house of 1916 was built for B. D. Marx Greene.[17] Although the office did not supervise the construction of the work, the house achieved an easy repose on the site. Located in Chabot canyon, southwest of the Chick house, its living and dining rooms opened into sunny southern terraces which provided garden spaces for eating and relaxation. Dormers and sleeping porches accented the outline of the building formed by two and three-story blocks, each gabled and roofed with red pan tiles. The eaves were wide and low. Darkened beveled siding covered the walls, and lush growth concealed much of the brick veneer that surrounded the entrance. From its entry, vistas through the house into the garden foretold of an open plan. The vines and creepers growing on the building accounted in part for its assimilation into the landscape, but the form of the house fitted both the ground which sloped towards the stream, and the tall trees which sheltered its northern entrance.

17. The house was destroyed in 1962 to create an eight lane freeway and rapid transit line adjacent to Chabot canyon. Ironically, the land was not used and was later sold for residential development.

B. D. Marx Greene house, view of stairway. William S. Ricco photograph.

The stairway off of the entry featured natural lighting from a bank of windows and combined linear and turned wood detailing.

A. E. Bingham house, 699 San Ysidro Road, Montecito,
Santa Barbara, 1916.
Documents Collection, C.E.D.

In response to the large, level site the Bingham house featured
long horizontal lines composed under crossed gable roofs.
Stone and shingled facings combined to present a most handsome exterior.

The most striking of the large houses of 1916 is the one
designed for A. E. Bingham in Montecito, near Santa Barbara.
Here, with an ample budget, Maybeck had for the first time a
reasonably level site of virtually unlimited size with which to
work. The house is composed of gabled roofs crossed over
one, two, and three-storied forms. Its exterior is covered with
dark-stained redwood shakes. Exterior Venetian blinds of
wood controlled the light and heat of the southwestern sun.
Strong masonry piers and facings of local stone contrast in
color with the walls and in form with the extended planes of
the roof. In his hillside houses Maybeck had emphasized the
rake of the gable roof in forms harmonizing with sloping
sites; in the Bingham house he allowed the long horizontal
lines of the ridges and the eaves to dominate in response to
its level and extended garden setting.

The house was laid out on a five-foot grid, but as the design
progressed and became more involved, Maybeck abandoned,

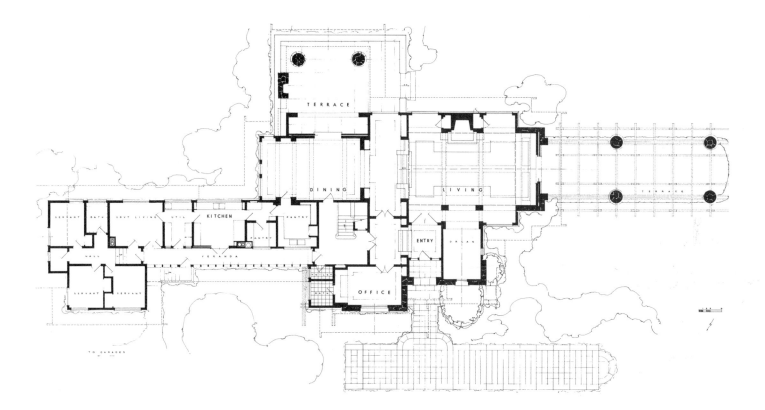

A. E. Bingham house, plan drawn by Alan Williams.
Documents Collection, C.E.D.

The linear plan featured cross vistas and changing floor levels while extending 130 feet including the large terrace covered by a pergola.

at least in part, his modular planning. The plan connects a series of spaces to create a vista one hundred and thirty feet long, over half within the house and the rest under an exterior pergola. The strong axis is composed with cross vistas through square seven-foot plate glass windows facing one another or opposite a principal entrance. Adding to the interest of the crossed axes, changes in the level of the floor plane, accents of the structural framing, and variations in interior shapes make the Bingham house a superb volumetric composition. Its formality may not be as appealing as Maybeck's more romantic interpretations, but it is no less surely handled.

The living room, designed for musical performances, once housed a pipe organ in addition to a grand piano. It is spanned by two heavy structural bents made of laminated lumber which carry beams the length of the room for support of the roof rafters. All of the structural members as well as the walls to normal ceiling heights are cased in white birch, watercolor stained. Raw silk dyed an ultramarine blue covers the frieze surrounding the upper portions of the room and the panels formed by the framing. A cornice conceals recessed lighting, and its gilded surface is highlighted by primary color accents wiped into the sculptured depths of its classical moldings. The richly decorated house was ornately furnished by the Binghams; yet its third-story contained a simple wood-framed game room reminiscent of the simple home. Grouped casement sash affording dramatic views of the coastline and the rugged Santa Ynez mountains, and a simple rhythm of exposed framing formed the decorative scheme.

A. E. Bingham house, view of entry.
Documents Collection, C.E.D.

A. E. Bingham house, view from living room to dining room.
Roy Flamm photograph.

Richly detailed, the formality of the decorative scheme is
enlivened by the varied axes and levels of the magnificent
volumetric composition.

It was a decade of change and diversity. The revitalized office work was interrupted by the United States entry into World War I. The slowing of private construction resulted, once again, in a drop of new commissions which came into Maybeck's office. He was asked to design a temporary Red Cross building in the San Francisco Civic Center; yet, although records indicate it was built, no drawings of it can be found. His former benefactress, Phoebe Hearst, commissioned him to make a general plan for Mills College in nearby Oakland, and his work on it, plus his appointment as supervising architect for the construction of a new town for shipyard workers at Clyde, California, kept him busy during the war years.

The first new construction with the full resumption of his practice in 1919 was a clubhouse built for the Forest Hills Association. The commission came through a former client and Bohemian Club friend, E. C. Young. In 1911 Maybeck had made preliminary drawings of a townhouse for Young, similar in detail to the Goslinsky residence, but it was never constructed. In 1913 he made a new design for a magnificient site in the newly opened Forest Hill district of San Francisco. The house commands a superb view of the Golden Gate to the north and the city to the east. It is an open-planned house with all of the charm and intriguing interior spatial effects of Maybeck's best work. However, the exterior treatment in shingles, half timbers, and aberrant Gothic details place it among those designs in which Maybeck seems not to have made all of the final decisions.

E. C. Young house, 51 Sotelo Avenue, Forest Hills, San Francisco, 1913.
Documents Collection, C.E.D.

The street elevation of the Young house presented a charming if somewhat erratic appearance through its varied details and form.

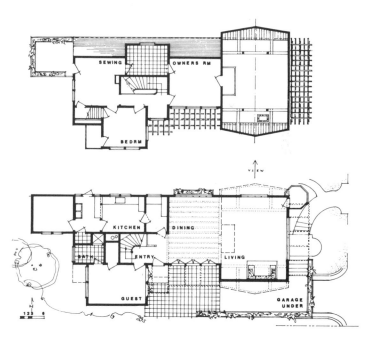

E. C. Young house, plan.
Documents Collection, C.E.D.

The open plan successfully related the house to the site while providing views of the surrounding areas.

Forest Hills Association club building, 381 Magellan Ave.,
San Francisco, 1919.
K. H. Cardwell photograph.

The varied exterior finishes and details gave the structure a
resemblance to traditional English architecture.

The same is true of the Forest Hill Clubhouse. In fact, the
drawings name E. C. Young as associate architect, but the
office records do not indicate the nature of the collaboration.
Exterior details of half-timber falsework, brick veneer panels,
and jigsawn barge boards lend an air of eclectic English architecture to the clubhouse. It consists of an assembly hall, club
room, balcony lounge area, kitchen, and independent living
quarters for a resident housekeeper. A flexible arrangement
of spaces form the assembly hall. The central portion is
covered by a high trussed roof and the north end diminishes
to a gabled alcove, rafter framed. At the south end, the balcony and the area below it may be used as part of the room.
Neither a dominant structural order, consistent patterning,
nor strongly composed vistas give the clubhouse organization.
Only the non-axial arrangement of the fireplace and openings
recalls the spatial quality of Maybeck's better work.

Forest Hills club building, interior.
Documents Collection, C.E.D.

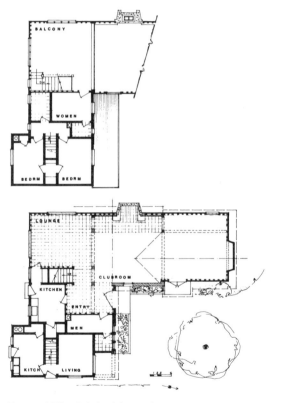

Forest Hills club building, plan.
Documents Collection, C.E.D.

Other office commissions received in the years following the end of the war took Maybeck up and down the state. An association with Mark Daniels involved Maybeck in several designs for the exclusive residential district of Pebble Beach near Monterey, California.[18] Daniels, a landscape engineer, had worked in many areas of the state in community development. The initial architectural project for Pebble Beach proposed to combine private luxury accommodations with common exquisite living rooms. However, the project never went beyond the preliminary stage. But Maybeck did meet Byington Ford, the manager of the Pebble Beach development, who gave him a commission to design his house and recommended his services to other property owners. Ford planned to create an artistic community by having architects of distinction employed to design the residences in the area. Although there was no strict architectural control in the subdivision, prospective home builders were urged to consider Mediterranean styles for their houses.

Maybeck's work in Pebble Beach did not meet with much success. A private school, proposed by the Del Monte Properties Company, for which Maybeck had been hired to do preliminary studies, was abandoned. And although the Byington Ford house (1922) and additions to the F. P. Thomas house (1922) were built, little remains of Maybeck's work. The Ford house has been remodeled beyond recognition and only the small Thomas addition remains to exhibit the simplicity of structural expression found in Maybeck's early work.

In addition to his trips to the Monterey area, Maybeck travelled to southern California to supervise the development of an outdoor theater in the Hollywood hills.[19] He also planned a residence for one of its sponsors, Christine Stevenson, on land overlooking the theater; but this work was terminated upon the death of his client. His residential designs after the war were mostly for locations outside the Berkeley area. One, a large rambling structure built in 1921 for Dr. Robert Peers in Colfax, California, is an extremely erratic performance executed in plaster, full of awkward details and proportions indicative of the inconsistent design that developed with his expanded practice.

But projects of special interest such as one for an old friend from the Bohemian Club captured Maybeck's full attention, and the results were as beguiling as ever. The James J. Fagan house (1920), a country retreat in the wooded knolls of southern San Mateo County, was planned as two units connected by a trellised entrance and passage. One unit contained a handsome living room with private sleeping quarters for the owners; the other provided four separate suites for guests. Each guest bedroom was entered directly from the outside and opened onto private gardens. In a plan reminiscent of the description of the Boynton camp, outdoor cooking, eating, and sleeping were featured in garden settings which took full advantage of the salubrious climate of Portola Valley. The construction was stucco and frame, with flat roofs over all but the living room. Trelliswork supported on rotund plaster columns of modified Tuscan design surrounded the structure. In recent years all of the trellises have been removed and the harmonious color scheme of tan, blue, and pink stucco has been obliterated by white paint, insensitively altering Maybeck's work.

James J. Fagan house, Portola Drive, Woodside, 1920. Documents Collection, C.E.D.

Stucco and frame construction was complemented by a profusion of trelliswork in this delightfully successful country retreat.

18.   Daniels was Superintendent of Parks for the State of California.
19.   E. Knight, "Outdoor Theaters and Stadiums in the West," *Architect and Engineer*, 78, (August 1924), p. 65.

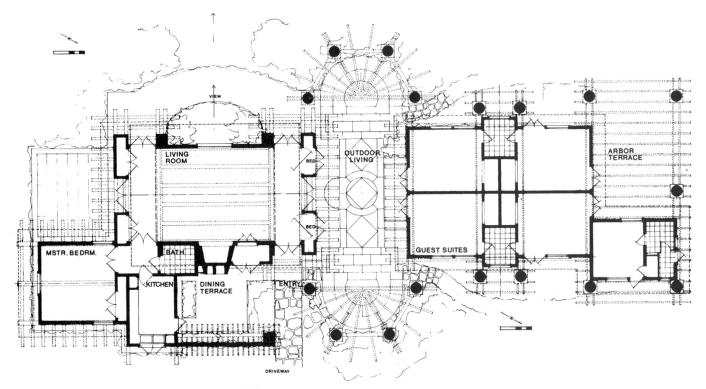

James J. Fagan house, plan drawn by Alan Williams.
Documents Collection, C.E.D.

The plan successfully relates the two separate units to each
other and the surrounding gardens. Each guest room features
its own outside entry.

James J. Fagan house, entrance breezeway.
Documents Collection, C.E.D.

The doorways on the left contained beds for outdoor sleeping.

Glen Alpine Springs resort buildings, El Dorado County, 1921.
Documents Collection, C.E.D.

Maybeck combined natural materials and industrial products
to produce a fire-proof resort complex excellently suited to the
rugged high Sierras.

While the large and elaborate house for Fagan was shaped
for the climate and terrain, one small project executed in 1921
better displays Maybeck's sensitivity to the natural environment and his ability to make sympathetic forms out of industrial products. The Maybecks habitually made outings to the
lake and mountain areas in northern California. At Glen
Alpine Springs, one resort they frequented, Maybeck traded
his design services for the costs of lodging his family. His
additions to the dining room had only been in use for a few
months when, in 1920, the entire complex was severely damaged by fire. E. G. Galt, the owner, thereupon engaged May-

beck to make a general plan for the summer resort and to
design a replacement for the destroyed dining room. Maybeck decided that the buildings should be fire resistant, and
his initial designs set the theme for the new development.

Glen Alpine Springs is located in a remote Sierra Nevada
valley near Lake Tahoe. Mountains tower above the timber-
line and their slopes are strewn with storm-broken trees, gla-
cial packed snows, and cascades of granite boulders. Using
stone, glass, and corrugated iron, Maybeck produced buildings uncomplicated by accepted notions of rusticity and
uniquely appropriate to the rugged contrasts of the high
Sierra country. His new dining room and kitchen are linked
pavilions, each with a distinctive shape formed by trussed
rafters supported on massive dry-laid stone piers. Walls are
made of industrial steel sash set with panes of glass or sheet
metal. Roofs are fashioned from standard sheets of corrugated iron with their ridges closed by curved culvert sections.

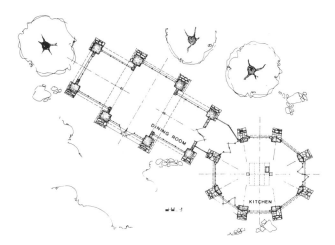

Glen Alpine Springs, dining room and kitchen plan.
Documents Collection, C.E.D.

The dining room and octagonal kitchen were linked pavilions with high trussed roofs supported on large stone piers.

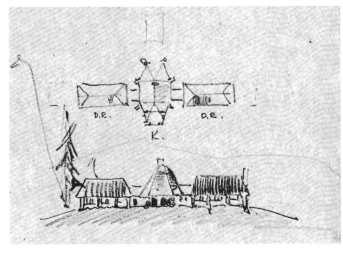

Bernard Maybeck, pencil sketch (4″ by 3″), dining rooms and kitchen, (no date).
Documents Collection, C.E.D.

This tiny preliminary sketch by Maybeck featured two separate dining rooms linked with the kitchen.

The dining room, seating sixty persons, is wide and high in the middle with lower sections at each end. The eight-sided kitchen is teepee-like in form and its rafters are strengthened by a compressive ring of timbers fastened to their interior surfaces. A lodge and cabins with board and batten walls covered by corrugated metal roofs with curved eaves were later added to the complex. Maybeck also designed a gate house, a new store, and a dance pavilion, but they were never constructed as the resort faltered when more accessible areas of the Lake Tahoe region were opened to year-round development.[20]

20. B. R. Maybeck DWGS, "E. G. Galt," C.E.D. Docs.

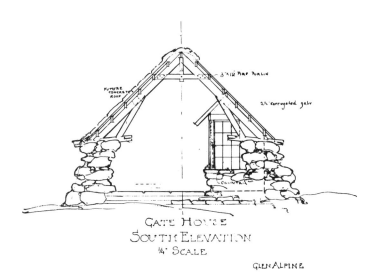

Bernard Maybeck, charcoal drawing (8″ by 6″), Gate house.
Documents Collection, C.E.D.

The Gate House was one of several buildings that Maybeck designed for the resort, but which were never constructed as the resort faltered when other more accessible areas around Lake Tahoe were opened for development.

Although Maybeck did not do any major new work in San Francisco immediately after the war, he was asked frequently to speak on architecture to civic groups. He turned away many requests, but when the San Francisco Chapter of the American Institute of Architects called upon him to serve as a juror of an architectural competition for a war memorial for the city of Honolulu, Hawaii, he accepted. He travelled by ship with two other architect jurors, Ellis F. Lawrence, Dean of the School of Allied Arts and Architecture of the University of Oregon, and W.B.R. Willcox, professor of architecture and journalist of their experiences. Willcox, or the Scribe, as he identified himself in his daily journal, records a number of anecdotes which add to the picture of Maybeck, the celebrated designer of the Palace of Fine Arts.

The description of the voyage opens with the Maybeck family's departing salutes at the pierside which, the Scribe notes, "they did with an effectiveness seldom matched."

> Mrs. Maybeck had worn a white cloth cape and as the boat drew away from the wharf she stood apart from the crowd of "farewellers" against the dark background of one of the great pierhead doors, and thus remained visible as a white spot, long after the crowd had merged with the gray surroundings. Even after the white spot was no longer visible, some sort of flashlight signals—frequently used by the family on mountain jaunts—were thrown and returned by Maybeck from the extreme stern of the boat ... by holding a large white handkerchief ... in such a way as to catch the sunlight. Exchanges continued until the pier was hidden by intervening buildings as the boat turned westward through the Golden Gate.[21]

Maybeck arrived on board with a pannier laden with fresh fruit, jars of honey, and marmalade which friends had given him. Upon opening his steamer truck, which Annie had packed, he found a paper with one word written on it in her firm hand, "Play." Lawrence and Willcox were congenial companions ready to discuss the arts, architecture, or the social and economic state of the nation; but while on board ship, Annie's admonition reigned. By the third day out, when radio messages could be transmitted to an eastbound ship of the Matson Line which would mail transmitted messages, Maybeck wired: "Sell land. Buy clouds in the Pacific. Have sloughed off sixty years. Using beard for a bib."[22]

Bernard Maybeck was sixty years old in 1922. He had practiced in the Bay area for more than thirty years and felt that he was nearing the end of his professional work. Some writers drawing from their contacts with him more than thirty years later have emphasized his gnome-like shrewdness and his

naivete. Most likely these contradictory qualities were heightened by the enervating effects of his age. Willcox, however, pictures a vigorous, outgoing personality, genial in action and sober in reflection. In his journal he refers to Maybeck's lovely character, his fertile imagination, his enthusiasm and insistence for doing, his sensible and interesting conversation, and his subtle and elusive humor. On the return trip from Honolulu Maybeck had penned a note to one of the shipboard companions remaining in the islands in which he had mused:

> Returning towards home and the land of fact is contrasting strongly with the drifting, carefree approach toward the land of unreality, Hawaii.
>
> I have learned on this trip the important lesson it is not necessary to die of hardening of the brain tissues, it is better to die young at three score years and ten.[23]

Even the San Francisco *Examiner* had seen fit to publish reminiscences of his career in 1921.[24] But no one could have foreseen the coming events which brought him architectural commissions in the fourth and last decade of active practice that would exceed in dollar value ten times the total of all his projects for the previous thirty years.

21. W.B.R. Willcox MSS, "Journal," C.E.D. Docs.
22. *Ibid.*
23. *Ibid.*
24. *San Francisco Examiner* (November 2, 1921), p. 6.

Bernard Maybeck, (ca. 1920), photograph by Mark H. White. Documents Collection, C.E.D.

Bernard Maybeck, ink and pencil drawing on tracing paper,
illustration of a hillside house with an open passage from lower
to upper garden, (no date).
Documents Collection, C.E.D.

IX

Welfare Of The City

Sooner or later cities will express the highest spiritual life and power that they are capable of. Through the spirit of self-preservation and in mutual protection the individuals will group themselves and in their combined efforts they will do those things that safeguard their holdings and in doing so they will develop the best they know for the welfare of the city.

Bernard Maybeck—1920

Maybeck's houses have long attracted attention and they make a strong contribution to American domestic architecture. But his ideas on site development and town planning, though little known, are also of interest to review for they are sometimes as unconventional as his approach to housing. Maybeck hoped to initiate general plans and architectural forms with a flexibility sufficient to make adaptation and change possible. He realized the difficulty of assessing needs in long-range planning, and he expected that plans and buildings would be modified as unforeseen factors appeared. However, as he had learned in the atelier from André, the landscape was less mutable. He felt that it should not be changed, but only enhanced by the forms which man added.

A refreshing attitude toward change and a practical view of buildings as mutable forms over a period of time were revealed in 1900 through Maybeck's words about the Phoebe Hearst International Competition:

> Fifty years from now the plan of the University will have become modified and softened; it will be transformed many times, because so easily done. The buildings will have undergone changes, so planned from the beginning that they could grow. This patchwork gives the same feeling to the whole composition as the new stones in a cathedral—the newness becomes tarnished, the monotony of exactness relieved. By that time the gardens will be older, and in places a vine may soften the harshness of perfection.[1]

Fifteen years after the Competition, John Galen Howard completed his plan for the University. It was not a modification of the Bénard plan, but one based on his own entry. The large open spaces, shaped by buildings and planting in the winning scheme, had disappeared. The sensitive combination of the natural landscape of the stream beds with formal terraces and parades was lost. Had Maybeck developed Bénard's proposal, the open squares defined by buildings would have been retained.

Although he had little influence on the physical outcome of the campus, Maybeck's activities with the Hillside Club were effective in the development of the north campus community. Other members of the club were also strong spokesmen for neighborhood planning, but Maybeck gave practical demonstrations through his buildings. In addition, the small pamphlet given to prospective residents of the area, which was reprinted in the 1906-07 Club Bulletin, appears to have been prepared by Maybeck. Its eight pages, unsigned, are illustrated with a dozen of his sketches, the text even repeating the phrasing of his writing:

> With neighborhood cooperation the roadside banks, terraces, etc., can be planted systematically in blocks instead of lots,—not fifty feet of pink geraniums, twenty-five of nasturtiums, fifty of purple verbena, but long restful lines, big, quiet masses,—here a roadside of grey olive topped with purple plum, there a line of willows dipped in flame of ivy covered walls,—long avenues of trees with houses back from roads, hidden behind foregrounds of shrubbery.... Grass on a hillside looks bare; the same strength and water put on trees and bushes will be more effective.[2]

1. Bernard Maybeck, *Blue and Gold* (San Francisco: 1900), pp. 17-20.

2. Hillside Club pamphlet. Original copies bear no title, date nor publisher's imprint. They are bound with hand sewing and were most likely produced by members of the club as a project.

The message of the pamphlet was simple—it urged residents motivated to leave the city to work instead for its maintenance and enhancement. It recommended contour planning of roads and lot subdivisions, coordinated planting of trees and street embankments, and houses shaped and pigmented to blend with the natural landscape. Maybeck's drawings of an ideal neighborhood show watercourses turned into public parks; streets ascend the hills with gentle curves and gradients, forming observation terraces at their switchbacks; houses, paralleling the contours of the land and varying in set-back lines, are surrounded by informal gardens. In the manner prescribed by the Hillside Club Bulletin, Maybeck designed Rose Walk as a public thoroughfare in a 1912 development of the property of W. W. Underhill. Rose Walk connects a portion of the hillside area with a street which is serviced with public transportation; private walks to residences blend with the public way "in an immense garden with nothing to show that it is not all one owned by each."[3]

3. *Ibid.*

Bernard Maybeck, cover design, Hillside Club booklet, 1907. Photograph courtesy of E. K. Davies.

This copy was signed by Maybeck and given to Lillian Bridgman.

Rose Walk and steps at Euclid Ave., Berkeley, 1912. Roy Flamm photograph.

A design by Maybeck which serves as an example of hillside planning in which contoured roadways are linked by crossing pedestrian paths. The houses shown were designed by Henry Gutterson.

Bernard Maybeck, pen and ink illustration for Hillside Club booklet.

The text reads: "Build around the hill on contour lines or step the house up against the hill, one story above and back of the other."

Maybeck gained practical experience in town planning in 1913, although circumstances conspired to leave almost all his designs on paper. J. L. Brookings, who had acquired a timber company in the southern coastal region of Oregon, approached Maybeck with a proposal to construct some housing and community buildings for his mill workers. However, Maybeck, true to his belief in comprehensive planning, countered with the idea that a town plan should be developed to prevent costly errors of erecting structures on ill-chosen sites. Brookings agreed and, prior to any construction, Maybeck prepared drawings for temporary buildings that would serve the community until a town plan was adopted.

The site of Brookings, named for its owner-developer, is a superb, scenic spot with a fine harbor at the mouth of the Chetco River. A number of wooded knolls are distributed on the broad coastal shelf that slopes up to the mountains where the principal logging operations took place. In 1913 its deep-water facilities and a promise of the North-Western Pacific Railway to extend its tracks northward from Eureka, presented ideal conditions for the growth of a healthy town.

Maybeck's plan for Brookings took advantage of the uneven contours of the land by using irregular parcels for public buildings or small parks and dedicating the steep slopes and crowning hills as permanent open spaces. The central spine of the residential community covered a mesa which connected the most distinctive knoll to the foothills. Individual lots were laid out in blocks curved to fit the contours. Pedestrian paths within the blocks led to schools, churches, and the town center. A commercial district around the base of the knoll formed a buffer between the residential area and the industrial sites adjoining the railway right-of-way at the western edge of the town.

Hotel, Brookings Lumber Company, Brookings, Oregon, 1914.
K. H. Cardwell photograph.

The simple, unpretentious hotel, planned as a temporary
structure, is all that remains of Maybeck's Brookings town plan.

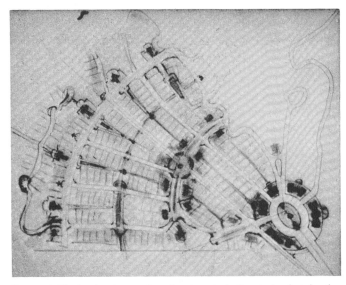

Bernard Maybeck, charcoal and colored chalk, study sketch of
a residential sector, Brookings Town plan, 1914.
Documents Collection, C.E.D.

The town center lies at the right, connected to the residential
subdivision by paths bisecting the blocks developed by a system
of radiating roadways.

Maybeck prepared drawings of neighborhood housing—
one and two-family cottages grouped around garden courts.
Some units were developed as bachelor houses with five or
six living-bedrooms combined with common dining and
kitchen areas. None of the grouped arrangements was built,
but some of the existing single-family houses located on the
streets of the original town are patterned after Maybeck's
designs. His house plans were modest, providing bedrooms, a
living room, and a large kitchen for family use. No allusions
to classic details or Gothic ornaments embellished the
designs—his approach called for common carpentry using
the products of the Brookings mill—but Maybeck provided
sketches of varied fencing which the owners themselves might
build in order to add an individual note to their homes.

Of all the community facilities that Maybeck planned for
Brookings, only the hotel exists today. The building, with
additions and alterations through the years, has an unpretentious character. It is a structure of few distinguishing features,
more properly described as a dormitory for mill hands than a
hostlery of elegance. Maybeck's notes to the contractor reveal
that he viewed the hotel as a temporary building. He expected
that it might be more handsomely finished at a later date or
even that it might be moved to a new site and put to a different
use. Maybeck's drawings of the town's school called for a
wooden framed assembly hall with two wings of clerestory-
lighted classrooms enclosing an open court—a variant form
of his Randolph School. However, the drawings of greatest
merit show a bold design in stock dimensioned lumber for
the Y.M.C.A. building or community hall. Completely detailed
in working drawings, it consisted of a thirty-by-fifty-foot room
spanned by a pair of modified "A-frame" trusses, finished in
a combination of exposed sheathing and applied shakes; but
Maybeck's records do not reveal if it was built.[4]

All of Maybeck's provisional designs and long-range planning were to no avail, for the inexperience of J. L. Brookings
in timber operations, augmented by mismanagement of funds
by a trusted assistant, led to the financial ruin of the lumber
company. To add to Brookings' troubles, the railroad decided
not to extend its tracks northward, and in a few years the state
highway, which Maybeck had planned to skirt the edge of the
town, was constructed through its commercial center, destroying forever the very heart of his ideal company town.

4. B. R. Maybeck DWGS, "Brookings," C.E.D. Docs.

Maybeck's use of temporary buildings in Brookings was not his only attempt to shorten the delay between conception and realization in large-scale planning. A postlude to his entry in the Canberra Competition records another try, no more successful, but interesting because of the correspondence it developed. The incident began in 1915 at a luncheon given to honor Australian Prime Minister Alfred Deakin at the Panama-Pacific International Exposition. Maybeck remarked to the minister's wife that he did not agree with Walter Burley Griffin's selection of a prominent hill for the site of the parliament buildings for Canberra. Within a few days Deakin called at Maybeck's office to hear more on the development of the capital. Maybeck proposed the use of temporary structures of wood and plaster to create an immediate visual impression of Griffin's design. He suggested that if major elements of the Canberra design could be built as rapidly as structures for the World's Fair, the vision of the artist would be palpably demonstrated and create public enthusiasm and pride which would assure the completion of the Federal City. Deakin found the proposal intriguing and encouraged Maybeck to pursue it. Maybeck did so and began a series of correspondence with three successive prime ministers, a premier, and the High Commissioner, which lasted over a period of more than seven years.[5]

In 1917 William Hughes, who succeeded Deakin as prime minister, referred all of Maybeck's correspondence to the architect of the Federal Capital for evaluation. Griffin's initial response to Maybeck was chilly. He stated that although he found points of interest in the suggestions offered, he felt "that some of the most important psychological elements of building a capital" had not been given due weight by Maybeck, "nor could they be" in distant San Francisco. Griffin explained that his immediate problem was one of politics and not one of construction. In any event, he continued, "plaster or stucco are hardly considered as temporary expedients (in Australia) for they are largely employed for buildings both commercial and governmental, already deemed to be permanent."[6]

In one letter, in an attempt to silence the criticism of some government engineers, Maybeck repeated his support of Griffin's preliminary effort but added:

I believe that the people themselves must determine how [the city] is to be used. A merchant selling silks, calico and ribbons is the best authority for determining where his shop is to be, a real estate man will know where people will buy for

their residences. I do not believe that the Parliament buildings should be the first ones to be located, for since all public business is conducted by human beings it is good to place them where it is most convenient for their work.[7]

After several years of Maybeck's efforts to influence the Australian parliament in the immediate implementation of the plan, Griffin's letters became cordial and he looked forward to meeting Maybeck after the war which had disrupted travel and, unfortunately, also the building of Canberra.

In the United States, too, the mobilization of industry had slowed private building; but in 1918 the war boom provided Maybeck with a limited opportunity for community planning when he became the supervising architect of a new town named Clyde. The Pacific Coast Shipbuilding Company had applied to the United States Government for a building loan to develop housing for its workers on the upper reaches of San Francisco Bay. The Clyde Company, its subsidiary organization, and the U.S. Shipping Board Emergency Fleet Corporation, became the responsible agents for the development of the new town. Maybeck was hired by the Fleet Corporation to oversee the government's interests.

Plans for the town site, including a residential hotel, houses, and a commercial district, had already been prepared for the Clyde Company by E. W. Cannon and G. A. Applegarth at the time of its application for the housing loan. Consequently, Maybeck's role in the layout was restricted. His contributions are the modification of a gridiron pattern of streets to one with gently curving roads adapted to the hillside site, the introduction of varying setbacks giving individual houses better exposures and views, and a modification of the hotel design.

Although the Clyde hotel was larger and more extensive than the one for Brookings, it was also workers' housing and again no fine materials or finishes were used in its construction. Designed and built in wood frame, its exterior walls were stuccoed and its openings were accented with Spanish Renaissance ornaments. Applegarth had been trained at the École des Beaux-Arts at the beginning of the century. He had done so at Maybeck's urging and in the design of the hotel it appears that he again welcomed Maybeck's suggestions.[8]

5. B. R. Maybeck MSS, "Canberra," C.E.D. Docs.
6. *Ibid.*
7. *Ibid.*
8. Interview by the author with George Applegarth.

Hotel at Clyde, California, G. A. Applegarth, Architect, 1918.
Stone and Stecatti photograph.

In his role as Supervising Architect, Maybeck's contribution to
the hotel design was limited. Although not elaborate, the
abandoned hotel had a kind of elegant grace surrounded by a
sea of weeds.

The public spaces of the hotel were most striking. The
lounge and dining room, robustly and confidently composed
of high, low, and extended volumes, were finished with wide
redwood boards and battens. A broad stairway with clerestory
lighting stepped up the hillside to connect to a three-storied
block of guest rooms. The tall piers of the pavilion lounge,
separated by windows formed of small-paned factory sash,
were capped with a wooden frieze ornamented with applied
band sawn motifs of swags and shields. Over the guest wings,
doubled ornamentally sawn rafters supported the broad flat
soffits of the hipped roof which were pierced with openings in
a manner reminiscent of other Maybeck work. Sun streamed
through the cut-outs and effectively modeled the deep shadows of the large overhangs.

The town of Clyde still exists—three residential streets in
an isolated corner of Contra Costa county. The close of the
war brought reductions in the shipbuilding industry and ended
the demand for nearby housing. And, during the short period
of its creation, no industry nor commercial enterprises other
than the shipbuilding had developed to assure Clyde's growth.
For more than four decades it remained a lonely suburb with
a derelict hotel cast aside in a field of weeds which covered
not only accumulating rubbish heaps but also the paths, roadways, and planting that were designed to be its civic center.[9]

9. The hotel has since been destroyed by fire.

Hotel at Clyde, stairway passage.
Stone and Stecatti photograph.

The simple interior board and batten finish and window
placement created a very attractive space. For several years
prior to the hotel's destruction, the residential wing was
divided into apartments and a temporary partition blocked the
opening into the public rooms.

Maybeck's interest in small house design can be followed from the days of the newcomers' editorials on the working-man's house in the *Architectural News* until the end of his career. What had happened in Brookings and what he saw in Clyde did not encourage him. He feared that the lack of concern for aesthetic elements in commercial housing could produce banal environments which in turn could produce dull people. He expressed his solution for the problem to the Land Settlement Board of California which, in 1918, was looking for an architect to work on a unit of subsidized housing for farm workers. Maybeck was not given the commission, but in expressing his disappointment in a letter to his friend and Chairman of the Board, Elwood Mead, he fortunately repeated his perceptively humane proposal:

> In this constant struggle for the lowest price the thing that suffers is the goods itself. . . . As a consequence, all the experience that we now have, is the haphazard growth under the pressure of economy. . . . Since there has never been a systematic worldwide study of the small house, it is a new problem. Therefore in visualizing the possibilities, I thought the United States would use this opportunity to establish a laboratory for the study of the small house . . . and the reaction on the people who are to use them.[10]

Maybeck proposed the development of the first unit of the farm housing as an architectural hypothesis which would be evaluated in human terms. Then each succeeding group of houses could be built as "an improvement over the first from the spiritual as well as the mechanical viewpoint." However, the federal government did not enter the housing field. Even its war-time efforts such as Clyde were sold to private interests. The Federal Housing Administration, established as a result of housing needs during the depression years, should have tried Maybeck's experiment, but it did not. Sociologists have recently made similar proposals, but the systematic study of the effects of housing on people suggested by Maybeck is yet to be done.

Maybeck viewed democracy as the form of government that allowed the greatest individual expression within the framework of the common social good. "I don't believe in putting fences around anything, least of all, the human mind," he once said. In his home community of Berkeley he worked constantly to create an architectural statement of this belief. He saw no conflict between the fulfillment of individual needs and the common good because he held that art had the power to make both goals compatible. He had the utmost respect for the worth of each man, and his overwhelming belief in the uniqueness of each person demanded that he create a singular architectural expression for every client. He feared that mass production would lead to a uniform, monotonous product and, in his own architectural solutions, he demonstrated the infinite variety of form obtainable using mass produced building materials. It is difficult to assemble, out of almost two hundred of his building designs in the Bay Area, more than five or six at a time that have enough architectural details in common to label them a "style." And while he was eager to experiment, he adopted no dogma and fostered no new architectural theories.

10. B. R. Maybeck MSS, "Land Settlement Board," C.E.D. Docs.

In 1918, Phoebe Apperson Hearst commissioned Maybeck to provide a general plan for Mills College. Originally founded as a young ladies' seminary in Benicia, the college had relocated in Oakland in 1873 at the base of the East Bay hills on the outskirts of the city. It had developed into a small but highly regarded liberal arts college for women, but had no plan to guide its physical growth. The college grounds are surrounded by hills. A small stream, flowing from a lake at the east, bisects the site and leaves the campus through an arroyo at the west. A strong, straight line of tall eucalyptus trees, marking an old boundary or roadway, traverses a meadow lying north of the stream. On a line generally perpendicular to the trees, the site opens to the north through a low gap in the hills. Maybeck composed courts and avenues around these strong lines, and although his plan indicated buildings of monumental scale and formal order, his thought was to establish a landscape design strong enough to dictate the shape of future building design.

Maybeck urged the immediate planting of various shrubs and trees so that they might grow even if the funds for buildings and equipment were not on hand. How and why this should be done he explained in a description of the plan in the college quarterly:

> The fundamental idea of the General Plan is a program of work to be done. If a building is to be built, the future architect may know where to place it and by that time the gardens of the ground will have shaped the landscape.... The landscape—I repeat—should be shaped at once, the avenues planted, the roads built, new bridges span the streams, and worthy gateways grace the campus portals.... The avenues can be marked in with planting and even remain ungraded with the wild grass growing and kept cropped with a lawn mower until the time has come to grade and pave the way. If necessary, in the beginning a two-foot pathway might run along the center of the path.[11]

Once again, however, Maybeck's hope for the grand scheme was not realized. Four years after the approval of his plan, he was asked to select some trees for planting on the site; but buildings he had envisaged as temporary are still in use, blocking the vistas and filling the open spaces he had hoped to create. The City of Oakland condemned a portion of the campus to complete a road into the hills, and only the line of the old eucalyptus trees and portions of the stream remain to identify elements of Maybeck's plan.

11. *Mills Quarterly*, October 1918, pp. 3-5.

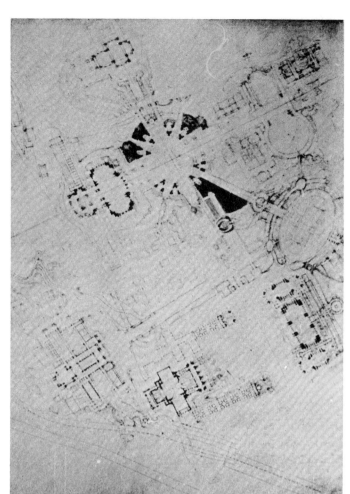

General Plan, Mills College, Oakland, 1918.
Photo courtesy of Mills College Library.

Maybeck's plan for the college was developed around (and emphasized) the natural features of the site.

Bernard Maybeck, colored chalk on brown kraft paper, Hearst Memorial auditorium, museum, and gymnasium buildings, 1924-1929.
Documents Collection, C.E.D.

Maybeck's original design featured a very large auditorium flanked by a museum and gymnasium.

In 1922, Hearst Hall, which had been so intimately connected with the development of the University of California plan, burned while Maybeck was judging the competition for the War Memorial in Honolulu. Upon his return he was handed a telegram from William Randolph Hearst commissioning the design of a permanent building for the University campus to honor his mother, Phoebe Apperson Hearst, who had died in 1919. The purpose of the building—other than a memorial— was never very clear. Old Hearst Hall had served the dual functions of social hall and women's gymnasium, and Maybeck's preliminary sketches for the new building show a barrel vaulted room of indeterminate use and location. The University authorities did not want to discourage Hearst in his efforts to add to the campus buildings, but suggested that their most urgent need was a women's gymnasium or an auditorium that would serve the studentbody.

Hearst Memorial gymnasium, Bernard Maybeck and Julia Morgan, Architects, University of California, Berkeley, 1925, south elevation.
Documents Collection, C.E.D.

Although the complete project was discontinued, the women's gymnasium was completed with Julia Morgan responsible for the construction drawings while Maybeck concentrated on the basic planning and design.

Hearst authorized Maybeck to prepare a second set of preliminaries to include not only a gymnasium and auditorium, but also an art gallery and a museum that would house the extensive collections already in possession of the University from the Hearst family bequests. Maybeck designed buildings in the image of his Palace of Fine Arts and proposed a large domed auditorium placed near Strawberry Creek on the north-south axis of the Campanile esplanade. A women's gymnasium was located at the south as its forecourt; colonnaded paths led to museums and art galleries to the east. The project stalled with delays created by Hearst's indecision as to whether he desired to contruct the whole, or only a portion, of Maybeck's expanded proposal. In addition, Maybeck's delay in completing drawings of the scheme allowed Hearst's interest to cool substantially. But in 1925 the University administration secured agreement for the construction of the women's gymnasium.[12] In order to expedite the design drawings, Maybeck entered into an arrangement by which Julia Morgan would be responsible for the construction drawings and functional details while he concentrated on the overall planning and design.

The sympathetic action of the two designers created a building of romantic beauty. Like the Palace of Fine Arts, the Hearst Memorial Gymnasium (1925) is Beaux-Arts design as Maybeck knew and practiced it, blending exterior and interior space into a unified composition. A number of large exercise rooms are joined to create courtyards which shelter one major and two minor outdoor swimming pools. California Live Oak trees planted in sculpturally ornamented boxes on the main floor and in open wells at the ground level complement the blocky massing of the individual elements of the gymnasium. The main pool, whose marble decks becom terraces and promenades surrounding the exercise rooms, is built above the ground level, bulwarked by service and locker facilities.

Maybeck used the Water Gardens at Nimes as a prototype and, for the first time in his work, details are copied from that design without the usual adaptation and restudy that enabled him to transform historical details into his personal ornamental pattterns. The interior of the building is generously daylighted with skylights and glazed walls that surround planted courts. Natural concrete interior surfaces were ornamented by stenciled patterns introducing color accents into the exercise rooms. Utilitarian incandescent fixtures are both protected and enriched by a framework of woven and bent rattan. The large rooms are linked by smaller ones and all open to the exterior galleries which adjoin the pool decks.

12. University of California, *President's Report* (1925).

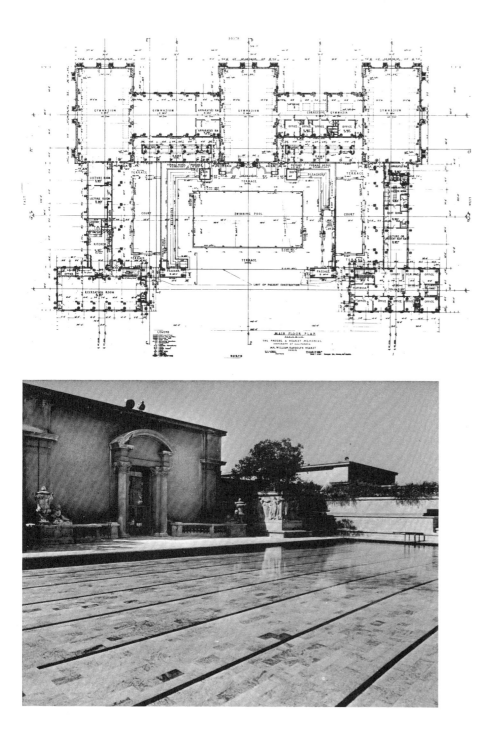

Hearst Memorial gymnasium, plan.
Documents Collection, C.E.D.

Hearst Memorial gymnasium, pool terrace.
Roy Flamm photograph.

The pool terraces were planned to also
serve as promenades and outdoor lobbies
for the auditorium of the original scheme.

It should be remembered that Maybeck designed his terraces not only as surfaces for everyday swimming areas but also as parts of a forecourt to the large auditorium which was to be sited directly to the north. The pool decks, connected with the principal floor of the auditorium planned to be one story above the natural grade level, would have then served as outdoor lobbies for the concert-goers. Whether or not funds would ever have been provided to erect the grandiose auditorium is quite dubious, but the location of a student union building by John Galen Howard blocking the access to the auditorium site from the central campus made the completion of Maybeck's scheme improbable.[13]

13. The General Development Plan for the University of California adopted in 1956 under the leadership of W. W. Wurster not only re-introduced the concept of planning around open spaces as in the Bénard Plan but also included the general development of buildings for art and architecture in the area proposed by Maybeck.

Hearst Memorial gymnasium, study of detail in clay.
Documents Collection, C.E.D.

Hearst Memorial gymnasium, view from pool terrace to ground
level court.
Roy Flamm photograph.

The gymnasium, successfully relating interior and exterior
spaces, was Beaux-Arts design as Maybeck knew it, and became
a building of romantic beauty.

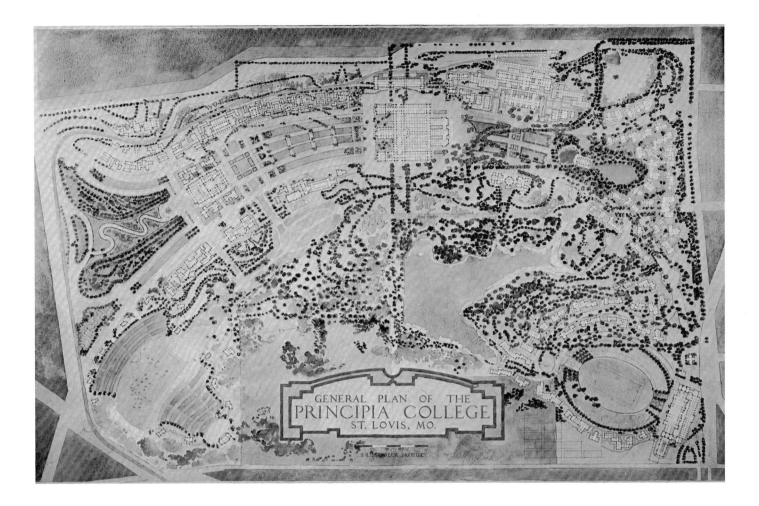

General Plan of the Principia College, St. Louis, Mo., 1927.
Documents Collection, C.E.D.

Maybeck's ambitious plan for the campus had to be abandoned when the city of St. Louis announced plans to build a highway through the campus property and form an industrial zone at its border.

Other major planning works which followed were May-beck's designs for The Principia—one for a campus in St. Louis (1923-30), and one for a new site at Elsah, Illinois (1930-38). The president of the college, Frederic E. Morgan, who had long admired the design of the First Church of Christ, Scientist, Berkeley, persuaded his Board of Trustees to have Maybeck prepare a general plan for the college. Numerous sketches and carefully delineated drawings were made for a handsome brochure which was used in fund raising throughout the United States.

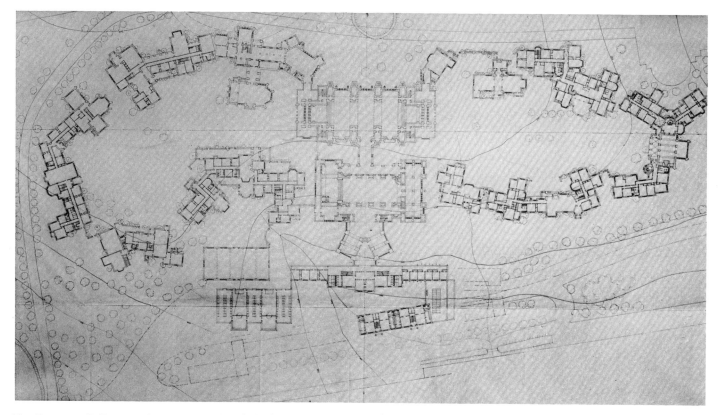

The Principia College, preliminary site plan, (1924).
Documents Collection, C.E.D.

Roughly patterned after the medieval plans of Oxford and
Cambridge, the college featured a large oval commons centered
around a great hall with residential units and academic departments grouped around the perimeter.

The first Principia College as conceived by Maybeck was a
variation on the medieval patterns of Cambridge and Oxford.
A large oval commons, planned on the back of a gentle rise
of the site, was surrounded by irregularly placed residential
and tutorial units. A great hall in the center created smaller
greens at each end of the oval and contained communal
rooms, library, assembly hall, and refectory. Individual academic departments were distributed throughout the residential buildings of the perimeter. Their general pattern consisted
of classrooms and common lounges on the ground floors with
living and tutorial areas above. Playing fields and sport facilities were planned beyond the oval of the academic units.
Maybeck's drawings show buildings with the character of
English structures of the Tudor period. Although some of his
studies for the great hall and gymnasium hint of exciting architectural concepts, time and events conspired in such a way
that the final development of The Principia has little interest
for the architect looking for inventive and imaginative design.

Bernard Maybeck, charcoal and colored chalk drawing of
museum, Principia College, (1925).
Documents Collection, C.E.D.

Bernard Maybeck, charcoal and colored chalk drawing of
residential units, Principia College, (1925).
Documents Collection, C.E.D.

Maybeck's drawings revealed structures in the character of
English Tudor design.

After the completion of the general plan for the St. Louis campus (1927), Maybeck arranged with the office of Julia Morgan for the production of technical drawings and specifications of his designs. The drawings for the initial buildings were started late in 1929; but before construction began the City of St. Louis announced its intention to build a new highway through the college property and to form an industrial zone on its border. Maybeck was summoned to St. Louis in November, 1930, by the Trustees of the College for his counsel, and he recommended the abandonment of their seven years of labor in favor of starting again at another location. His advice was accepted and within two weeks, with his assistance, a new site was acquired. These hurried events were reported to Julia Morgan by Annie Maybeck, who had travelled to St. Louis with her husband to act as his secretary. She wrote:

> Ben told [the Trustees] the College should be moved before it is begun,—told them to go into Illinois, at least an hour's ride from St. Louis.... He drew a plan of what they should have....
>
> In 1840 several families bought along the east bank of the Mississippi, above Alton on the bluffs 335 feet above the river.... In the middle of it, down by the river, is a quaint little old village, Elsah... and now Principia has contracted to buy 2,000 acres, three or more miles along the bluffs, [with views of] the Missouri, the Mississippi, and the Illinois rivers...—if Ben had seen it and drawn it from memory he could not have hit it better. It is superb... it would have been easier for him if they had only 50 acres,—for once he's got land enough.[14]

Ironically, this time land was not the problem. Maybeck had drawings for permanent buildings, the Trustees had money for building construction, but no one had a general plan. There was no time for organic growth using temporary structures or planting as Maybeck had urged for Canberra and Mills College, the Trustees having set the spring of 1931 for the dedication of their first building. Therefore, Maybeck arranged for the establishment of an architect's office in Elsah—staffed by Charles Lundgren from his office and Edward Hussey from Julia Morgan's—to expedite on-site construction while the San Francisco draftsmen hastily modified the drawings of the St. Louis campus buildings for the new location. Maybeck concentrated his efforts on the chapel, one of the buildings of the first group funded for construction. It had been decided that the chapel should be in the American Colonial style.[15] In the years that followed the construction of Maybeck's Berkeley church, most Christian Science building committees had chosen the New England meeting house or village church as a model for their structures and had avoided the Gothic and Renaissance forms widely used by the older Protestant and Catholic sects. The Colonial buildings had few symbolic or ritualistic elements and therefore were deemed appropriate for a religion which made no use of traditional sacred forms.

14. A. W. Maybeck MSS, "Principia," C.E.D. Docs.
15. Maybeck had toured eastern college campuses and chapels with President F. E. Morgan of The Principia in 1925.

John White, pencil drawing, residential unit, Principia College, (no date).
Documents Collection, C.E.D.

Residential unit, Principia College, Elsah, Ill., 1932.
Documents Collection, C.E.D.

The campus was built at Elsah, Illinois with Julia Morgan as supervising architect and Maybeck as design consultant. The basic designs developed for the St. Louis campus were modified for the actual construction.

The Principia chapel, sited near the edge of the high bluffs, commands a view of the confluence of the Missouri and Mississippi rivers. Its spire, resembling those found on New England churches and their Christopher Wren prototypes, rises high above the trees, marking the chapel's position on the campus. Its exterior is finished with walls of dressed sandstone, a white, wood cornice, and details of modified classic forms. It has a bold scale and simplicity characteristic of Maybeck's early work; but none of the imaginative play of light and form or skillful display of structure and pattern that occur in the Berkeley church are to be found in The Principia chapel.

By 1932 the first unit of The Principia buildings was sufficiently complete to permit removal of the college to the new campus. But the rush in design and construction, orders and counter orders emanating from San Francisco and St. Louis had caused friction between Maybeck, his associates, and the client. He therefore proposed that Julia Morgan take full control of the work and that he act as designer-consultant. This arrangement continued until 1938 when Maybeck, at the age of seventy-six, relinquished his interest in The Principia, and recommended that Julia Morgan and Henry Gutterson be hired to continue his work.[16]

Maybeck's continuous effort and enthusiasm for long range and organic development has been overshadowed by his association with Beaux-Arts design which has been criticized as grandiose, unreal, and impractical. But his ideas on site planning were actually very sound. For the University of California he advocated a scheme capable of organic growth, for Brookings he followed the principles of the garden city, and for Canberra and Mills College his imaginative proposals using temporary structures or landscape masses still seem intriguingly inviting. Maybeck never wanted to eliminate the politician, the entrepreneur, and the engineer from the direction of a project shaping the environment; he only wanted to place the artist, the sculptor, and the architect on a footing equal with them. He believed it was in the best interests of society to do so, for beautiful surroundings help create social health. In Maybeck's view, city planning must combine the dreams of artists with the practical ideas of artisans into an "expression of the highest spiritual life and power" of their society. Although complete realization of his proposals was often forestalled by factors beyond his control, Mills College awarded Bernard Ralph Maybeck an honorary degree in 1926 in recognition of his contribution to the physical development of the campus. In 1930, though somewhat tardily, the University of California did the same.

Bernard Maybeck, charcoal and colored chalk drawing of chapel, (no date).
Documents Collection, C.E.D.

Maybeck designed the chapel for the campus in the American Colonial style preferred by the building committee.

16. B. R. Maybeck MSS, "Principia," C.E.D. Docs.

Berkeley hillside, vicinity of La Loma Ave. and Buena Vista Way, 1923.
Documents Collection, C.E.D.

While the R. H. Mathewson house escaped the Berkeley fire of 1923, the Maybeck house (#2) on Buena Vista Way lies in ashes in the foreground.

X

All That Surrounds Us

You and I are moulded by the land, the trees, the sky and all that surrounds us, the streets, the houses, and men. Our hearts are shaped by the plaster walls that cover us and we reflect plaster wall ideals and that by repetition to the Nth power. When I make a vase, a cup, or a saucer they will be my expression and they will tell you who I am and what I am.
Bernard Maybeck—1927

In September of 1923 a grass fire originating in dry brush canyons reached the ridge forming Berkeley's eastern border. Fanned by strong winds contrary to the prevailing westerlies and fed with added fuel from shingled houses, trees, and shrubs, the fire cut a broad path to the southwest toward the University campus and the center of the city. The masonry commercial structures and the greenbelt of the campus (aided by a change in the wind direction) stopped the fire, but not until it had destroyed the heart of the district which Maybeck and members of the Hillside Club had worked for twenty years to make an ideal community. Among the charred ruins, hundreds of chimneys stood as memorials to a residential development of modest homes highly individualistic yet unusually harmonious.

Maybeck's own home on Buena Vista Way, the Hillside Clubhouse, and more than fifteen additional structures of his design were among the many that burned. Since Maybeck already considered himself to be near the end of his career, the destruction of his home and neighborhood might well have made him lose heart in architectural practice; but it did not. Most likely, Maybeck's natural optimism led him to view the devastation caused by the fire as an opportunity to improve the community it had destroyed. In any case, the immediate work provided by his neighbors who wanted to rebuild left him no time for remorse. Indeed, his last significant contributions to residential design are related to the work he did as a result of the fire. In addition to rebuilding houses,

Maybeck developed a one-room house and experimented with incombustible construction.

Long before the disastrous Berkeley fire, Maybeck had become acutely aware of the vulnerability of wooden structures. The San Francisco fire that had destroyed his office and early records, and perhaps even buildings he had designed, had been aggravated by the mixtures of frame and timber building existing in the city at the turn of the century. Although he preferred to build with wood, he could develop designs in concrete which were rich and satisfying, as he had for the Lawson house. His reaction to the destruction of Glen Alpine had been to work with stone, steel sash, and corrugated metal in unique forms that were as responsive to the environment as those usually associated with wooden mountain buildings. And when rebuilding in Berkeley, his replacement of trelliage with tiles on the Alma S. Kennedy studio (1923) and his design of stucco walls and tile roofs for the McMurray house were more than his adoption of a current Mediterranean mode— they were designs to reduce the hazards of fire.

Orin Kip McMurray house, 2357 Le Conte Ave., Berkeley, 1924.
William S. Ricco photograph.

A low-pitched gable roof echoes the slope of the land and
covers both the one-story and two-story portions of the house.

Professor Orin Kip McMurray was one of the first who came to Maybeck to ask him to rebuild. He was not a former client, but had purchased the F. B. Dresslar chalet which Maybeck had designed in 1902.[1] Through the years his family had so enjoyed it that when the house burned they wanted it reconstructed. The drawings of the original chalet had also been burned many years earlier in the San Francisco fire. This fact, however, was not what led Maybeck to persuade the McMurrays that they should have a house tailored to their current needs and to the present time. The cost of reproducing a redwood house would not have been economically reasonable and, furthermore, Maybeck could not believe that a design executed for one individual would serve as well for another.

The Dresslar chalet had been built on a piece of sharply sloping property rising more than twenty-five feet in elevation in its diagonal dimension. Located near the street, it had occupied the flattest area of the land. Maybeck's new design, retaining the basement area of the burned house as a sunken garden in front of the new one, freed his planning from the limits of existing foundations and made their costly removal unnecessary. Also, by using the higher portions of the property for building, Maybeck could arrange for better views of San Francisco.

The McMurray house (1924) is one of Maybeck's best. It is the climax of his Mediterranean design which has roots in his classic Maurer studio. A one-storied living area and a two-storied bedroom wing combined, not as linked pavilions as in the early Gothic houses, but as one unit, strongly composed under a sweeping, low-pitched gabled roof. The roof extends over the broken perimeter of the plan, echoes the rising slope of the land, and shelters an entrance which lies intriguingly concealed yet enticingly indicated beyond the sunken garden. The roof is tiled and the walls of a stucco dash coat are rendered in tones of tan and Indian red. Eave rafters, stained blue-green, support ochre colored soffits. Stenciled patterns ornament a tie-beam at the entrance, and a wrought iron railing guards the balcony overlooking the garden. Tile, stucco, and wrought iron were common materials in residential designs of California in the twenties, but few architects who used them attained the rich and bold effects achieved by Maybeck.

---

1. There are scant records revealing its character. Poor photographs show it to be similar to the Flagg chalet.

Orin Kip McMurray house, garden and entrance detail.
E. Born photograph.

Maybeck rebuilt the house higher up on the site and used the existing basement foundations to create a sunken garden.

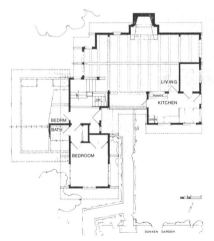

Orin Kip McMurray house, plan, drawn by Alan Williams.
Documents Collection, C.E.D.

The McMurray house plan featured a kitchen overlooking the garden and also containing serving access to the living room balcony and dining space.

In planning the McMurray house, Maybeck introduced features that reflected the changing living patterns of middle-class Americans after World War I. He thought that the housewife, no longer aided by servants, should have a pleasant work space. Consequently, he placed the kitchen at the front of the house to command a view of the garden and neighborhood activities. The kitchen also served a balcony off the living room. A large sliding panel opened to join the kitchen counter to the dining space, permitting Mrs. McMurray to both prepare food and entertain her guests directly and informally. Maybeck placed the cooking elements from an electric range into the tiled counter top—an early prototype for modern drop-in stove units—and installed its oven in the opposite wall. While his inventive design was convenient for the housewife, it was unprofitable for the office, as Mark White later pointed out. In order to obtain the individual cooking units, Maybeck had to purchase a complete stove and have the office staff disassemble it. But when it was charged to the client it was billed as a new stove without adding any of the costs incurred by taking it apart.[2]

A split-level plan accommodates the house to the hillside. The entry leads to bedrooms and an open stairwell which connects to the living pavilion at a half-level above. The combination living-dining room is spanned by two bents built of carved and bolted timbers supporting a ridge beam loaded by paired rafters. The framing is organized on a rectangular grid. As in the Mathewson house, Maybeck concentrated his efforts to create one handsome living space. The principal room is finished in fine, vertically-grained redwood. Unfortunately, the view of the Bay to the west is now blocked by multi-storied apartment houses, but the balcony and its view of the garden at the south is accessible through industrial steel sash sliding doors. A large concrete fireplace—its andirons and tools also designed by Maybeck—is obliquely opposed to the balcony, making a strong diagonal line to contrast with the rectangular patterning of the ceiling framing. The room is a bold, dynamic space, but one with intimate areas and humanly-scaled parts.

2. Conversations between Mark White and the author.

Orin Kip McMurray house, view from dining space to kitchen counter range top.
William S. Ricco photograph.

A sliding panel provided serving access from the kitchen to the dining area.

Orin Kip McMurray house, view of living room fireplace.
E. Born photograph.

The living room was finely finished in woods and featured a large concrete fireplace.

The E. F. Geisler house (1924) on Buena Vista Way was the second one built by Maybeck as the direct result of the fire. It was constructed on, and most likely from, the remains of a house at the same location. The name of the original designer has not been determined, but it seems possible that the burned house might have been one of Maybeck's early, unrecorded designs. In contrast with the McMurray house, Maybeck chose to repeat the steeply-pitched, gabled roofs and shingled exteriors of the Gothic houses which he had designed thirty years before. The Geisler house also incorporated new features, such as built-in cooking units and the integration of the kitchen with the dining area. But, in addition, the new plan included within the bulk of the house a garage which also functioned as a service and family entry.

The large living room dominates the house. A gallery serving upstairs bedrooms passes through its upper reaches. Its interior is finished in redwood wire-brushed to emphasize the pattern of its grain. This finish made it possible for Maybeck to use salvage materials scorched in the fire. Indeed, to obtain the *sugi* finish that he had recommended to Keeler for interior treatments in *The Simple Home*, the wood surface first had to be charred and then brushed.

E. F. Geisler house, 2563 Buena Vista Way, Berkeley,
1924, plan.
Documents Collection, C.E.D.

The Geisler house utilized the existing foundations from its burned predecessor and consisted of three levels composed under steeply-pitched gable roofs.

E. F. Geisler house, view of interior finish.
K. H. Cardwell photograph.

Maybeck salvaged material from the earlier house which was destroyed by the fire and obtained the *sugi* finish by wire-brushing the charred wood.

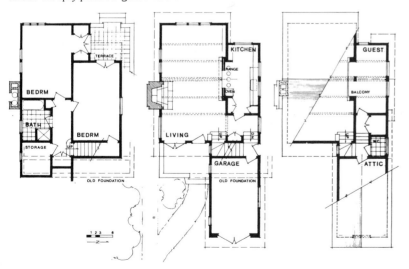

Since the war, the rise in construction costs had made the simple, well-designed house more difficult to obtain. In 1923 *Sunset Magazine* published an article entitled "The Maybeck One-Room House," in which he proposed the incorporation of house and garden into one entity, concentrating time and effort as well as cost on one handsomely proportioned and beautifully furnished space.[3] Service rooms were to be reduced to such a minimal size that they would become mere alcoves. Maybeck had no fixed ideas concerning materials or style to be used, preferring to put the personal tastes and preferences of the owner foremost in the hopes of achieving an individual expression. The kitchen of his one-room house was to be equipped with the best labor-saving devices to take the place of a hired girl. Both the McMurray and the Geisler designs were servantless houses; but it was the studio built on the site of his own burned house which initiated the pattern of his one-room designs.

The Maybeck studio (1924) on Buena Vista Way had no fine finishes. In fact it was an experimental structure, as much a laboratory as it was a house. Three large, glazed industrial doors opened its one room to the surrounding garden. There was neither kitchen nor dining room, and the open sleeping loft over the low entryway filled one side of the room's one-and-one-half-story height. The house has undergone many modifications which have obscured its original form, so that today it is better known for its use of lightweight concrete as a wall surface than it is for its planning.

In his own one-room studio Maybeck experimented with a new material, producing a unique, low cost, fire resistive construction system. His friend, John A. Rice, had been trying for several years to clear patent rights to a light-weight, air-entrained concrete named "Bubblestone." Maybeck, prophesying its broad use in low-cost housing, had interested a newly formed cement company in marketing Rice's product, once his right to patent was settled.[4] Maybeck tested the material in the building in his studio. His method of utilizing the "Bubblestone" was a simple one. On a conventional wood stud frame, strung horizontally with wire, burlap bags that had been saturated in the light-weight concrete mixture were hung shingle-fashion over the wires and left to harden into a serviceable, fire-resistant exterior. Window openings, corners, and flarings were easily negotiated with shears or by modeling the material in its plastic state. It was a technique that required no skilled labor and one that produced an interesting textural finish.

3. M. A. Maclay, "The Maybeck One-Room House," *Sunset Magazine*, 51, (July 1923), pp. 64-66.
4. B. R. Maybeck MSS, "J. A. Rice," C.E.D. Docs.

Bernard Maybeck studio, 2745 Buena Vista Way, Berkeley, 1924, plan.
Documents Collection, C.E.D.

Maybeck's studio served as a prototype for his one room houses as well as a laboratory for experimenting with materials and finishes.

Bernard Maybeck studio, elevation.
Documents Collection, C.E.D.

Bernard Maybeck studio, detail of wall surface.
Roy Flamm photograph.

The lightweight "Bubblestone" concrete provided a uniquely
rustic finish enlivened by the industrial sash of the doors and
windows.

R. I. Woolsey house, 20 Sunset Drive, Kensington, Contra
Costa County, 1927.
William S. Ricco photograph.

Maybeck used "Bubblestone" as a roofing material, with results
very reminiscent of an English thatch-roof cottage.

Maybeck also experimented with "Bubblestone" as a roofing material on the 1927 residence of Dr. R. I. Woolsey. The concrete was colored a deep plum; however, its rough surface encouraged the growth of creepers and vines which accelerated its cracking and made it permeable. How long the concrete roofing material was effective is difficult to determine; it is now surfaced with an aluminized waterproofing coat. The roof form recalls an image of the thatch on an English cottage, yet it is not contrived. Its shapes developed out of the method of construction and the nature of the material, and its recall of the hominess of a vernacular architecture illustrates why Maybeck believed in the associative values of older architectural forms.

The finish of Maybeck's own cement sack studio has survived the exposure of forty years, even though there has been some rotting of the jute fabric where moisture has been able to penetrate the surface.[5] Maybeck had searched as far as China and Japan for a suitable netted fabric to replace the low quality jute of the gunny sack material. He experimented with grass cloths and woven paper products, proposing to use his sack system for some structures in Glen Alpine. He even thought of experimenting with it in the construction of The Principia; but his experimentation ceased when Rice was unable to establish exclusive rights to his "Bubblestone."[6]

Maybeck designed several one-room houses. The first built was the Warren P. Staniford house (1925) on Ocean View Avenue in Oakland. While not completely contained in one room, it adhered to the principles Maybeck had prescribed in his *Sunset* article. The house consisted of a living space, one end of which was arranged with a large fireplace, view window, and dining area. Across the other end a low platform served as a sleeping alcove with beds and linens placed in a storage wall. The kitchen, bath, and dressing room were planned as a small lean-to addition along one side of the room. The kitchen served the main room through a large hatch. The room with its high-raftered ceiling is pleasant, but extensive additions have been made which make it difficult to sense its original scale and its relation to the garden setting.

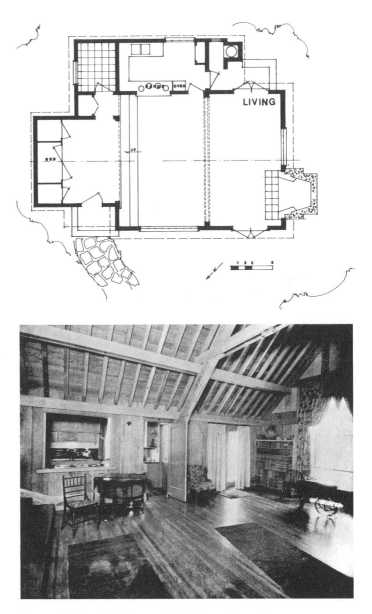

Warren P. Staniford house, 6130 Ocean View Drive, Oakland, 1925.
Documents Collection, C.E.D.

Although not technically one room, the Staniford house was basically contained in one area and formed a pleasant utilitarian space.

5. Annie also chided Ben for his habit of tearing off sample pieces which he gave to many of their visitors during their years in retirement.
6. B. R. Maybeck MSS, "J. A. Rice," C.E.D. Docs.

Maybeck saw that functional activities, with man as their measure, gave shape to architectural forms. An architect ordered the functional needs into an architectural program and designed a structure to house them. Maybeck's own awareness that man's daily activities and social patterns were constantly modified by economic and technological change led to his early experimentation with the servantless house. His creative development was enhanced by his willingness to consider what his clients' needs truly were and not what he thought they ought to be. Hence he insisted that buildings must be fitted to their users as well as to their environment.

A more ambitious project than the Staniford house was designed for Charles Duncan in Sausalito in 1925. Although it was not constructed, it was the ultimate in open planning of indoor and outdoor spaces using alcoves and sliding and folding doors to achieve a variety of open and closed effects. Only the most private areas, the dressing rooms and baths, were fully enclosed. The kitchen facilities of built-in counter cabinets at an end wall of the studio room could be screened from view by vertically sliding panels. Everything in the house was subordinant to the large living area. A long, glazed gallery, overlooking a wooded canyon, provided open or closed space for sleeping. Entry, studio, gallery, and exterior courts, articulated by changes in levels or by large openings spanned by beams, were arranged in axial lines in a free but strongly ordered spatial composition. The architecture became a single unit encompassing all activities of its occupants, day or night, winter or summer. The one-room house, handsomely proportioned and beautifully appointed, had been achieved in design even though it failed to reach translation into physical form.

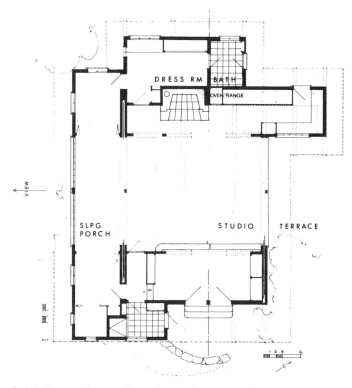

C. W. Duncan house, Santa Rosa Ave., Sausalito, 1925 project, plan drawn by Alan Williams.
Documents Collection, C.E.D.

The Duncan design featured excellent open planning with only the most private areas being fully enclosed.

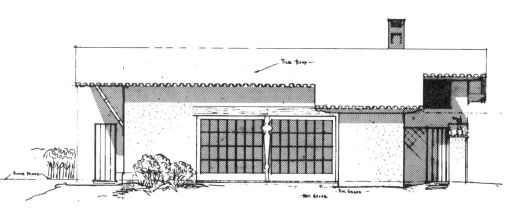

C. W. Duncan house, elevation.
Documents Collection. C.E.D.

Bernard Maybeck, ca. 1930.
Documents Collection, C.E.D.

This charred photograph is one piece of memorabilia which survived the fire in the Maybecks' third house in 1939.

The small structures built in the first years after the 1923 fire formed only a minor portion of Maybeck's work during his fourth decade of practice. However, they are among the most interesting. In them invention or experiments in the building process continued with greater freedom than in the large-scale projects, even though the results seldom achieved the clarity or brilliance found in pre-fire buildings.[7] Beginning in 1924 Maybeck organized his office for work on commissions received from The Principia, William Randolph Hearst, and Earle C. Anthony. Although his staff never grew very large, at times he employed more than a dozen men. Charles Lundgren (who had started with the firm in 1915) and Mark Manning (who was hired in 1923) became the principal draftsmen, and Annie White Maybeck became the office manager. Most of Maybeck's time was devoted to the creation of designs.

In the early years Maybeck's interest in structure and the craft of building had dominated his design, as in Hearst Hall. In his architectural triumph, the Christian Science church, he had blended structure with form and feeling, while in the Palace of Fine Arts emotions held sway. And in the fourth decade of practice, as his interest in inventive structural ideas waned, Maybeck became more an artist producing images that others would develop into drawings of buildings for construction. His concern narrowed, noticeably so in his larger projects, to abstract qualities of architecture—color, light, and texture. Although he was less completely involved in the total scope of the work, Maybeck worked assiduously, searching for and selecting materials and colors, designing light fixtures and hardware, and improvising building techniques. It was a pattern which began with the design of the Hearst Gymnasium and The Principia with Julia Morgan and continued with Henry Gutterson for the Christian Science Sunday School. But it is most vividly illustrated in the designs of buildings for Earle C. Anthony, the major distributor of Packard automobiles on the Pacific Coast.

7. Conversations between Maybeck and the author. The only regret Maybeck ever expressed about his active professional life was that it ended before he could experiment with plastics and light metals.

Packard automobile showroom, Van Ness Ave., San Francisco, 1926, Powers and Ahnden, Associate Architects. Wayne Andrews photograph.

The Packard showrooms in San Francisco (1926) and Oakland (1928) were built in conjunction with the firm of John H. Powers and John H. Ahnden. Maybeck prepared schematic drawings which his associates used to make preliminary structural, mechanical, and electrical drawings for his approval. Maybeck then concentrated on the decorative features of the design and charged Anthony a straight fee for his "art work."[8] It was a system which left no give and take as the design progressed; and the decorative schemes, rather than growing out of the spatial order and the patterns of structures as they had in the Christian Science church, were restricted to surface treatments and added ornament. The showrooms became stage sets, where automobiles or "magic carpets" were sold "to carry one away to faraway places." In a decade that first brought wide ownership of individual vehicles, many people shared Maybeck's romantic vision.[9]

The San Francisco showroom, on Van Ness Avenue, was opened in 1927 with a gala array of motion picture actresses and a special radio broadcast. Anthony also owned two broadcasting stations and the San Francisco building was designed to carry large steel towers for transmitting antennae on its roof. The building is a four-story rectangular block, its front third contains a two-story high showroom with mezzanine sales offices. Maybeck chose to design in the free, classical style he had learned in André's atelier. But his combination of the temple-like salesroom with the frankly utilitarian service section, and the brutal penetration of the overscaled frieze for service floor windows, combined with unorthodox unfluted Corinthian columns produced a mannerist design even less admired by his Beaux-Arts colleagues than his design for the Palace of Fine Arts.

8. B. R. Maybeck MSS, "E. C. Anthony," C.E.D. Docs.
9. Advertisements for automobiles in magazines published contemporarily with the construction of the showrooms portray the same romantic image.

Screen walls of black tiles lie between red columns and are penetrated by richly sculptured doorways. A large, sand-colored entablature crowns the salesroom. Color is carried into the interior with pigmented stains worked into the wood ceiling of the sales room. Maybeck had intended to use a waste cedar product for this ceiling—boards mottled with areas of unsound wood cut from trees infested with a fungus growth—but when this material was not available, a similar disfigured cypress shipped from Florida was substituted. Pigments were also worked into the crevices of ornamental plaster brackets and the moldings of the column capitals which housed colored spotlights illuminating the automobiles on the salesroom floor with theatrical effectiveness.

Packard automobile showroom, interior details.
Roy Flamm photograph.

In his later years, Maybeck concentrated on basic design schemes and decorative effects while relegating the actual structural planning to other architects. The results were usually dramatic but less unified and effective than his earlier work.

Packard automobile showroom, Harrison St., Oakland, 1928.
California Arts and Architecture, February, 1929.

The pointed arches of the exterior suggest Islamic architecture.

In Oakland, Maybeck's sales building was medieval in mood. Sited near the edge of Lake Merritt, it also combined a utilitarian garage section with a richly modeled sales pavilion. A square-based tower terminating in a round form enriched by arched and balconied openings joined the service and sales sections. The lakeside facade was dominated by three large pointed arches whose flaring spring lines suggested Islamic sources. Tall lanterns softly illuminated the intradoses of the arches which could be seen reflected in the lake.

The picturesquely composed exterior was strongly accented by lines of stout wooden corbels supporting tiled roof overhangs. The sales room floor, consisting of three tiled and tiered platforms, was spanned by low, pointed arches springing from squat, black scagliola columns with capitals of Romanesque design. The scale of the architecture was large and heavy and, as in the San Francisco showroom, became a make-believe setting rather than a straightforward housing for the display of motorcars.

Packard automobile showroom, interior view.
California Arts and Architecture, February, 1929.

Maybeck's automobile showrooms were fantastic
structures—a suitable setting for the "magic carpet"
automobile advertising world of the 1920s.

On the Oakland Packard building—a concrete structure—Maybeck applied a technological development of plastering to create a new finish. The dull surfaces of plastered walls had never appealed to him and when he used stucco for reasons of economy he always attempted to enrich it by some means. The Jockers house (1911) had rough cast and contrasting troweled surfaces; the Kennedy studio used variously colored plasters without restraint. Most late houses, like the McMurray and the Staniford, had stucco exteriors modeled in several colors of plaster applied in successive dash coats. This method rendered the wall with light pinks at its top to dark earth browns at its bottom and produced a lively finish. But the hand-controlled application was not economical for use on large structures. A new technique, which covered concrete surfaces with a coat of plaster blown by air guns, took quantities of cement, pigment, and water, and mixed them as they were driven against the surface of the building. Maybeck saw that with this method he could vary the pigmentation of the plaster almost at will. He did so on the Oakland building, first stationing himself across nearby Lake Merritt where he conducted the finishing operations by field telephone.[10] Prior to the destruction of the building in 1974, the mottled wall treatment so subtlely contrived by Maybeck had been painted a garish raspberry hue, a large neon sign blanketed the three great arches of the facade while another twirled idiotically on the round tower, turning Maybeck's fantasy into farce.

10. Irving F. Morrow, "The Packard Building at Oakland," *California Arts and Architecture*, 32, (February 1929), pp. 54-59.

Packard automobile showroom and office interiors, John and Donald B. Parkinson, building architects, Los Angeles, 1928. William Current photograph.

Richly decorative, the Los Angeles showroom still effectively housed automobiles of the 1970s.

In the Los Angeles Packard building, designed by John and Donald B. Parkinson, Maybeck's work was limited to the interior finishes and the styling of the executive office suite. However, late in 1928, he established temporary residence in southern California to oversee its construction and the development of the Anthony's residential property at the eastern end of the Santa Monica mountain range.

224

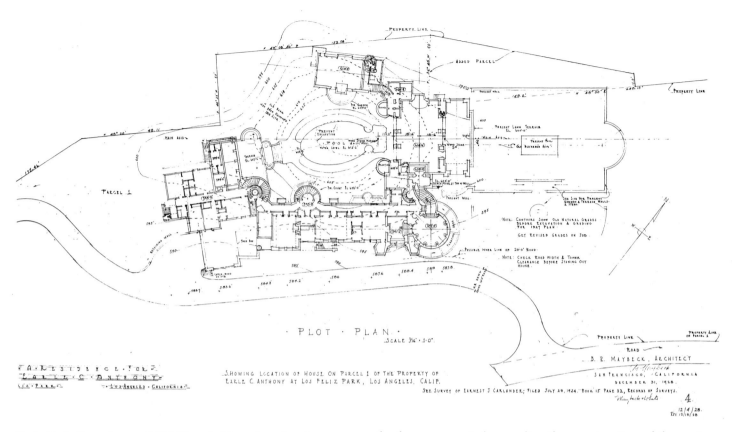

· PLOT · PLAN ·

SCALE 3/16" = 1'-0".

SHOWING LOCATION OF HOUSE ON PARCEL 1 OF THE PROPERTY OF
EARLE C ANTHONY AT LOS FELIZ PARK, LOS ANGELES, CALIF.

SEE SURVEY OF EARNEST J CARLANDER; FILED JULY 28, 1924, BOOK 15, PAGE 32, RECORDS OF SURVEYS.

B. R. MAYBECK, ARCHITECT
SAN FRANCISCO, CALIFORNIA
DECEMBER 31, 1928.

Earle C. Anthony house, 3435 Waverly Place, Los Angeles,
1928, plan.
Documents Collection, C.E.D.

The huge estate was set in a commanding position on its
8 acre site.

The Anthony residence (1928) in Los Feliz Park was the
last large house that Maybeck built. He had started its plan
in 1924, and at that busy period had asked John White to be
his associate architect for its design and construction. The
house is situated on an eight-acre hilltop site and commands
an unobstructed view in all directions. Prior to the construction
of the main house, two smaller structures were built, one in
1925 for temporary living quarters and later guest house
accommodations and the other in 1927 as a playroom with
motion picture facilities. The site was extensively landscaped
by building retaining walls to create garden terraces and by
planting more than ten carloads of trees and shrubs during

the four-year period preceding the construction of the main
residence. The living rooms of the house surround a patio
containing an elliptical swimming pool, planting, and dining
terrace. Large windows frame vistas across the patio and
through the gardens to the mountains beyond.

An unsigned typescript among the Maybeck records, evidently written as an article for a contemporary journal, states:

The Los Angeles home of Earle C. Anthony in Los Feliz
Park expresses the catholicity of taste of the owner and architect Bernard R. Maybeck. Its long low roof lines and stone
battlements, crowned with a huge Norman tower, are at first
glance reminiscent of the hill towns of Italy. Closer inspection
discloses a surprising combination of architectural orders
and national elements used apparently without any regard
for chronological continuity or academic conventions. These
"studied differences" as the architect phrases them are vigorously, intelligently and skillfully combined to the satisfaction
of the most fastidious, to form a most comfortable and livable
home.[11]

11. B. R. Maybeck MSS, "E. C. Anthony," C.E.D. Docs.

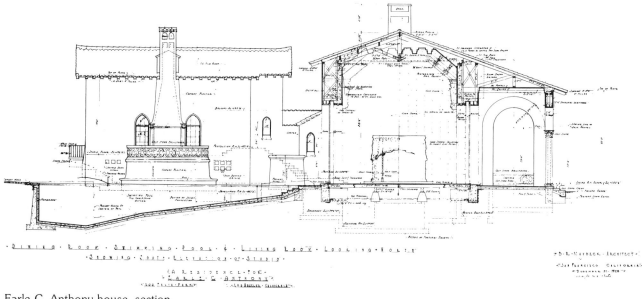

The Anthony mansion was richly finished and handsomely detailed, but its eclectic assemblage of forms and decoration was antithetical to Maybeck's earlier practice.

The house was redesigned every time Anthony made a visit to Europe, where he gathered materials and new ideas for its construction, and its final form in 1928 became the antithesis of the kind of buildings Maybeck had promulgated thirty years earlier. Whereas Wyntoon (1902) and the Roos house (1909), both luxurious designs, have an affinity with the principles of the Gothic house, the Anthony house has none. It is the epitome of historical pastiche and artifice, even though well-proportioned and carefully detailed. In spite of fine materials, handsome spaces, and intriguing vistas, Maybeck's use of anachronistic architectural forms, such as the portcullis guarding the entrance, the crenellated tower, and groined masonry vaults and arches executed in plaster, demonstrate an approach to architectural design contrary to every maxim proclaimed in *The Simple Home*.

Of course, in all of Maybeck's work there had been borrowed details. Even his earliest residences had the flavor of southern German or early Greek forms, but during those years his interest in structure and invention in building form made a contribution worthy of note. The Anthony residence, like the automobile agency buildings, created a make-believe world. Maybeck believed that an architect can only reflect the spirit of his time. On the eve of the great economic depression

Earle C. Anthony house, dining room.
K. H. Cardwell photograph.

From the exterior the house reminds many viewers of a lavish
Italian villa.

and in a decade which focussed on material values, the acquisition and exhibition of wealth was an end in itself. Maybeck
characterized Earle C. Anthony as a "merchant Prince" serving mankind with "flying carpets" to carry one to enchanted
lands. Perhaps it is no coincidence that the architecture Maybeck created for him was as illusive as his image of Anthony—
entrepreneur, purveyor of automobiles, and promoter of
radio advertising.

Earle C. Anthony house, drawing room and study.
K. H. Cardwell photograph.

Earle C. Anthony house, bedroom wing.
K. H. Cardwell photograph.

Earle C. Anthony house, detail.
K. H. Cardwell, photograph.

Bernard Maybeck, ca. 1948.
Esther Born photograph.

While staying in Los Angeles to supervise some construction details for the Anthony house, Maybeck underwent minor surgery. Unfortunately, he developed a severe post-operative infection, and for almost two months it was doubtful whether he would survive. Annie traveled to Los Angeles to be at his bedside, but during his convalescence she became distraught with her husband who irrepressibly insisted on continuing with drawing and approving details of the Anthony construction.[12] Annie had taken over the financial management of Maybeck's practice in 1924. Under her direction it had shown a good profit and she saw no reason why Ben, now sixty-eight, should not begin to end his professional career. He had little liking for the idea, but when his vigor did return, he soon found that the ensuing financial depression forced other unwanted changes in his practice.

At the conclusion of the Anthony work, Maybeck did not seek or take on any new commissions. He reduced his office staff to Mark White, Charles Lundgren, and Mark Manning, and even they took leaves of absence without pay. Maybeck's work on the University auditorium and art galleries had ceased when the stock market collapse forced Hearst to reconsider his plan to fund their construction. Late in 1929 The Principia had ordered the start of drawings for the initial buildings of the Saint Louis campus, but these were being developed in Julia Morgan's office. Maybeck had already completed his design studies. Annie had almost convinced Ben to retire; but the change in the campus location of The Principia from St. Louis to Elsah in 1930, calling for the development of a new general plan, made her arguments futile.

12. B. R. Maybeck MSS, "Illness," C.E.D. Docs.

Designing buildings for the new campus of The Principia filled Maybeck's days from 1930 to 1938. After his stay in Elsah to oversee the completion of the college chapel, Maybeck returned to Berkeley. He built a second studio house on his Buena Vista property, where he worked on his large charcoal and pastel sketches, foregoing his daily trips to San Francisco. His residential designing was restricted to the development of his Berkeley property where he constructed a third house for J. B. Tufts (1931), one for himself known as Annie's house (1933), and one for his son Wallen and his wife, Jacomena, (1933). As the Berkeley property filled with construction, Annie purchased undeveloped land lying to the north of Berkeley and Maybeck's first structure on this property was for his son, Wallen. Its isolated position above dry grass hills beyond the area of city fire protection was one of the factors that led Maybeck to his final demonstration of fireproof building.

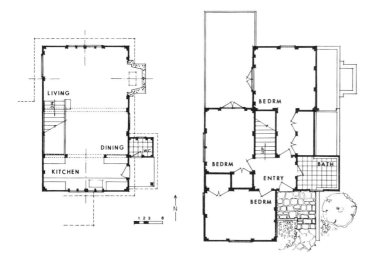

Wallen W. Maybeck house (#1), 2751 Buena Vista Way, Berkeley, 1933.
K. H. Cardwell photograph of north elevation.

Wallen W. Maybeck house, plan.
Documents Collection, C.E.D.

The two-story plan featured living areas above enclosed in one large space.

Steep roofs, woodwork, abundant windows and a terrace over the garage was again found in Maybeck's house built after the destruction by fire of his earlier home.

Wallen W. Maybeck house, interior view.
Esther Born photograph.

The high-ceilinged, well-lit interior provided a fine space for
Maybeck's work tables.

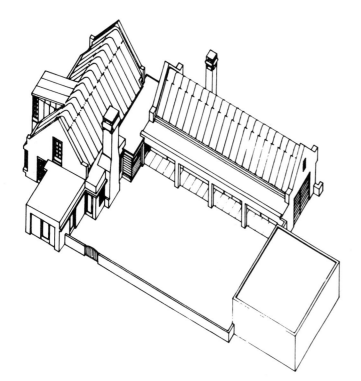

The Wallen Maybeck house (1937), located on the ridge of the Berkeley Hills, commands magnificient views. Built in two separate blocks, it shelters an eastern court overlooking Wildcat canyon. The plan is derived from early California prototypes where rooms are joined into one volume with exterior circulation. Maybeck's bold design in concrete and corrugated iron roofing incorporates a sandwich of precast concrete panels separated by insulation made of waste rice hulls. The interior panels are finished with an exposed aggregate and the exterior ones left with a natural concrete surface.

Wallen W. Maybeck house (#2), Purdue Ave., Kensington, Contra Costa Co., 1937.
Drawing by Thomas Gordon Smith.

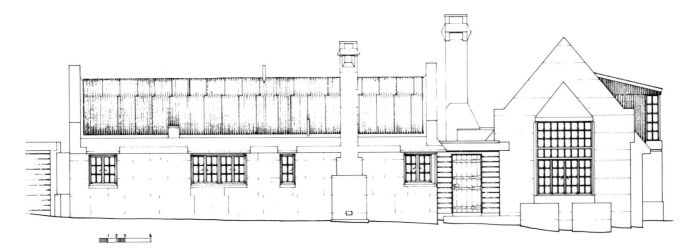

Wallen W. Maybeck house, west elevation.
Drawing by Thomas Gordon Smith.

Wallen W. Maybeck house, view from court.
William S. Ricco photograph.

The Wallen Maybeck house boldly employed concrete and
corrugated iron roofing to create a fire-proof structure of
unique character.

In designing a small sales and workroom structure for the
Mobilized Women of Berkeley (1937), a community service
organization with which Annie had worked for many years,
Maybeck again experimented in building with pre-cast concrete panels, using a product being developed by a local firm.
He used the panels—glazed with obscure glass—for walls,
factory metal sash for windows, and corrugated metal for a
frieze and the roof. Maybeck enjoyed experimenting, and his
imaginative handling of materials often transposed a common
item into one of distinction. But the experiments of the later
years suffer from a refinement of detail and a lack of precision
in execution that mar the quality of the work. Such was the
case with the Mobilized Women's Building, where the panels
and trim materials were crudely joined. Even its broad canopy,
which originally sheltered the entrance, was the victim of
faculty construction, necessitating a row of pipe columns to
support it.

Mobilized Women of Berkeley store building, University Ave.,
Berkeley, 1937 (destroyed 1975).
Documents Collection, C.E.D.

The architect himself, complete with top hat, poses outside of
his pre-cast concrete, industrial sash and corrugated metal
building for a community service club.

At the age of seventy-six Maybeck relinquished his interest in The Principia. And, although he was associated with William G. Merchant for some designs for the Golden Gate International Exposition of 1939 and did other designs as late as 1941, Maybeck had ended his professional career. He and Annie lived a simple, independent life in retirement; dividing their time between their mountain retreat in Twain Harte and the second Berkeley studio which Maybeck had enlarged in 1938. And while Bernard did an occasional design for a friend or a family member, Annie astutely managed the sales and development of their real estate holdings in Berkeley and Kensington. Annie was always an integral part of the family ventures. From the early days of private practice, she had acted as secretary and general assistant for Bernard and her brother Mark. The monogram "A" in Maybeck's architectural ornament was more than a sentimental device; it was his recognition of the close understanding and cooperation that Annie gave him in his quest for beauty.

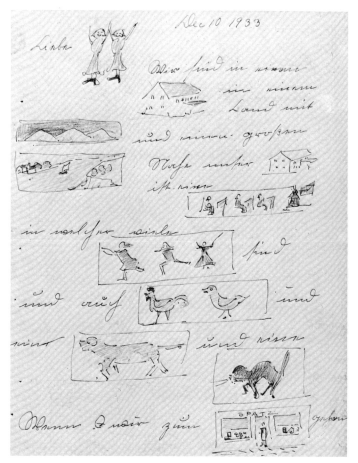

Bernard Maybeck, letter to grandchildren, 1933.
Documents Collection, C.E.D.

Maybeck's charming, illustrated letters to his grandchildren not only served to delight the recipients but also facilitated their learning of the German language.

Bernard Maybeck, at work on the Charles Aikin house, 2750 Buena Vista Way, Berkeley, 1940.
Photograph courtesy of Charles Aikin.

Annie White Maybeck died in 1956; a year later, on October 3, 1957, Bernard Ralph Maybeck followed. On his trip to Hawaii many years before, at the passing of his vessel and its sister ship bound for California, he had commented to the Scribe, "How like it is to life in its larger aspects."

> ...Man lives out his human experience and passes on, and we say he is no more, but like the passing ship, is simply out of sight. As for man himself, he goes on, ever sailing across new seas, which doubtless shall seem to him not very unlike those he sailed before. Thus a man's life here comes to appear in its true character, as a mere flash in the immensity of eternity.[13]

Maybeck's career was seen by his colleagues as a beacon rather than a mere flash and, in 1951, they awarded him the highest honor they could bestow, the Gold Medal of the American Institute of Architects. The announcement brought visitors from all parts of the world to pay their respects to the gifted architect. They usually found him in his favorite retreat on the Buena Vista property, an open-air atelier outside his studio home, where he spent his days sketching his ideas for the improvement and beautification of the San Francisco Bay region.

When Bernard Ralph Maybeck received the Gold Medal of the American Institute of Architects it was more than the recognition of one man and his architectural achievements. It demonstrated the maturity of a modern architecture which could acknowledge growth from the roots in American practice as well as European theory. Many Pacific Coast designs had achieved a national and international recognition as a logical development of the International Style into one more expressive of the nature of man and his environment. When questioned about their designs, the architects of the San Francisco Bay region almost unanimously denied anything unique about their work and pointed to the architecture of Bernard Maybeck which, at the beginning of the century, had demonstrated similar characteristics.

13. W.B.R. Willcox MSS, "Journal," C.E.D. Docs.

ANNO DOMINI MCMLI

IN OUR TIMES GREAT PIONEERS HAVE COURAGEOUSLY STEERED THEIR WAY TO THE FOUR CORNERS OF THE SPIRIT: COURSING EVER ON WITH FREE WILLS THEIR SOULS—IN ADVENTUROUS PATHS. OVER SEAS, OVER THE VAST PLAINS, THE HIGH MOUNTAINS, HEWING THE GREAT FORESTS—HAVE FOUND NEW BEAUTY AND FURTHER UNDERSTANDINGS OF HUMAN ASPIRATIONS. WHILE CASTING LOOSE THE ANCHOR CHAINS OF TRADITION, THEY HAVE GUARDED HUMAN HOPES AS PRECIOUS CARGOES.

THE AMERICAN INSTITUTE OF ARCHITECTS

IS PRIVILEGED TO ACKNOWLEDGE IN AWARDING ITS

GOLD MEDAL OF HONOR

A PIONEER WHOSE LIFE AND WORK GIVE LUSTROUS DISTINCTION TO OUR PROFESSION

BERNARD RALPH MAYBECK

EVER FREE IN SPIRIT: "EVER SEEKING A SAD FEELING, A HUNGER OF AN ARTIST AFTER BEAUTY, A HUNGER THAT IS NEVER SATISFIED",— HE HAS CREATED THE STURDY BEGINNINGS OF AN ARCHITECTURE TRULY REPRESENTATIVE OF AMERICAN LIFE IN A CIVILIZATION, WE HOPE, TO BE EVER PIONEERING. INSPIRED TO FURTHER SEEKINGS "WE TOO TAKE SHIP, O SOUL!"

SECRETARY   PRESIDENT

Citation of Gold Medal award, American Institute of Architects, 1951.
Courtesy of Jacomena Maybeck, (Mrs. Wallen W.).

The immediate reaction was to look at Maybeck as a forerunner of the modern movement. It is true that some of his architectural innovations broke with the immediate past and used products of a machine technology in fresh and imaginative solutions to building problems. However, in the sense of "out with the old order and in with the new," Maybeck was not a revolutionary. The architect's primary function, he reasoned, was to fulfill one of man's greatest yearnings—to be surrounded by beauty. As an architect he strove to produce, with modern materials and techniques, an architecture as beautiful and meaningful as that which had been created in past times and for past cultures.

> The artist... suspects that it is not the object nor the likeness to the object that he is working for, but a portrayal of the life that is behind the visible.
>
> Here he comes face to face with the real things of this life; no assistance can be given him; he cannot hire a boy in gold buttons fashionably to open the door to the Muse, nor a clerk nor an accountant to do the drudgery. He is alone before his problem and drifts away from superficial portrayals. After this he strives to find the spiritual meaning of things and to transmit that secret to the layman.[14]

Maybeck and his work represent an inventive, independent stream of American design. After World War II, in a reaction to the mechanistic and collectivist expression of the International Style, American architects looked with more favor on the more organic developments in their own past. In an area such as the San Francisco Bay region, which was relatively uninfluenced by the International Style, there had been a continuing amalgamation of the romantic tradition with the technological present. And to the architects practicing in this tradition Bernard Ralph Maybeck stood out as the most imaginative creator of an individualistic architecture from which they could draw inspiration. Maybeck's application of contemporary technology and materials, his direct structural expression, his creative development of plan to suit changing social needs or geographical location, his masterly handling of the elements of architecture, and his prime concern for the individual mark him as a strong, vital contributor to an architecture distinctively American.

14. Bernard Maybeck, *Palace of Fine Art and Lagoon*, pp. 6-7.

Bernard Maybeck, 1930, at the Bohemian Grove, Russian River. Documents Collection, C.E.D.

The twinkle in the eyes, the little grin, the casual clothes, the flame burning in the rustic setting combine to picture the happy, creative spirit of Bernard Ralph Maybeck.

238

Chronological List of Executed Work and Projects

The earliest list prepared on the work of the firm of Maybeck and White was compiled in 1947 by Mark White more than ten years after the close of Maybeck's active practice. It was made in response to a request by Jean Murray Bangs, who through her articles published in architectural journals was one of the first writers to present Maybeck's designs to a nation-wide audience. White's list contained 157 items and we are indebted to him for most of our knowledge of the work done prior to the San Francisco earthquake and fire which destroyed Maybeck's early office records and drawings. White listed only a few street addresses, many of his entries were incomplete, a few were inaccurate, and the majority lacked the construction date and the full names of the clients; but, fortunately, Maybeck's gift of his papers and drawings to the College of Environmental Design, Documents Collection provided one means to supplement the list and to verify the work of the firm.

The chronology of Maybeck's work presented here is derived from White's list, the Maybeck and White office records, tax records, and directories. Project and building listings are restricted to documented works. Many buildings in the San Francisco Bay area have been popularly attributed to Maybeck, or the Maybeck and White firm, but none of these are included unless its design and construction has been verified by an original owner, or an immediate family member of the original owner of the project in question. The work of the firm of Maybeck, Howard, and White is listed separately.

The dates listed represent as accurately as possible the start of the construction of a project. Most of Maybeck's drawings are not dated; but contract records, specifications, and the first Certificate of Payment (issued by the architect) have been used to determine the completion of the office design phase of a project or the beginning of its construction. These dates appear in the list with both year and month. Dates shown by year only, and listed alphabetically, have been derived from secondary sources, such as directories and newspaper notices. Bracketed dates, based on inferences from secondary sources, have been assigned by the author to designs for which we have no evidence to date the project other than the evaluation of stylistic characteristics. They are the least reliable and may vary greatly in their degree of accuracy. There are items in the College of Environmental Design, Documents Collection which do not appear on the list. They are photographs or sketches for projects with no names, dates, or geographic location. It is also likely that a few structures dating between 1892 and 1906 remain undiscovered. It is hoped that individuals with documentary evidence of other work by Bernard Maybeck will add to this list and correct any errors which must be presumed to exist in it.

1892 May — Bernard R. Maybeck house (#1), Grove and Berryman St., Berkeley, CA. (Purchased as a one story cottage in 1892, remodeled and extended during the years 1892-1902. Remodeled and converted into a multiple dwelling by subsequent owners.

[1895] — Charles Keeler house, Ridge Road and Highland Place, Berkeley, CA. (Extensively remodeled and divided into apartments, but some room interiors remain unchanged.)

1896 — Emma Kellogg house (#1), Palo Alto, CA. (Destroyed, 1899)

[1896] — Laura G. Hall house, 1745 Highland Place, Berkeley, CA. (Destroyed, 1956)

[1896] — Andrew C. Lawson house (#1), 2461 Warring St., Berkeley, CA. (Destroyed)

[1897] — Williston W. Davis house, 2305 Ridge Road, Berkeley, CA. (The living room planned as a pavilion on the front of the property was never completed. Destroyed, 1957)

1899 July — Town and Gown Club building, 2401 Dwight Way, Berkeley, CA. (Extensive additions by other architects, but much of the original building remains unaltered)

1899 — Emma Kellogg house (#2), 1061 Bryant, Palo Alto, CA.

1899 — Reception building, Phoebe A. Hearst, Channing Way near College Ave., Berkeley, CA. (Moved to the University of California campus and refitted as a gymnasium. See 1901)

1899 — William P. Rieger house, 1901 Highland Place, Berkeley, CA. (Destroyed, 1958)

1900 — Lillian Bridgman house, 1715 La Loma, Berkeley, CA.

1900 — G. H. G. McGrew house, 2601 Derby St., Berkeley, CA.

1901 — Hearst Hall gymnasium, University of California, Berkeley, CA. (Destroyed, 1922)

[1901] — Isaac Flagg house (#1), 1200 Shattuck Ave., Berkeley, CA.

1902 June — Project: Barn, University of California, Berkeley, CA.

1902 July — Irving Whitney house, 1431 Hawthorne Terrace, Berkeley, CA. (Destroyed, 1923)

1902 August — Faculty Club building, University of California, Berkeley, CA. (Extensive remodeling and additions, but some original work remains.)

1902 Sept. — Hiram D. Kellogg house, 2608 Regent St., Berkeley, CA. (House relocated at 2960 Linden St., Berkeley.)

1902 Nov. — Miss Stockton house, Le Roy Ave., Berkeley, CA. (Destroyed, 1923)

1902 Nov. — T. J. Bunnell, living room addition, San Francisco, CA.

1902 — Project: Barnett house, [San Francisco, CA.] (Preliminary drawings)

[1902] — George H. Boke house, 23 Panoramic Way, Berkeley, CA.

[1902] — F. B. Dresslar house, 2327 Le Conte Ave., Berkeley, CA. (Purchased by O. K. McMurray, 1909. Destroyed, 1923)

[1902] — Charles Keeler studio, 1736 Highland Place, Berkeley, CA.

1902-03 — Phoebe A. Hearst country estate, "Wyntoon", McCloud River, Siskiyou Co., CA. (Destroyed)

1903 March — Project: Cooley house, Haste St., Berkeley, CA.

1903 April — Grove Clubhouse, Bohemian Club of San Francisco, Bohemian Grove, Russian River, CA. (Second scheme, Dec., 1903)

1903 April — Newhall Brothers store building, George and Irving Newhall, San Jose, CA. (Remodeled)

1903 April — W. C. Jones house, [Berkeley]. (Preliminary drawings)

1903 July — J. W. Thomas house additions, Berkeley, CA. (Destroyed, 1923)

1903 Sept. — Drawing: University of California Hospital, [San Francisco, CA.]

1904 March   Howard B. Gates house, 62 S. 13th St., San Jose, CA.

1904 March   California Wine Association exhibit, St. Louis Exposition, St. Louis, Missouri.

1904 July   George Newhall house remodeling, 2340 Pacific St., San Francisco, CA. (Additional remodeling, July, 1906)

1904 August   Bettys house, [Berkeley, CA.] (Preliminary drawing)

1904 Sept.   T. J. Bunnell house, Broadway near Pierce St., San Francisco, CA. (House moved to this location and remodeled)

1904 Sept.   George Newhall house, El Camino Real near Oakgrove, Burlingame, CA. (Remodeling, destroyed)

1904 Sept.   William W. Underhill house (#1), 1403 Le Roy Ave., Berkeley, CA. (Purchased by Simeon D. Hutsinpillar, 1908. Destroyed, 1923)

1904 Sept.   Outdoor Art Club building, 1 West Blithedale Avenue, Mill Valley, CA.

1904 Oct.   Ranson E. Beach house, 110 Sunnyside Ave., Oakland, CA.

1905 June   Frederick E. Farrington house, 1829 Arch St., Berkeley, CA. (Destroyed, 1923)

1905 June   C. S. Diggles house, Lomita Park, San Mateo, CA.

1905 Oct.   J. B. Tufts house (#1), 14 Entrata Ave., San Anselmo, CA.

1906 March   Project: Hamilton Church, Belvedere and Waller, San Francisco, CA. (Preliminary drawings)

1906 March   School, Morgan Hill, CA.

1906 March   Hillside Club building, 2286 Cedar St., Berkeley, CA. (Additions, 1922, destroyed 1923. Existing structure designed by John White.)

1906 April   Imogene L. Sanderson house, 1610 Lookout Place (Le Roy Ave.), Berkeley, CA. (Destroyed, 1923)

1906 May   Project: Francis E. Gregory house, Hilgard St., Berkeley, CA.

1906 May   J. B. Elston house, Aberdeen, Washington. (Office records indicate plans and specifications of Boke house duplicated.)

1906 June   Unitarian Church, Cowper and Channing St., Palo Alto, CA. (Destroyed)

1906 July   Isaac Flagg studio, 1208 Shattuck Ave., Berkeley, CA.

1906 August   Project: Miall house, Burlingame, CA. (Preliminary drawings)

1906 August   George H. Robinson house, 528 El Camino Real, Burlingame, CA. (Destroyed)

1906 Sept.   Project: Frey house, [Berkeley, CA.]

1906 Sept.   Project: George R. Stiles house, Piedmont, CA.

1906 Sept.   Project: William C. Tait house, East Oakland, CA.

1906 Oct.   J. H. Hopps house, Winding Way, Ross, CA. (Additions, 1925)

1906 Oct.   Paul Elder Bookstore, Van Ness and Pine, San Francisco, CA. (Building constructed on foundations of building burned in the 1906 fire. Destroyed)

1906 Oct.   Project: de Lemascheffsky house, Le Conte Ave. nr. LeRoy, Berkeley, CA.

1906 Oct.   George Hansen houses, [Berkeley, CA.] (four speculative house designs)

1906 Nov.   Project: Ernest H. Evans house, Arch St. near Virginia St., Berkeley, CA.

1906 Dec.   Telegraph Hill Neighborhood house, 1734 Stockton St., San Francisco, CA.

1906 Dec.   Project: Samuel B. Welch house, Larkin St. near Chestnut, San Francisco, CA.

1906 Dec.   Project: L. W. Read house, Stockton, CA.

[1906]   William Rees house, La Loma and Virginia, Berkeley, CA.

1907 Feb.	F. M. French house, 2236 Summer St., Berkeley, CA.
1907 March	J. H. Senger house, 1321 Bay View Place, Berkeley, CA.
1907 April	Albert C. Kern house, Dormidera nr. Pacific, Piedmont, CA.
1907 July	Stebbins house, Berkeley, CA. (Remodeling)
1907 July	Photographic Studio building, Oscar Maurer, 1772 Le Roy Ave., Berkeley, CA.
1907 Sept.	Francis E. Gregory house, 1428 Greenwood Terrace, Berkeley, CA.
1907 Oct.	Project: Victor Robinson house, Burlingame, CA.
1907 Oct.	Albert Schneider house, 1325 Arch St., Berkeley, CA.
1907 Nov.	Andrew C. Lawson house, 1515 La Loma Ave., Berkeley, CA. (Reinforced concrete construction)
1907 Dec.	Dudley Saeltzer house, 2100 West Street, Redding, CA.
1907 Dec.	William W. Underhill house (#2), 1350 Tamalpais Road, Berkeley, CA. (Destroyed, 1923)
1907	Hearst Hall bath house, University of California, College Ave., Berkeley, CA. (Destroyed, 1922)
1908 Feb.	J. B. Tufts house (#2), 245 Culloden, San Rafael, CA.
1908 Feb.	Eliza R. Roman house, 245 Laurel Place, San Rafael, CA.
1908 May	P. H. Atkinson house, 2735 Durant Ave., Berkeley, CA.
1908 June	Frank C. Havens house, 101 Wildwood Gardens, Piedmont, CA. (Extensively remodeled by Tiffany Company of New York.)
1908 June	R. H. Briggs house, Library addition, Los Gatos, CA.
1908 Nov.	Paul Elder Bookstore, 239 Grant St., San Francisco, CA. (Destroyed)
1908	Social hall, Unity Church, Bancroft and Dana St., Berkeley, CA. (Destroyed)
1909 Feb.	Project: H. P. Goodman, Berkeley, CA.
1909 March	Isaac Flagg summer house, vicinity of Orr's Creek, Ukiah, CA. (Destroyed, 1921)
1909 March	Leon L. Roos house, 3500 Jackson St., San Francisco, CA. (Living room additions, May 1913, Garage, Jan. 1916, Dressing room, July 1919, Second floor study, Dec. 1926)
1909 July	Randolph School, Flora B. Randolph, 2700 Belrose Ave., Berkeley, CA. (Currently used as a residence.)
1909 August	Samuel Goslinsky house, 3233 Pacific Ave., San Francisco, CA.
1909 August	Chester N. Rowell house, Mildreda and Forthcamp St., Fresno, CA. (Destroyed)
1909 Sept.	R. Fry house, 32nd Ave., [San Francisco] CA.
1909 Sept.	A. W. Thomas house, 315 Eldridge Ave., Mill Valley, CA.
[1909]	Bernard R. Maybeck house (#2), 2701 Buena Vista Way, Berkeley, CA. (Destroyed, 1923)
[1909]	Project: School, Flora B. Randolph, Shattuck and Berryman, Berkeley, CA.
1910 Feb.	J. W. Thomas studio, Greenwood Terrace, Berkeley, CA. (Destroyed, 1923)
1910 Feb.	L. P. Dyer house, Los Gatos, CA.
1910 April	Project: Edyth H. Decker house, Buena Vista Way, Berkeley, CA. (Preliminary drawings)
1910 April	Project: Apartment house, Pine Realty Co., T. J. C. Jacques, Lombard and Leavenworth St., San Francisco, CA.
1910 May	E. B. Power house, 1526 Masonic Ave., San Francisco, CA.
1910 July	Percy L. Shuman house, 144 Sycamore Ave., San Mateo, CA.
1910 July	Club building, San Francisco Settlement Association, 2520 Folsom St., San Francisco, CA. (Destroyed)

1910 August	Church building, First Church of Christ, Scientist, Dwight Way and Bowditch St., Berkeley, CA.
1911-13	Field houses, Oakland Playground Commission,

de Fermery Playground 1911 Jan.
Mosswood Park Playground 1912 Jan.
Bella Vista Playground 1913 April

1911 Feb.	Project: E. C. Young house, Green St., San Francisco, CA.
1911 May	Charles C. Boynton house, 2800 Buena Vista Way, Berkeley, CA. (Maybeck completed a temporary house on this site, the existing house, "Temple of the Wings," was completed by A. R. Monro. See 1912 Nov.)
1911 May	Elsa Jockers house, 1709 La Loma Ave., Berkeley, CA.
1911 May	Project: Strawberry Canyon bath house, University of California, Berkeley, CA.
1911 August	Leigh Towart house, Buena Vista Way and La Loma Ave., Berkeley, CA., (Destroyed, 1923)
1911	Competition drawings, Canberra City, Canberra, Australia.
[1911]	Competition drawings, Courthouse, Dayton, Nevada.
[1911]	Project: Schwartz house, Oakland, CA.
1912 March	Isaac Flagg (Ransome) house (#2), 1210 Shattuck Ave., Berkeley, CA.
1912 Sept.	Project: Mary Runyon house, Los Molinas, CA.
1912 Sept.	S. C. Irving house, Sonora, CA.
1912 Nov.	Charles C. Boynton house, "Temple of the Wings", 2800 Buena Vista Way, Berkeley, CA. (A. R. Monro completed the design of this house after the columns had been placed. Destroyed and rebuilt after the 1923 fire.)
1912 Dec.	Project: Church and School, Pacific Unitarian School, Dana and Allston Way, Berkeley, CA.
1912 Dec.	Steps and Walk, (Wm. Underhill), Rose Path and Euclid Ave., Berkeley, CA.
[1912]	Competition drawings, San Francisco City Hall, San Francisco, CA.
1913 May	Competition drawings, Alameda County Infirmary, Alameda County, CA.
1913 August	George A. Scott house, Vine and Scenic Ave., Berkeley, CA. (Destroyed, 1923; the original concrete chimney rebuilt into a new house not by Maybeck.)
1913 Nov.	E. C. Young house, 51 Sotelo Ave., Forest Hills, San Francisco, CA.
1913	Parsons Memorial Lodge, Sierra Club, Tuolumne Meadows, CA.
1913-14	Exposition buildings, Panama-Pacific International Exposition, San Francisco, CA.

Palace of Fine Arts 1913
Livestock Pavilion 1914
(See also House of Hoo-Hoo 1914

1913-15	Town plan and buildings, Brookings Lumber Company, Brookings, Oregon.

Town plan May 1914
Hotel
Cottages Project
Y.M.C.A. Club Project
School Project

1914 March	F. K. McFarlan house, 1428 Hawthorne Terrace, Berkeley, CA. (Destroyed, 1923)
1914 July	Drawings, The Chinese Village and Pagoda Company, (Fung Ming, Secretary) San Francisco, CA.
1914 Sept.	Guy Hyde Chick house, 7133 Chabot Road, Berkeley, CA.
1914 Nov.	Exposition building, "House of Hoo-Hoo," Pacific Lumbermen's Association, Panama-Pacific International Exposition, San Francisco, CA.
1914 Dec.	Alma S. Kennedy studio, 1537 Euclid Ave., Berkeley, CA. (Destroyed, 1923; rebuilt and annex added, 1923)

1915 May   Thomas F. Hunt house, 1800 Spruce St., Berkeley, CA. (House relocated at 53 Domingo Ave., Berkeley, CA.)

1915 May   R. H. Mathewson house, La Loma and Buena Vista Way, Berkeley, CA.

1915 June   C. W. Whitney house, 1110 Keith Ave., Berkeley, CA.

1916 Feb.   B. D. Marx Greene house, 7240 Chabot Road, Berkeley, CA. (Destroyed)

1916 May   S. Erlanger house, 270 Castenada, Forest Hills, San Francisco, CA.

1916 May   H. F. Jackson house remodeling, Orchard Lane, Berkeley, CA.

1916 August   A. E. Bingham house, 699 San Ysidro Road, Montecito, Santa Barbara, CA.

1916 Oct.   J. A. Owens house, 1041 Ashmount Ave., Oakland, CA. (Addition, 1920)

1917 July   Dahlia Loeb house, 275 Pacheco St., St. Francis Woods, San Francisco, CA. (Additions for J. L. Mears, 1922)

1917 Nov.   Alice Gay house, 196 Clarendon Ave., San Francisco, CA.

1918 Jan.   Project: Thomas R. Hanna speculative houses, [36 Ceres St.] Crockett, CA.

1918 August   Red Cross building, Civic Center Plaza, San Francisco, CA. (Temporary)

1918 Dec.   General Plan, Mills College, (Phoebe A. Hearst), Oakland, CA.

1918-19   Town plan, Clyde, California (Supervising Architect)
        Hotel   G. A. Applegarth, Architect

1919 May   Hazel P. Hincks garage and service rooms, Rancho Lomo, Live Oak, Sutter County, CA.

1919 May   Forest Hills Association club building, 381 Magellan Ave., San Francisco, CA. (Associate Architect E. C. Young)

1919 Dec.   M. P. Freeman Memorial Seat, Tucson, Arizona. (Beniamino Bufano, Sculptor)

1920 Jan.   Sidney H. Greeley house additions, 2600 19th Ave., Bakersfield, CA.

1920 Feb.   Project: Christine W. Stevensen house, Hollywood, Los Angeles, CA.

1920 April   Drawing, Oakland Memorial, Oakland, CA.

1920 June   Project: J. F. O'Keefe house, San Jose, CA.

1920 Nov.   Project: Community house, (S. F. B. Morse), Del Monte Properties, Pebble Beach, CA. (Associate, Mark Daniels)

1920   James J. Fagan house, Portola Drive, Woodside, CA.

[1920]   Drawings for Colonel Powers house, executed for Mark Daniels.

[1920]   Drawing, California Branch of the National Conservatory of Music.

1921 Jan.   Cedric Wright house, 2515 Etna St., Berkeley, CA.

1921 Feb.   Drawing, Reconstruction for San Carlos de Borromeo Mission, Carmel, CA.

1921 March   Project: C. E. Floete house, Pebble Beach, CA. (Associate, Mark Daniels)

1921 May   Project: J. A. Landsberger house, Carmel, CA.

1921 July   Resort buildings, E. G. Galt, Glen Alpine Springs, El Dorado County, CA.

1921 August   Outdoor theater, Pilgrimage Play, (Christine W. Stevensen), Hollywood, Los Angeles, CA.

1921 Oct.   Robert A. Peers house, Old Truckee Road, Colfax, CA.

1921 Dec.   J. Wilbur Calkins house, 601 Rosemont, Oakland, CA.

1921 Dec.   Estelle S. Clark house, 1408 Hawthorne Terrace, Berkeley, CA.

1922 April   Byington Ford house, Pebble Beach, CA.

1922 May   Frances Potter Thomas house, additions and remodeling, Pebble Beach, CA.

1922 June   Project: School, Del Monte Properties (Byington Ford), Pebble Beach, CA.

1922 June   Camp Curry kitchen additions, Yosemite Valley, CA.

1922 July   Project: School building, San Francisco Teachers College, Department of Education, State of California (Proposal for the site of the 1915 fair.)

1922 August Project: J. A. Manning house, Pebble Beach, CA.

1922 Sept.   Project: Wheeler Beckett house, [Berkeley] CA.

1922-23   Project: Phoebe Hearst Memorial building, University of California, Berkeley, CA.

1923 May   Ira B. Joralemon house and studio, 168 Southampton Ave., Berkeley, CA.

1923 Oct.   Mary D. Loy (W. E. Chamberlain) house, 2431 Ellsworth St., Berkeley, CA.

1923 Nov.   Project: E. R. Sturm house, E. Orange Grove Ave., Glendale, CA.

1923   Project: Laurence J. Kennedy house, Redding, CA.

1923-30   General Plan and buildings, Principia College, East St. Louis, Illinois. (General Plan, published 1927)

1924 May   Orin Kip McMurray house, 2357 Le Conte Ave., Berkeley, CA. (Constructed to the rear of the Dresslar house; destroyed by fire, 1923)

1924 June   E. F. Giesler house, 2563 Buena Vista Way, Berkeley, CA.

1924 August J. H. Burnett house, 2680 Hilgard Ave., Berkeley, CA.

1924   Bernard R. Maybeck house (#3), "Sack house," 2745 Buena Vista Way, Berkeley, CA. (Experimental house finished with gunny sacks dipped in lightweight concrete.)

1924-29   Project: Auditorium-Gymnasium-Museum buildings, William Randolph Hearst, University of California, Berkeley, CA.

1925 Jan.   Phoebe A. Hearst Memorial Gymnasium, University of California, Berkeley, CA. (Julia Morgan, Associate Architect)

1925 Jan.   Project: Office building, Dr. Robert A. Peers, Colfax, CA.

1925 March   Project: Charles W. Duncan house, Santa Rosa Ave., Sausalito, CA.

1925 March   L. F. de Angulo house, 2815 Buena Vista Way, Berkeley, CA.

1925 March   Project: Robert Legge, Panoramic Way, Berkeley, CA.

1925 July   Project: Chevy Chase School library and recreation hall, F. E. Farrington, Chevy Chase, Md.

1925 July   Earle C. Anthony house (#1), 3405 Waverly Place, Los Angeles, CA. (First house of the Anthony development)

1925 Oct.   Warren P. Staniford house, 6130 Ocean View Drive, Oakland, CA.

1925 Oct.   Project: Dr. James F. Smith house, [San Francisco] CA.

1926 April   Packard Automobile showrooms, Earle C. Anthony, Van Ness Ave., San Francisco, CA. (Powers and Ahnden, Associate Architects)

1926 Oct.   Project: Hemet Hotel, Hemet, CA. (M. E. Manning, designer)

1926 Dec.   Project: Caroline W. Hollis house, La Loma Ave., Berkeley, CA.

1927 March   Earle C. Anthony house (#2), 3347 Waverly Drive, Los Angeles, CA.

1927 Oct.   Associated Charities building, Gough and Eddy St., San Francisco, CA.

1927 Oct.   R. I. Woolsey house, 20 Sunset Drive, Kensington, Contra Costa County, CA.

1928 March   Harrison Memorial Library, Carmel, CA.

1928 May   Packard Automobile sales room and office

interiors, Earle C. Anthony, Los Angeles, CA. (John Parkinson and Donald B. Parkinson, Architects)

1928 May First Church of Christ, Scientist, Sunday School, Dwight Way, Berkeley, CA. (Henry Gutterson, Associate Architect)

1928 July Edwin S. Pillsbury house, 220 Alvarado Road, Berkeley, CA.

1928 Sept. Packard Automobile showrooms, Earle C. Anthony, Harrison St., Oakland, CA. (Powers and Ahnden, Architects; destroyed 1974)

1928 Dec. Earle C. Anthony house, studio, and gardens (#3), 3435 Waverly Place, Los Felix Park, Los Angeles, CA. (Mark Daniels, Consultant on land development)
    Original Scheme   Sept. 1924
    Revised   March 1925
    Revised   Sept. 1926

1930-38 General Plan and buildings, Principia College, Elsah, Illinois (Julia Morgan, Associate Architect)
    Chapel   June 1931

1931 Dec. A. W. Maybeck cabin, Twain Harte Mountain Club, Twain Harte, CA.

1931 J. B. Tufts house (#3), 2733 Buena Vista Way, Berkeley, CA.

[1932] Paul Elder Book Store, Geary St., San Francisco, CA.

1933 Wallen Maybeck house (#1), 2751 Buena Vista Way, Berkeley, CA.

1933 Annie Maybeck house, 2780 Buena Vista Way, Berkeley, CA.

1935 House, 2786 Buena Vista Way, Berkeley, CA.

1935-37 Drawings, Ninth Church of Christ, Scientist, San Francisco, CA.

1936 Wells cabin, Fuller Road, Twain Harte, CA.

1936 Drawings, Cole Chemical Company, B. L. Cole, St. Louis, Missouri.

1937 Nov. Project: Paul Staniford house, Fresno, CA.

1937 Mobilized Women of Berkeley building, University Ave., Berkeley, CA.

1937 Wallen W. Maybeck house (#2), Purdue Ave., Kensington, Contra Costa County, CA.

[1938] Bernard R. Maybeck studio, Maybeck Twin Drive, Berkeley, CA.

1939 Mark Morris house, 39 Edgecroft Road, Berkeley, CA. (Mark White, Architect)

1940 June Project: Cemetery, A. H. Darbee, (South San Francisco), CA. (Julia Morgan, Architect)

1940 Charles Aikin house, 2750 Buena Vista Way, Berkeley, CA.

Maybeck, Howard, and White, Architects.

1907 Dec. San Mateo Polo Club building, San Mateo Realty Investment Company, San Mateo, CA.

1907 Project: Balfour house, San Mateo, CA.

1907 Charles Josselyn house, 400 Kings Mountain Road, Woodside, CA.

[1907] R. Y. Hayne office building, Washington and Stockton Streets, San Francsco, CA.

[1907] Project: J. H. P. Howard office building addition, Battery and Commercial Streets, San Francisco, CA.

Selected Bibliography

Ackerman, James. "Report on California," *Architectural Review*, (October, 1956), pp. 237-239.

Allen, Harris. "Two Nature Lovers," *The Building Review*, (May, 1919), pp. 46-47.

Anderson, Timothy J.; Moore, Eudorah M.; Winter, Robert W. *California Design, 1910*. Pasadena: California Design Publications, 1974.

The Architectural News, San Francisco, (November, 1890), p. 10.

Baird, Joseph Armstrong. *Time's Wondrous Changes; San Francisco Architecture, 1776-1915*. San Francisco: California Historical Society, 1962.

Bakewell, John, Jr. "The San Francisco City Hall Competition," *Architect and Engineer*, (July, 1912), pp. 46-53.

Bangs, Jean Murray. "Bernard Ralph Maybeck, Architect, Comes into his Own," *Architectural Record*, (January, 1948), pp. 72-79.

_____. "Maybeck—Medallist," *Architectural Forum*, (May, 1951), pp. 160-162.
(*See also* Harris, Jean)

Battu, Zoe A. " 'The Man on the Street' Speaks on the Packard Building," *California Arts and Architecture*, (July, 1927), pp. 32-35. ·

Bell, Mary. "Hearst Hall," *The University of California Magazine*, (February, 1900), pp. 10-14.

Besinger, Curtis. "After 50 Years this House is Newer than Many Moderns," *House Beautiful*, (May, 1962), pp. 150-57.

Bohemian Club. "Description of the Grove Clubhouse," *Annual Report, 1903-04*. San Francisco: 1904.

Brown, A. Page. "Bungalow at Burlingame for J. D. Grant, Esq.," *American Architect and Building News*, (June 8, 1895), p. 95.

Brune, Emmanuel. *Cours de Construction*. Paris: Librarie des imprimeries reunies, 1888.

Bullock, John. *The American Cottage Builder*. New York: Stringer and Townsend, 1854.

Burchard, John and Bush-Brown, Albert. *The Architecture of America—A Social and Cultural History*. New York: Little, Brown and Co., 1961.

"The California Building at the World's Columbian Exposition in 1893," *American Architect*, (March, 1892), p. 187.

California World's Fair Commission. *California at the World's Columbian Exposition, 1893*. Sacramento: State Printing Office, 1894.

Cardwell, Kenneth H. "Bernard Maybeck: San Francisco Genius," *Bulletin*, Northern California Chapter, A.I.A., (April, 1960), pp. 22-25.

Cardwell, Kenneth and Hays, William C. "Fifty Years from Now," *California Monthly*, (April, 1954), pp. 20-26.

Carrère, J. M. and Hastings, T. "Gatelodge and Farm House, E. H. Johnson, Alta Crest, Greenwich, Connecticut," *American Architect and Building News*, (August 11, 1888), p. 63.

_____. "Plans of the Hotel Ponce de Leon, the Alcazar, and the

Methodist Episcopalian Church, St. Augustine, Fla.," *American Architect and Building News*, (August 25, 1888), pp. 87-88.

————. "Competitive Design for the Cathedral of St. John the Divine, New York, N.Y.," *American Architect and Building News*, (October 5, 1889), p. 158.

Cheney, Charles H. "The Art of the Small House," *House Beautiful*, (September, 1910), pp. 34-38.

Cheney, Sheldon. *The New World Architecture*. New York: Longmans, Green, 1930.

Clark, Arthur Bridgman. *Art Principles in House, Furniture and Village Building*. Stanford, Ca.: Stanford University Press, 1921.

Clark, Robert Judson (ed.). *The Arts and Crafts Movement in America, 1876-1916*. Princeton: Princeton University Press, 1972.

Condit, Carl W. *American Building*. Chicago and London: The University of Chicago Press, 1968.

————. *American Building Art*. New York: Oxford University Press, 1960.

Cornelius, Brother Fidelis. *Keith, Old Master of California*. New York: G. P. Putnam's Sons, Inc., 1956.

Craft, Mable Clare. "A Sermon in Church Building," *House Beautiful*, (February, 1901), pp. 125-132.

Craig, Robert M. "Bernard Ralph Maybeck and the Principia: Architecture as a Philosophical Expression," *Journal of the Society of Architectural Historians*, (October, 1972), p. 234.

Dana, William S. B. *The Swiss Chalet Book*. New York: The William T. Comstock Co., 1913.

Delaire Edmond A. and de Penanrun, David. *Les Architectes Eleves de l'Ecole des Beaux-Arts*. Paris: Librairie de la Construction Moderne, 1907.

"An Early Glimpse of the Panama-Pacific Exposition Architecturally," *Archiectect and Engineer*, (October, 1912). pp. 46-55.

Embury, Aymar, II. *One Hundred Country Houses: Modern American Examples*. New York: The Century Company, 1909.

Flagg, Ernest. "The Ecole des Beaux-Arts," Part I (January-March, 1894), pp. 302-313. Part II (April-June, 1894), pp. 419-428.

Freudenheim, Leslie Mandelson and Sussman, Elisabeth Sacks. *Building with Nature: Roots of the San Francisco Bay Region Tradition*. Santa Barbara and Salt Lake City: Peregrine Smith, Inc., 1974.

Garnier, Charles. *L'habitation humaine*. Paris: Hachette et Cie., 1892.

Gebhard, David and Von Breton, Harriette. *1868-1968: Architecture in California*. Santa Barbara: The Art Galleries, University of California, Santa Barbara, 1968.

Gebhard, David et al. *A Guide to Architecture in San Francisco and Northern California*. Santa Barbara and Salt Lake City: Peregrine Smith Inc., 1973.

Gout, Paul. *Viollet-le-Duc, sa vie, son oevre, sa doctrine*. Paris: E. Champion, 1914.

Gray, David. *Thomas Hastings, Architect*. Boston: Houghton Mifflin, 1933.

Griffin, Walter Burley. "Commonwealth of Australia Federal Capitol Competition," *The Western Architect*, (September, 1912), p. 91.

Guadet, Jules. *Elements et Theorie de l'Architecture*. Paris: Librairie de la construction moderne, [1905].

Hamlin, Talbot. *Architecture Through the Ages*. New York: G. P. Putnam Sons, 1940.

Harris, Jean. "Bernard Ralph Maybeck," *Journal*, The American Institute of Architects, (May, 1951), pp. 221-228.
(See also Bangs, Jean M.)

Harvey, Lawrence. "Semper's Theory of Evolution in Architectural Ornament," *Transcripts*, Royal Institute of British Architects, London, 1885.

Hastings, Thomas. "Reminiscence of Early Work," *American Architect and Building News*, (July 7, 1909), pp. 3-4.

Hays, William C. "Some Interesting Buildings at the University of California: The Work of Bernard Maybeck, Architect," *Indoors and Out*, (May, 1906), pp. 68-75.

Hegemann, Werner. *Report on a City Plan for the Municipalities of Oakland and Berkeley*. Oakland: Municipal Governments of Oakland and Berkeley, 1915.

Hitchcock, Henry-Russell. *Architecture of the 19th and 20th Centuries*. Baltimore: Penguin Books, 1958.

"House of Mrs. Elsa Jockers, North Berkeley, Cal.," *Architectural Record*, (October, 1916), pp. 338-340.

Howard, John Galen. "Country House Architecture on the Pacific Coast," *Architectural Record*, (October, 1916), pp. 323-355.

"Is There a Bay Area Style?" *Architectural Record*, (May, 1949), pp. 92-97.

Jones, William Carey. *Illustrated History of the University of California*. San Francisco: Frank H. Dukesmith, 1895.

Jordy, William H. *American Buildings and their Architects: Progressive and Academic Ideals at the Turn of the 20th Century.*

Garden City, N.Y.: Doubleday and Company Inc., 1972.

Keeler, Charles A. *The Simple Home*. San Francisco: Paul Elder and Co., 1904.

_____. "Thoughts on Home Building," *Architect and Engineer*, (October, 1905), pp. 19-28.

Kelham, George William. "Will the Panama Pacific International Exposition Be an Architectural Influence?" *Pacific Coast Architect*, (February, 1915), pp. 55-75.

Kirker, Harold. *California's Architectural Frontier*. San Marino: The Huntington Library, 1960.

Knight, Emerson. "Outdoor Theaters and Stadiums in the West," *Architect and Engineer*, (August, 1924), pp. 52-91.

"Lumbermen's Building," *The Western Architect*, (September, 1915), p. 25.

Maclay, Mira A. "The Maybeck One Room House," *Sunset Magazine*, (July, 1923), pp. 65-66, 80.

Macomber, Ben. *The Jewel City: Its Planning and Achievement; Its Architecture, Sculpture, Symbolism, and Music: Its Gardens, Palaces, and Exhibits*. San Francisco and Tacoma: John H. Williams, Publisher, 1915.

"Mark Hopkins Institute of Art," *Architect and Builder*, (August, 1895).

"B. R. Maybeck: Designer of the Palace of Fine Arts—P.P.I.E.," *Sunset Magazine*, (November, 1915), pp. 951-952.

Maybeck, Bernard Ralph. "A Dream that Might Be Realized," *Merchant's Association Review*, San Francisco, (November, 1903), pp. 1-2.

_____. "Fine Arts Palace Will Outlast Present Generation," *Architect and Engineer*, (November, 1915), p. 53.

_____. "House of Mrs. Phoebe A. Hearst in Siskiyou Co., Cal.," *Architectural Review—Boston*, (January, 1904), pp. 64-66.

_____. "The Palace of Fine Arts," *Transactions, Commonwealth Club of California*, (August, 1915), pp. 369-374.

_____. *Palace of Fine Arts and Lagoon*. San Francisco: Paul Elder and Company, [1915].

_____. "The Planning of a University," *Blue and Gold*, University of California Yearbook, 1900, pp. 17-20.

_____. *The Principia College Plans*. Saint Louis: Trustees of the Principia, 1927.

_____. "Reflections on the Grauman Metropolitan Theater, Los Angeles," *Architect and Engineer*, (June, 1923), pp. 99-101.

_____. Untitled booklet on *Hillside Building* issued by the Hillside Club, Berkeley. South Berkeley: Richard J. Orozco, [1907].

_____. "Willis J. Polk, 1867-1924," *American Architect*, (November 5, 1924), p. 422.

McCoy, Esther. *Five California Architects*. New York: Reinhold Publishing Corporation, 1960.

_____. *Roots of Contemporary Architecture*. (Exhibit Catalog) Los Angeles: Los Angeles Art Commission, The Municipal Art Department, 1956.

McLaren, John. *Gardening in California*. San Francisco: A. M. Robertson, 1909.

Mock, Elizabeth. *Built in U.S.A.: Since 1932*. New York: Museum of Modern Art, 1944.

Moore, Charles C. *Daniel H. Burnham*. (2 vols.) Boston: Houghton Mifflin, 1921.

Mooser, John. "Search for American Style," *American Architect and Building News*, (January 8, 1887), p. 16.

Morrow, Irving F. "Earle C. Anthony Packard Building, San Francisco," *Architect and Engineer*, (July, 1927), pp. 60-67.

_____. "The Packard Building at Oakland," *California Arts and Architecture*, (February, 1929), pp. 54-59.

Moyle, Gilbert. "Mr. Maybeck's Suggestion for a California Branch of the National Conservatory of Music and Art," *Architect and Engineer*, (January, 1921), pp. 64-65.

Mullgardt, Louis Christian. *The Architecture and Landscape Gardening of the Exposition*. San Francisco: Paul Elder and Company, [1915].

Mumford, Lewis. *Roots of Contemporary American Architecture*. New York: Reinhold, 1952

_____. "The Skyline, Status Quo," *The New Yorker*, (October 11, 1947), pp. 94-99.

Nichols, F. D. "A visit with Bernard Maybeck," *Journal of the Society of Architectural Historians*, (October, 1952), p. 30.

Noffsinger, James P. *Influence of the Ecole des Beaux-Arts*. Washington: Catholic University of America Press, 1955.

Osbourne, Katherine D. *Robert Louis Stevenson in California*. Chicago: A. C. McClurg and Co., 1911.

Pevsner, Nicolaus. *Pioneers of Modern Design*. New York: Museum of Modern Art, 1949.

Polk, William H. *Polk Family and Kinsmen*. Louisville: Bradley and Gilbert, 1912.

Polk, Willis J. "Preservation of the Palace of Fine Arts," *Architect and Engineer*, (January, 1916), pp. 100-103.

"Presentation of Institute's Gold Medal to Bernard Ralph Maybeck," *Journal*, The American Institute of Architects, (July, 1951), pp. 3-8.

"Residence of Dr. J. W. Calkins, Oakland, California," *The Building Review*, (December, 1923), pp. 72-74.

San Francisco Museum of Art. *Domestic Architecture of the San Francisco Bay Region*. (Exhibit Catalog) San Francisco, [1949].

"San Francisco the Home of Mission Type of Furniture," *Architect and Engineer*, (August, 1906), pp. 67-68.

Sargeant, Winthrop. "Bernard Ralph Maybeck," *Life*, (May 17, 1948), pp. 141-153.

_____. *Geniuses, Goddesses and People*. New York: E. P. Dutton, 1949.

Saylor, Henry H. *Architectural Styles for Country Houses*. New York: R. M. McBride and Company, 1919.

Schuyler, Montgomery. "State Buildings at the World's Fair," *Architectural Record*, (July-September, 1893), pp. 55-71.

Scott, Mel. *The San Francisco Bay Area: A Metropolis in Perspective*. Berkeley and Los Angeles: University of California Press, 1959.

Scully, Vincent, J., Jr. and Downing, Antoinette F. *Architectural Heritage of Newport, R. I. 1640-1915*. Cambridge, Mass: Harvard University Press, 1952.

Scully, Vincent J., Jr. *The Shingle Style; Architectural Theory and Design from Richardson to the Origins of Wright*. New Haven: Yale University Press, 1955.

Semper, Gottfried. *Der Stil*. Munich: Friedrich Bruckmann's Verlag, 1863.

Telegraph Hill Neighborhood Association. *Fourth Annual Report*. San Francisco, 1907.

The Trustees of the Phoebe Apperson Hearst Architectural Plan for the University of California. *The International Competition for the Phoebe Hearst Architectural Plan for the University of California*. San Francisco: H. S. Crocker Co., [1899].

Thompson, Elizabeth K. "The Early Domestic Architecture of the San Francisco Bay Region," *Journal of the Society of Architectural Historians*, (October, 1951), pp. 15-21.

"Three Houses by Maybeck and White, Architects," *Architectural Record*, (November, 1916), pp. 488-489.

Tobisch, Othmar. *Historical Recollections*. San Francisco Society of the New Jerusalem, Centenary Edition, 1950.

Todd, Frank Morton. *The Story of the Exposition*, *The Panama-Pacific International Exposition*. New York and London: G. Putnam's Sons, 1921.

United States Patent Office. "Toilet Fan, Bernard R. Maybeck," *Official Gazette*, (July 22, 1890), p. 476.

University of California. *President's Report*, (November 16, 1923).

_____. "The Visit of the Jurors in the Phebe [sic] A. Hearst Architectural Competition, University of California," *University Chronicle*, (October, 1899).

Viollet-le-Duc, E. "Medieval Houses," *American Architect and Building News*, (June 16, 1888).

Ware, William R. "St. Louis City Hall Competition," *Inland Architect and News Record*, (March, 1890), pp. 35-37.

Wastell, A. B. "Bernard R. Maybeck," *Pacific Coast Architect*, (March, 1916), p. 154.

_____. "Lumbermen's Building and House of Hoo-Hoo," *Pacific Coast Architect*, (July, 1915), p. 40.

The Wave, San Francisco, (October 18, 1890), p. 7; (November 22, 1890), p. 5; (February 4, 1893), p. 5.

Weeks, Charles Peter. "Brickwork on the Pacific Slope," *The Brickbuilder*, (September, 1904), pp. 178-180; (October, 1904), pp. 205-207; (November, 1904), pp. 235-236.

White, John. "Painting and Sculpture," *Homes and Grounds*, (May, 1916), p. 155.

Woodbridge, Sally (ed.), *Bay Area Houses*. New York: Oxford Area. New York: Grove Press, 1960.

Woodbridge, Sally (ed.), *Bay Area Houses*, New York: Oxford University Press, 1976.

Woolett, William L. "Scene Painting in Architecture, Maybeck's Palace of Fine Arts," *Architectural Record*, (November, 1915), pp. 571-574.

Wurster, William W. "San Francisco Bay Portfolio," *Magazine of Art*, (December, 1944), pp. 300-305.

Index